ETHEROW OF THE WHITE DIAMOND BEAM

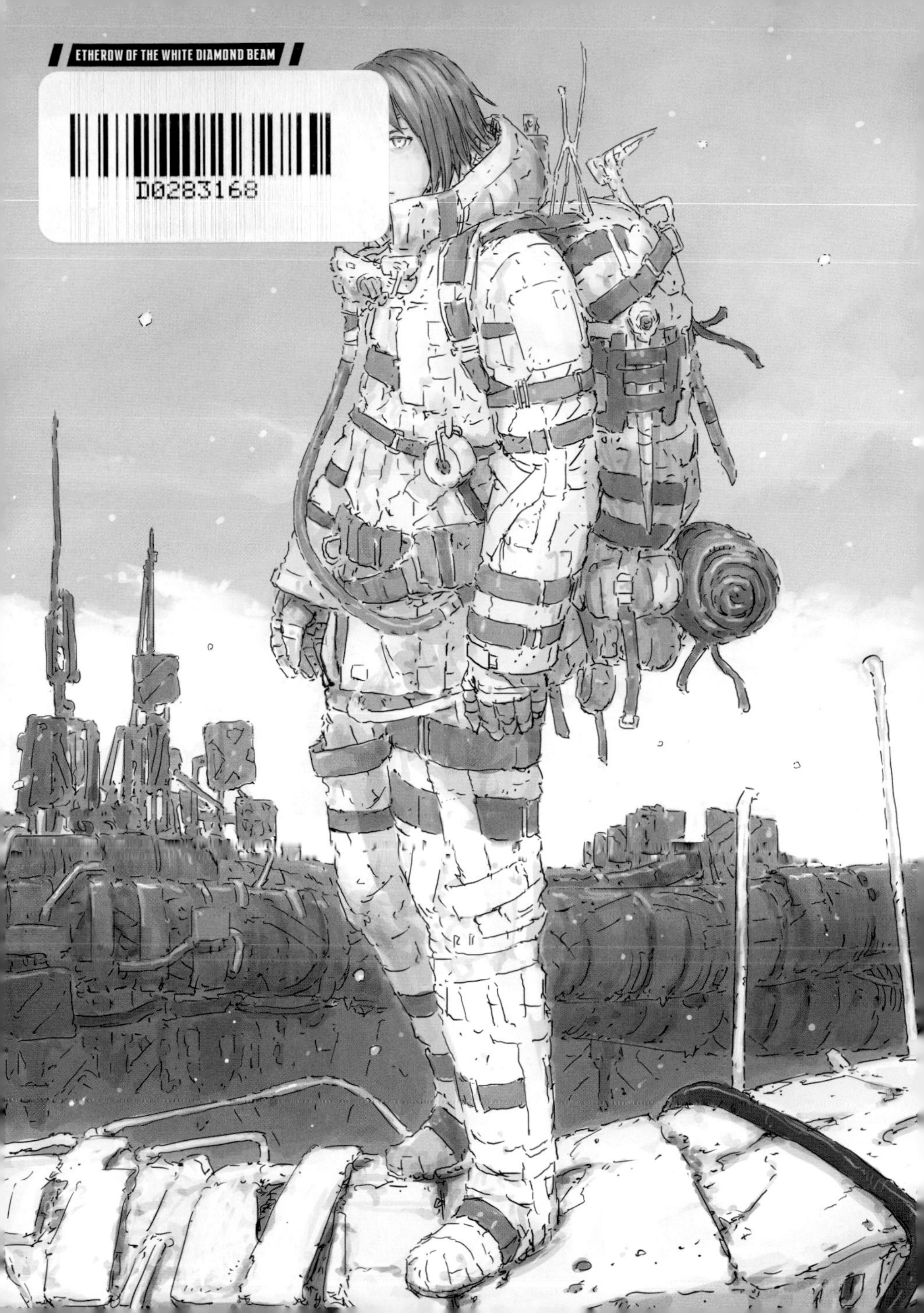

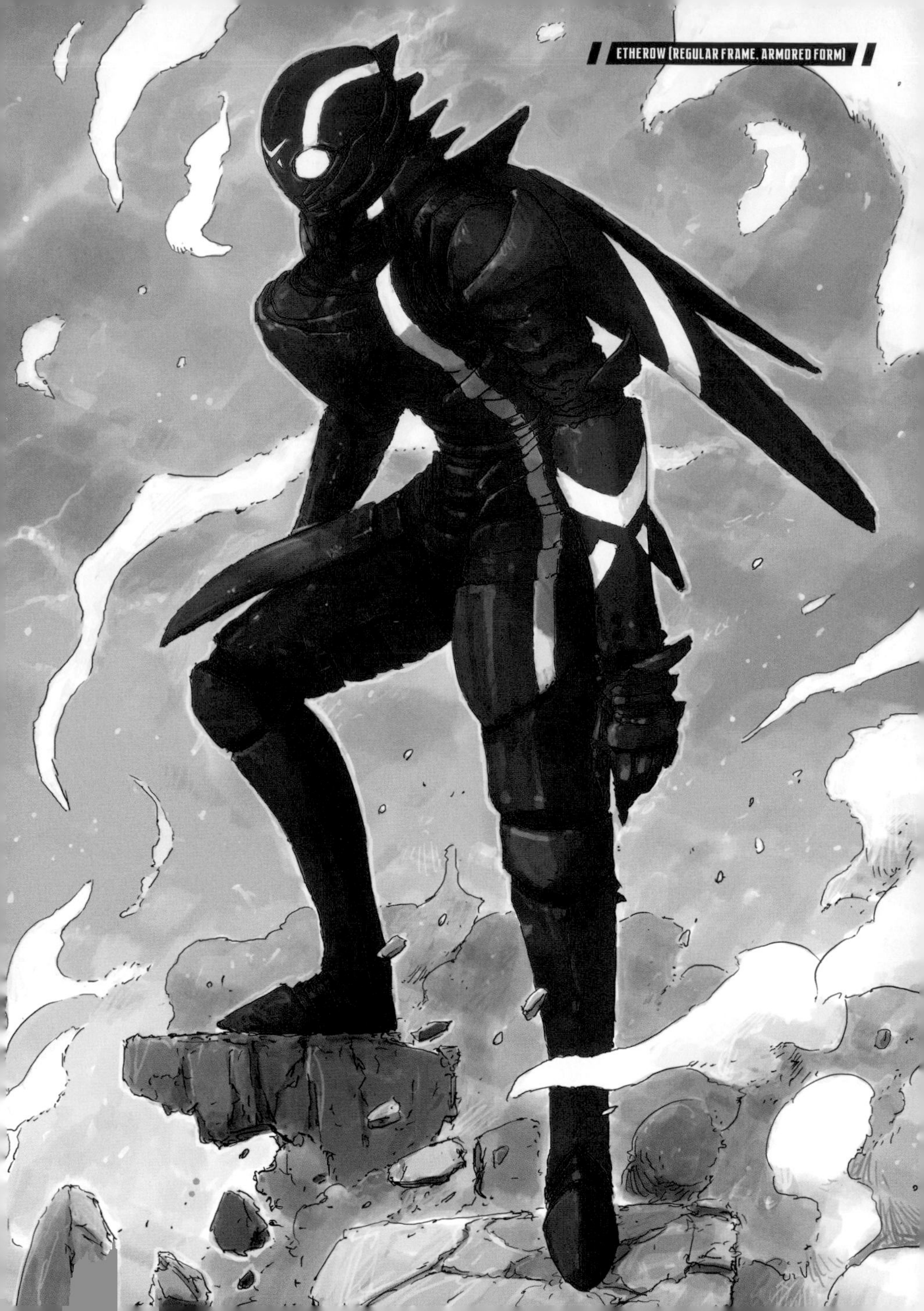
ETHEROW (REGULAR FRAME, ARMORED FORM)

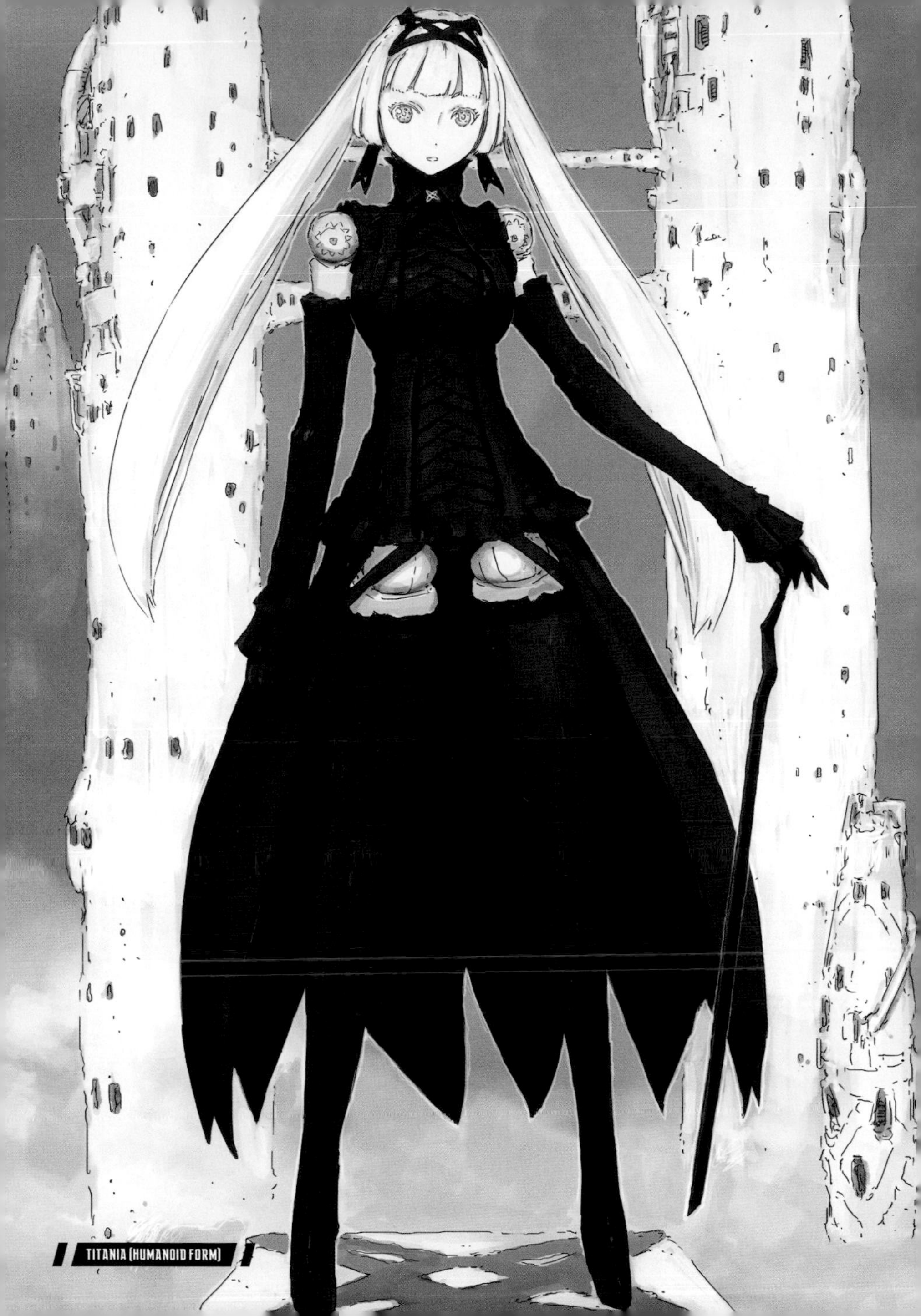
TITANIA (HUMANOID FORM)

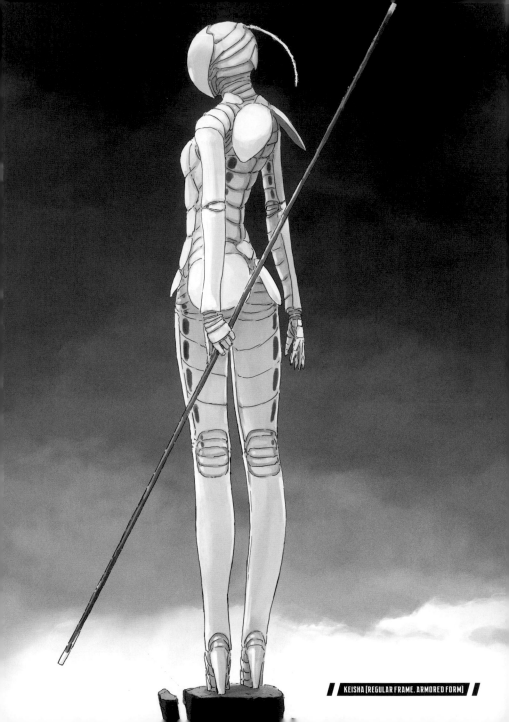

KEISHA (REGULAR FRAME. ARMORED FORM)

A P O S I M Z

02

TSUTOMU
NIHEI

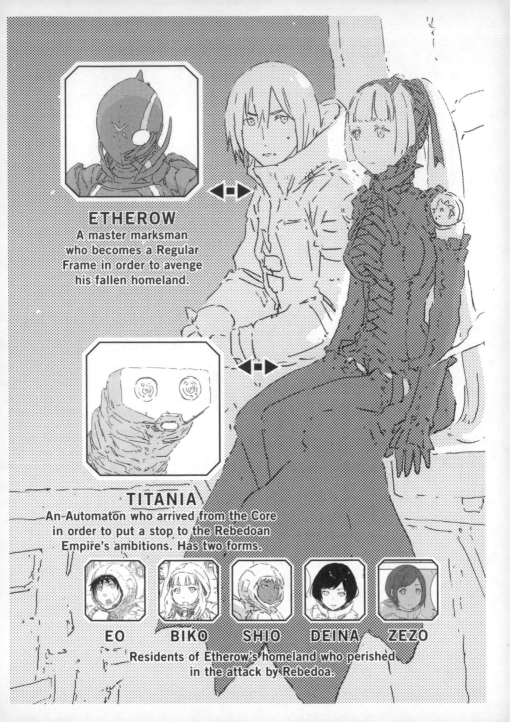

ETHEROW
A master marksman who becomes a Regular Frame in order to avenge his fallen homeland.

TITANIA
An Automaton who arrived from the Core in order to put a stop to the Rebedoan Empire's ambitions. Has two forms.

EO   **BIKO**   **SHIO**   **DEINA**   **ZEZO**

Residents of Etherow's homeland who perished in the attack by Rebedoa.

PLOT AND CHARACTER INTRO

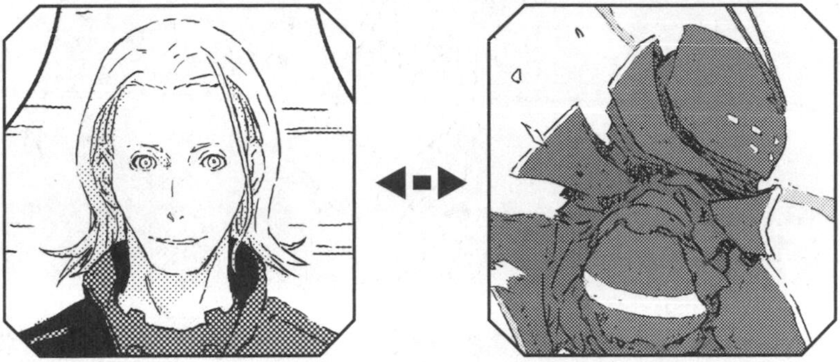

YIYU

A Rebedoan Regular Frame (Reincarnated) responsible for the destruction of Etherow's homeland.

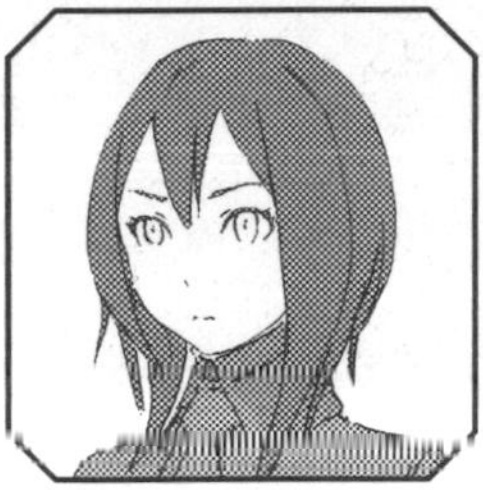

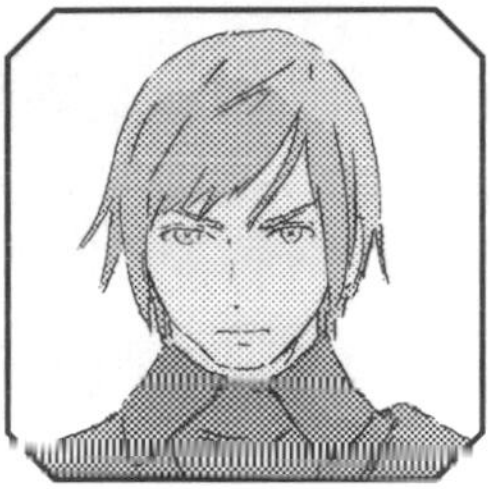

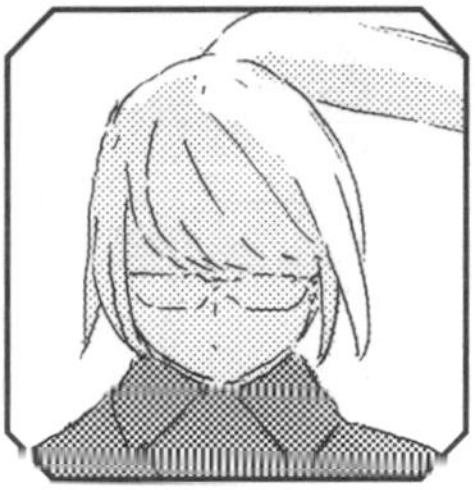

JATE **FYUMA** **UNKNOWN**

Rebedoan Regular Frames (Reincarnateds) that came to aid Yiyu in his mission.

Previously

Etherow's homeland, the White Diamond Beam, was destroyed by the Rebedoan Empire's Regular Frame Yiyu. Vowing revenge, Etherow becomes a regular frame himself and joins Titania on her journey to put an end to Rebedoa's ambitions. In order to become more powerful, they hunt down the Regular Frames under Yiyu's command....

APOSIMZ

CHAPTER 04

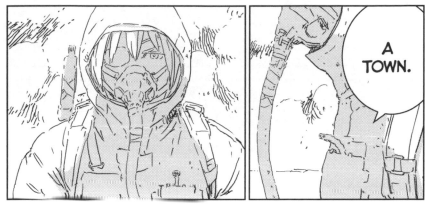

A TOWN.

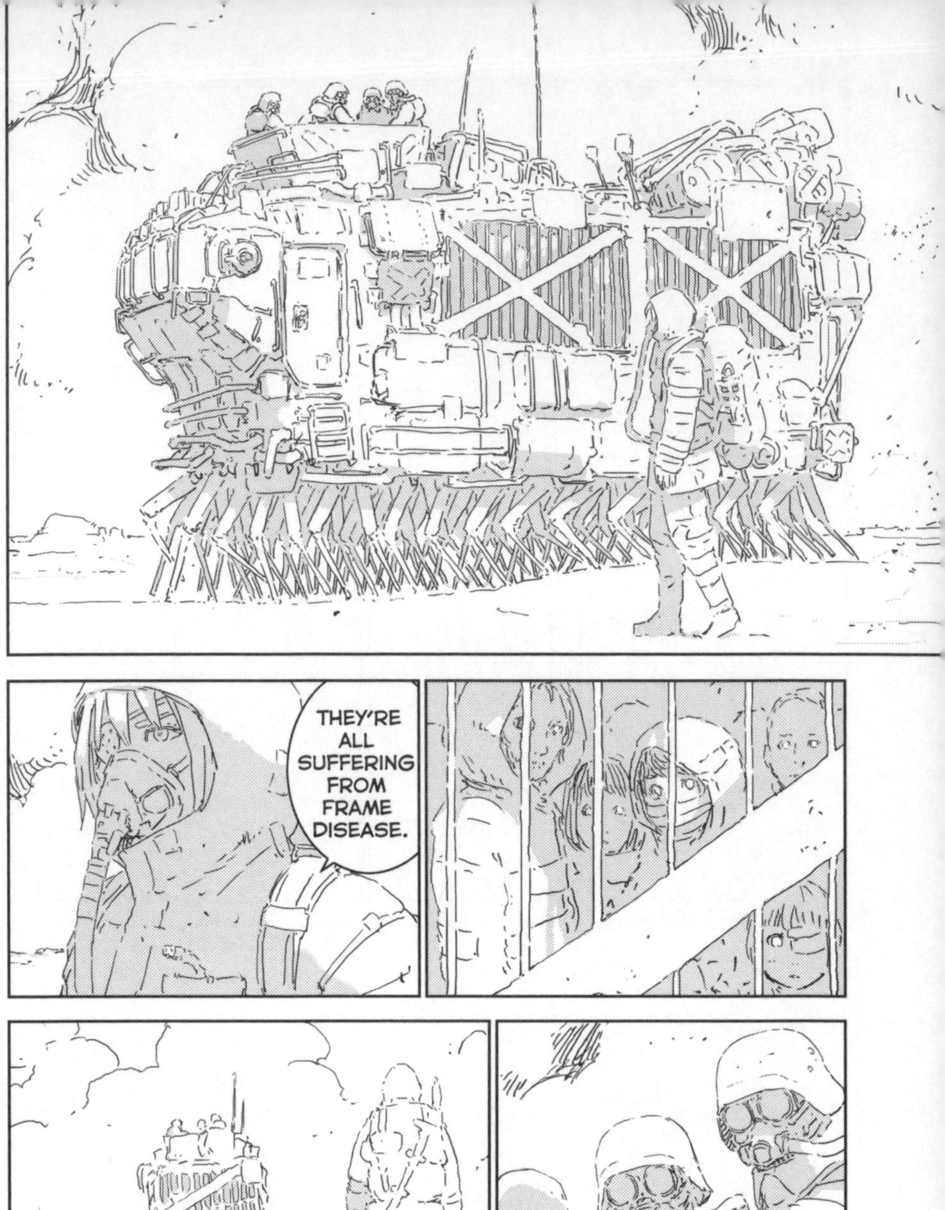
THEY'RE ALL SUFFERING FROM FRAME DISEASE.

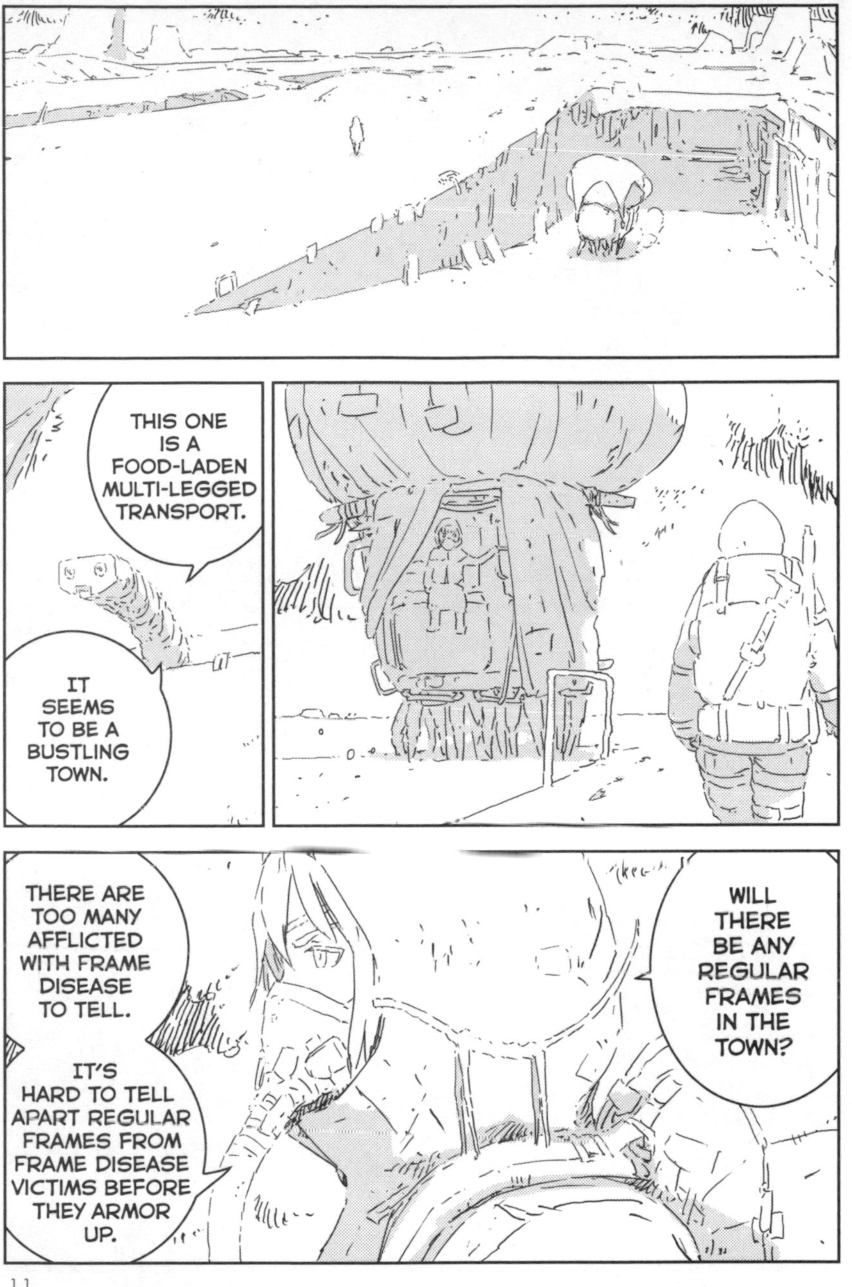

THIS ONE IS A FOOD-LADEN MULTI-LEGGED TRANSPORT.
IT SEEMS TO BE A BUSTLING TOWN.
WILL THERE BE ANY REGULAR FRAMES IN THE TOWN?
THERE ARE TOO MANY AFFLICTED WITH FRAME DISEASE TO TELL.
IT'S HARD TO TELL APART REGULAR FRAMES FROM FRAME DISEASE VICTIMS BEFORE THEY ARMOR UP.

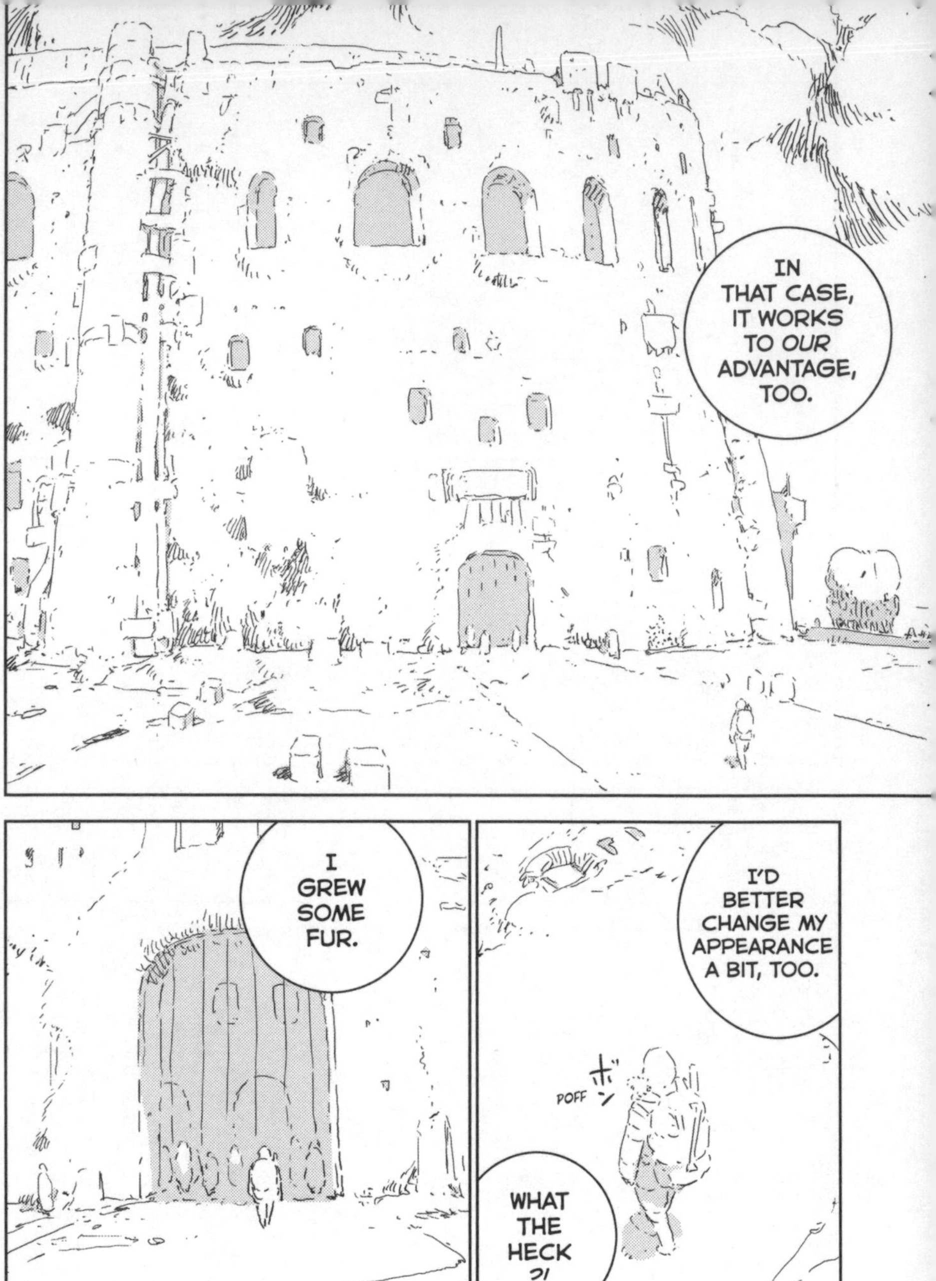
IN THAT CASE, IT WORKS TO *OUR* ADVANTAGE, TOO.
I GREW SOME FUR.
I'D BETTER CHANGE MY APPEARANCE A BIT, TOO.
POFF
WHAT THE HECK ?!

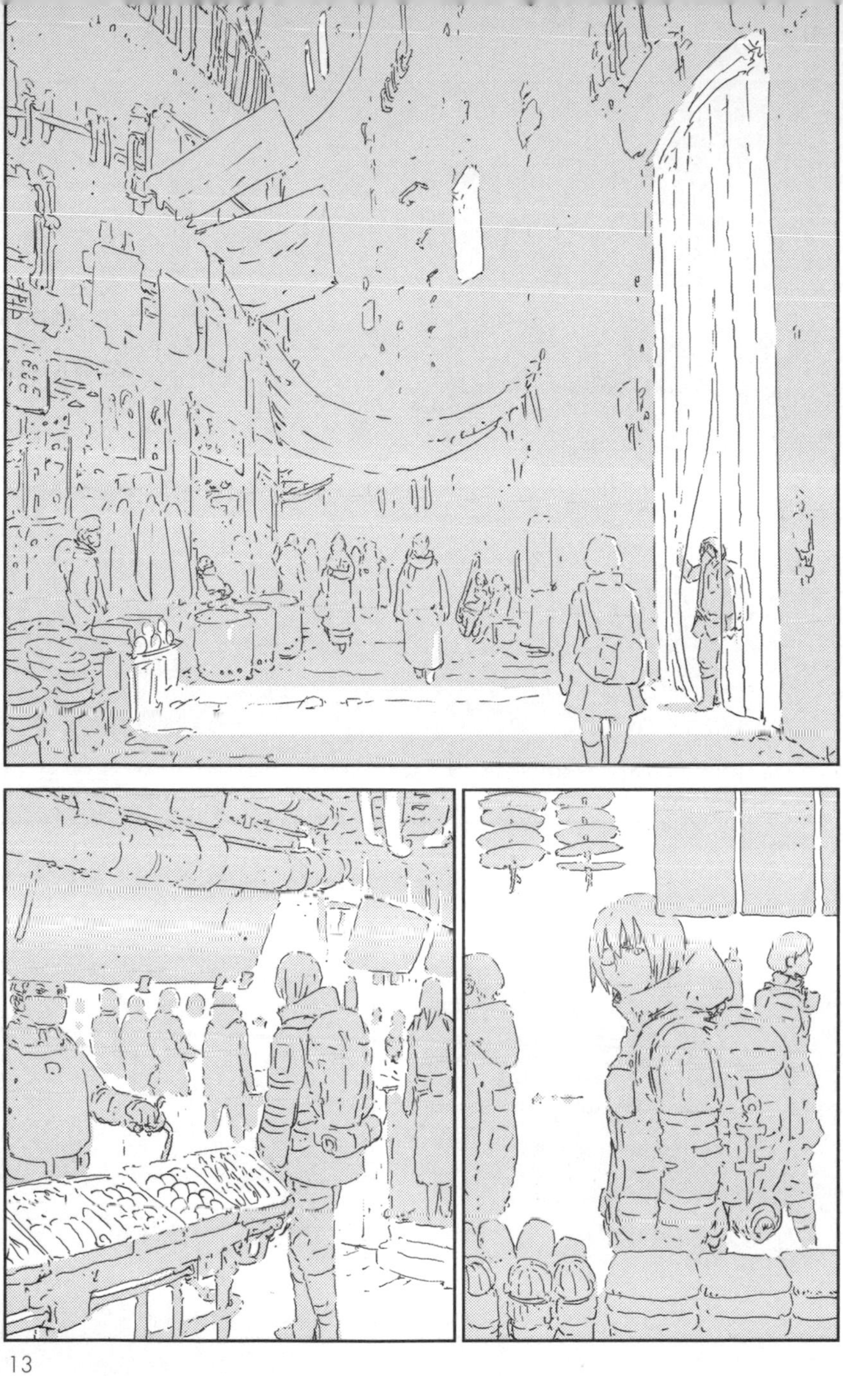

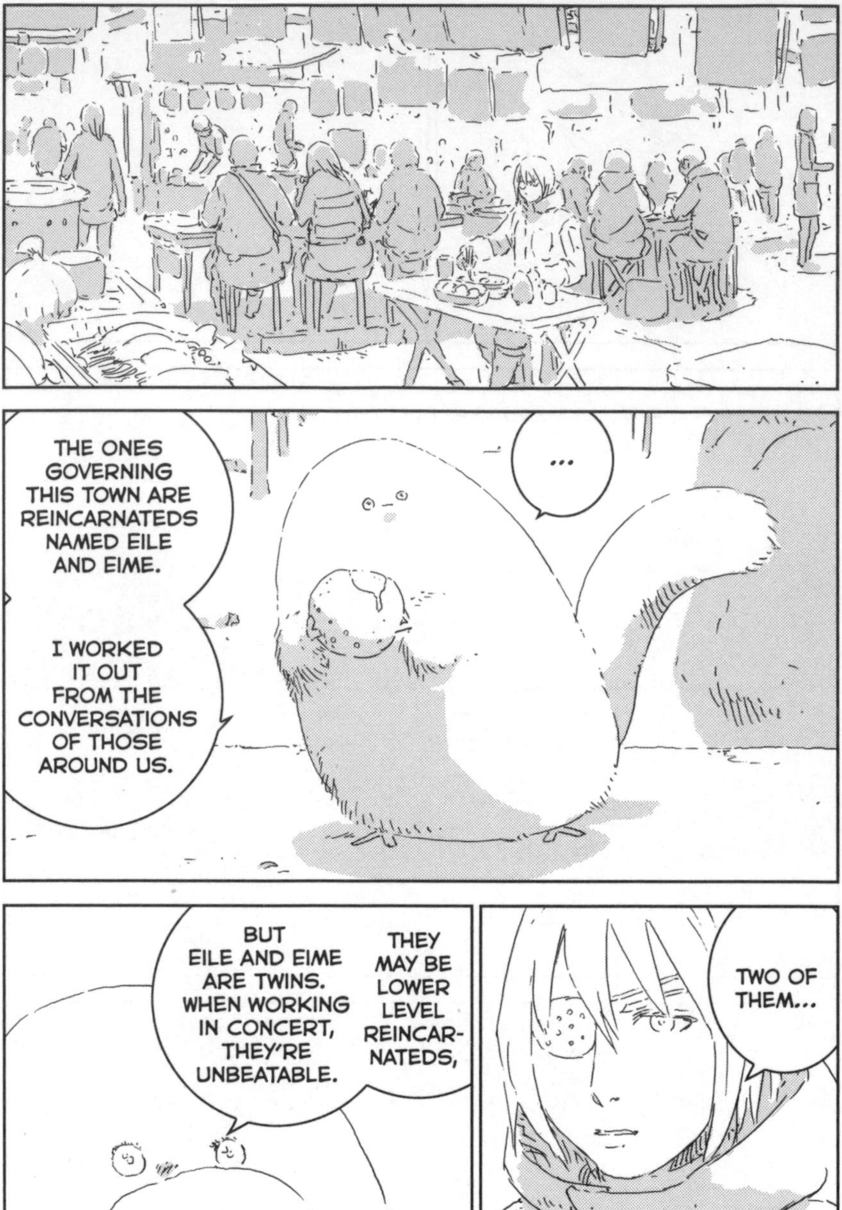
THE ONES GOVERNING THIS TOWN ARE REINCARNATEDS NAMED EILE AND EIME.
I WORKED IT OUT FROM THE CONVERSATIONS OF THOSE AROUND US.
...
THEY MAY BE LOWER LEVEL REINCARNATEDS,
BUT EILE AND EIME ARE TWINS. WHEN WORKING IN CONCERT, THEY'RE UNBEATABLE.
TWO OF THEM...

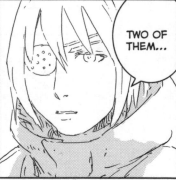

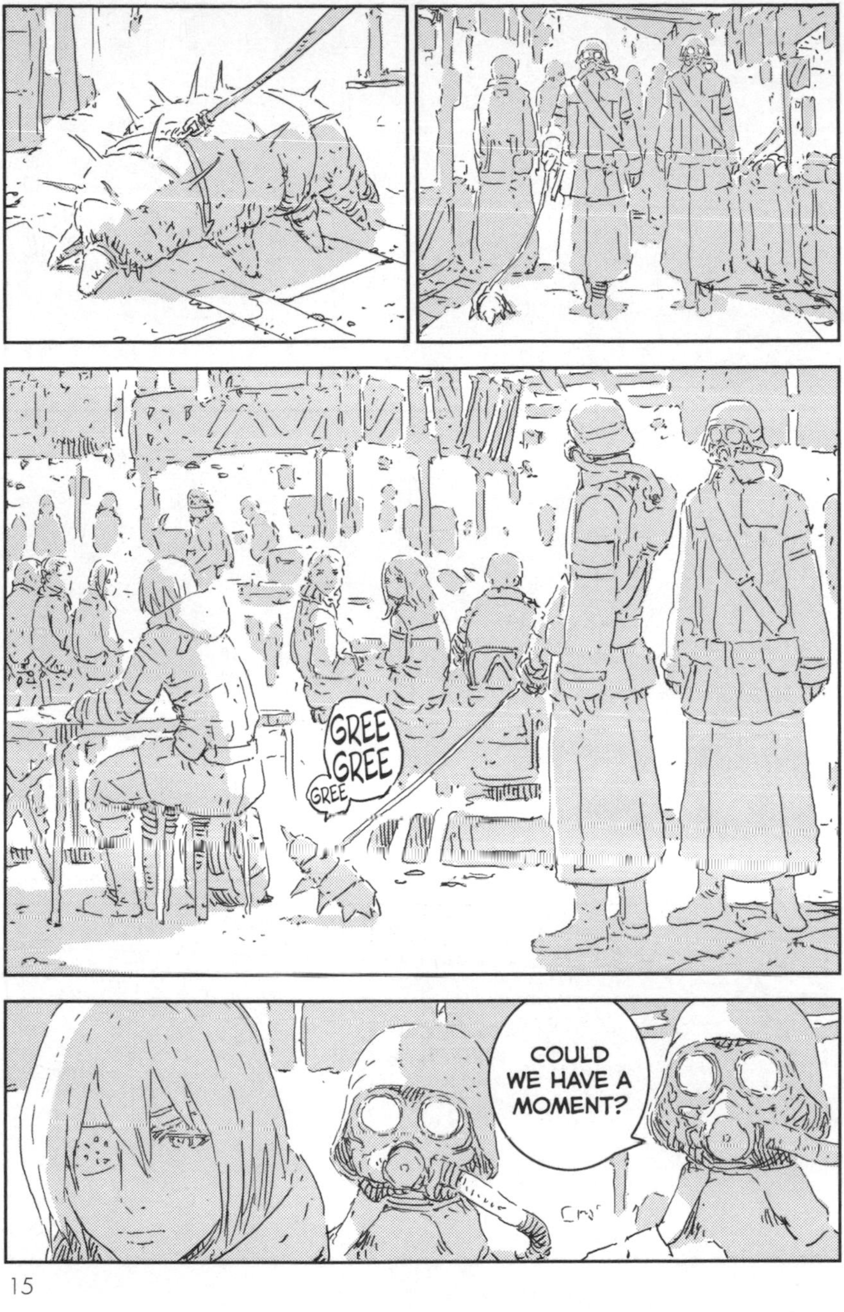
GREE
GREE
GREE
COULD WE HAVE A MOMENT?

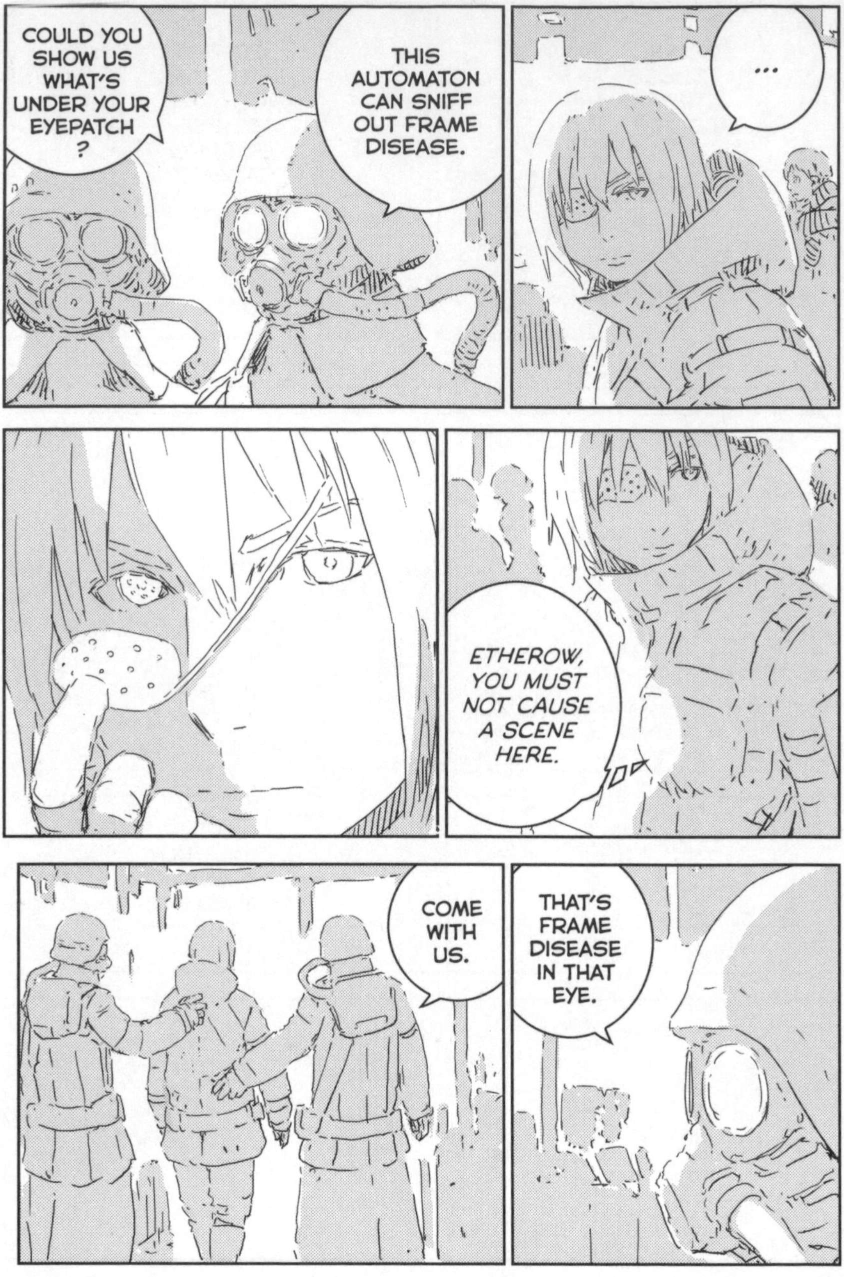
COULD YOU SHOW US WHAT'S UNDER YOUR EYEPATCH ?
THIS AUTOMATON CAN SNIFF OUT FRAME DISEASE.
...
ETHEROW, YOU MUST NOT CAUSE A SCENE HERE.
COME WITH US.
THAT'S FRAME DISEASE IN THAT EYE.

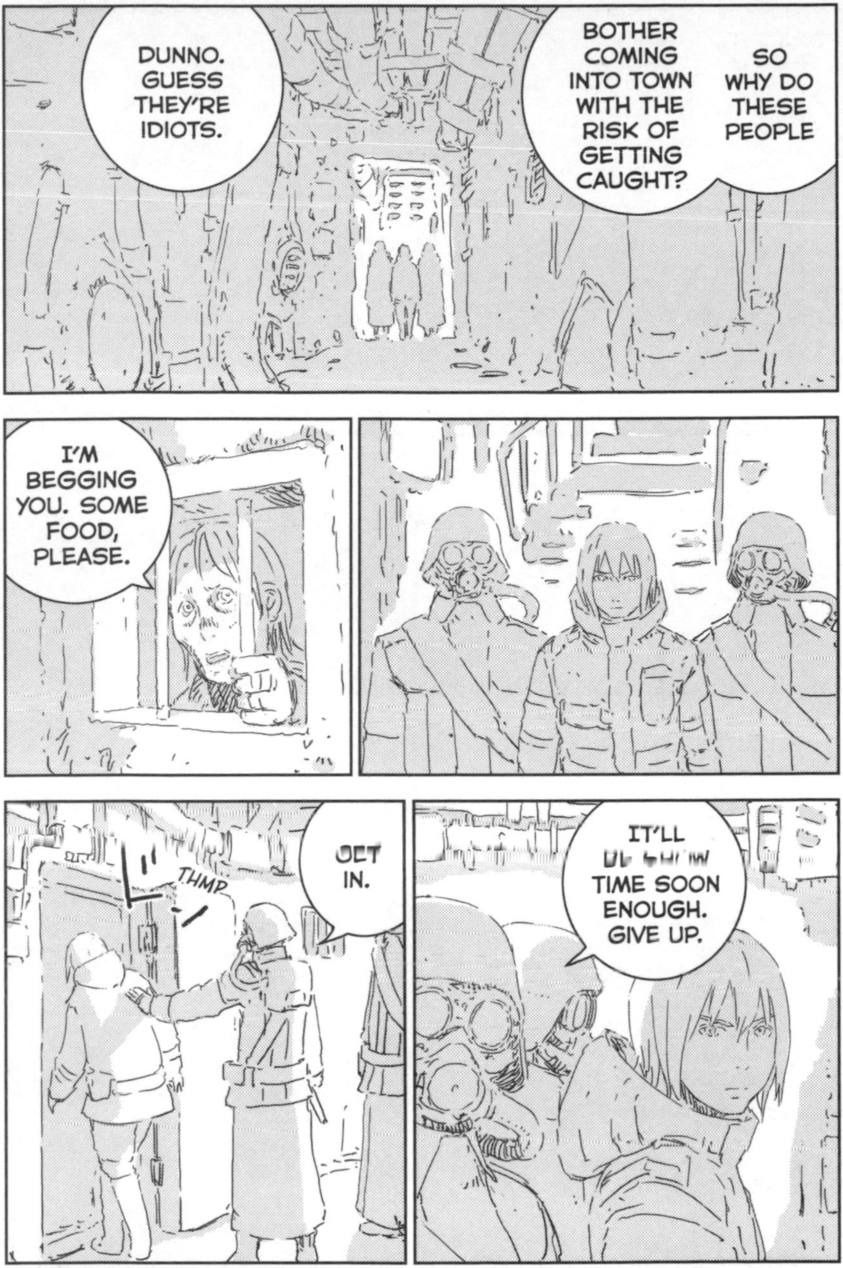
SO WHY DO THESE PEOPLE
BOTHER COMING INTO TOWN WITH THE RISK OF GETTING CAUGHT?
DUNNO. GUESS THEY'RE IDIOTS.
I'M BEGGING YOU. SOME FOOD, PLEASE.
THMP
IN.
IT'LL
TIME SOON ENOUGH. GIVE UP.

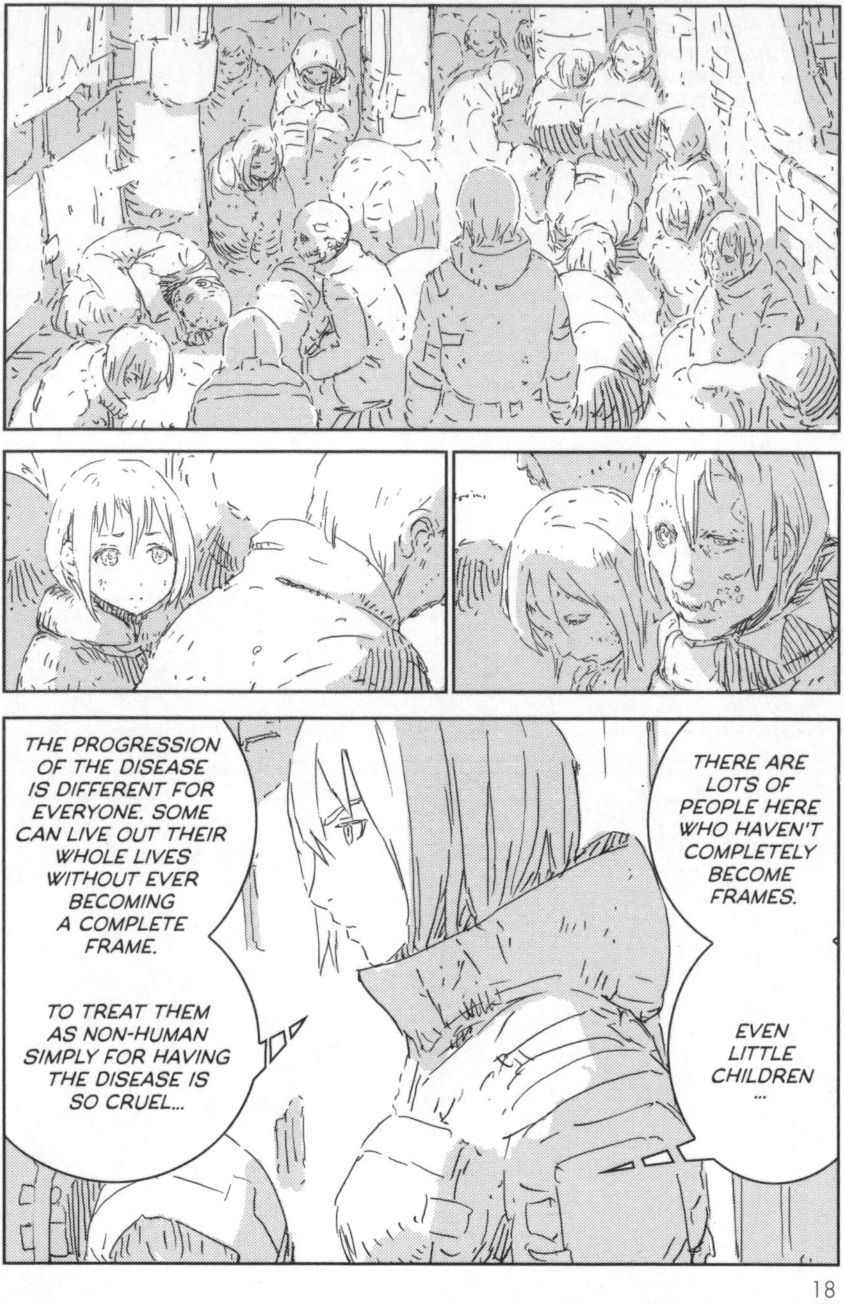
THERE ARE LOTS OF PEOPLE HERE WHO HAVEN'T COMPLETELY BECOME FRAMES.
EVEN LITTLE CHILDREN ...
THE PROGRESSION OF THE DISEASE IS DIFFERENT FOR EVERYONE. SOME CAN LIVE OUT THEIR WHOLE LIVES WITHOUT EVER BECOMING A COMPLETE FRAME.
TO TREAT THEM AS NON-HUMAN SIMPLY FOR HAVING THE DISEASE IS SO CRUEL...

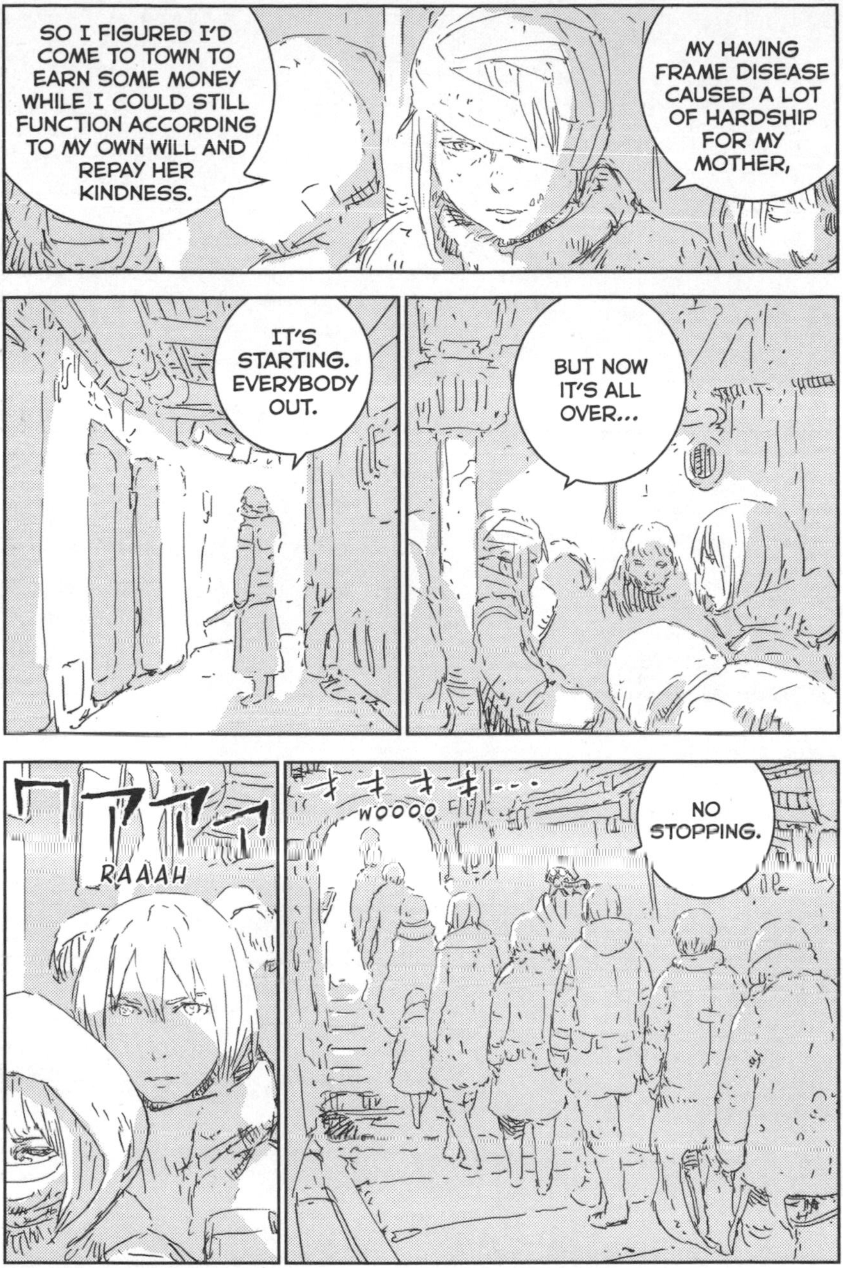
MY HAVING FRAME DISEASE CAUSED A LOT OF HARDSHIP FOR MY MOTHER,
SO I FIGURED I'D COME TO TOWN TO EARN SOME MONEY WHILE I COULD STILL FUNCTION ACCORDING TO MY OWN WILL AND REPAY HER KINDNESS.
BUT NOW IT'S ALL OVER...
IT'S STARTING. EVERYBODY OUT.
WOOOO
NO STOPPING.
RAAAH

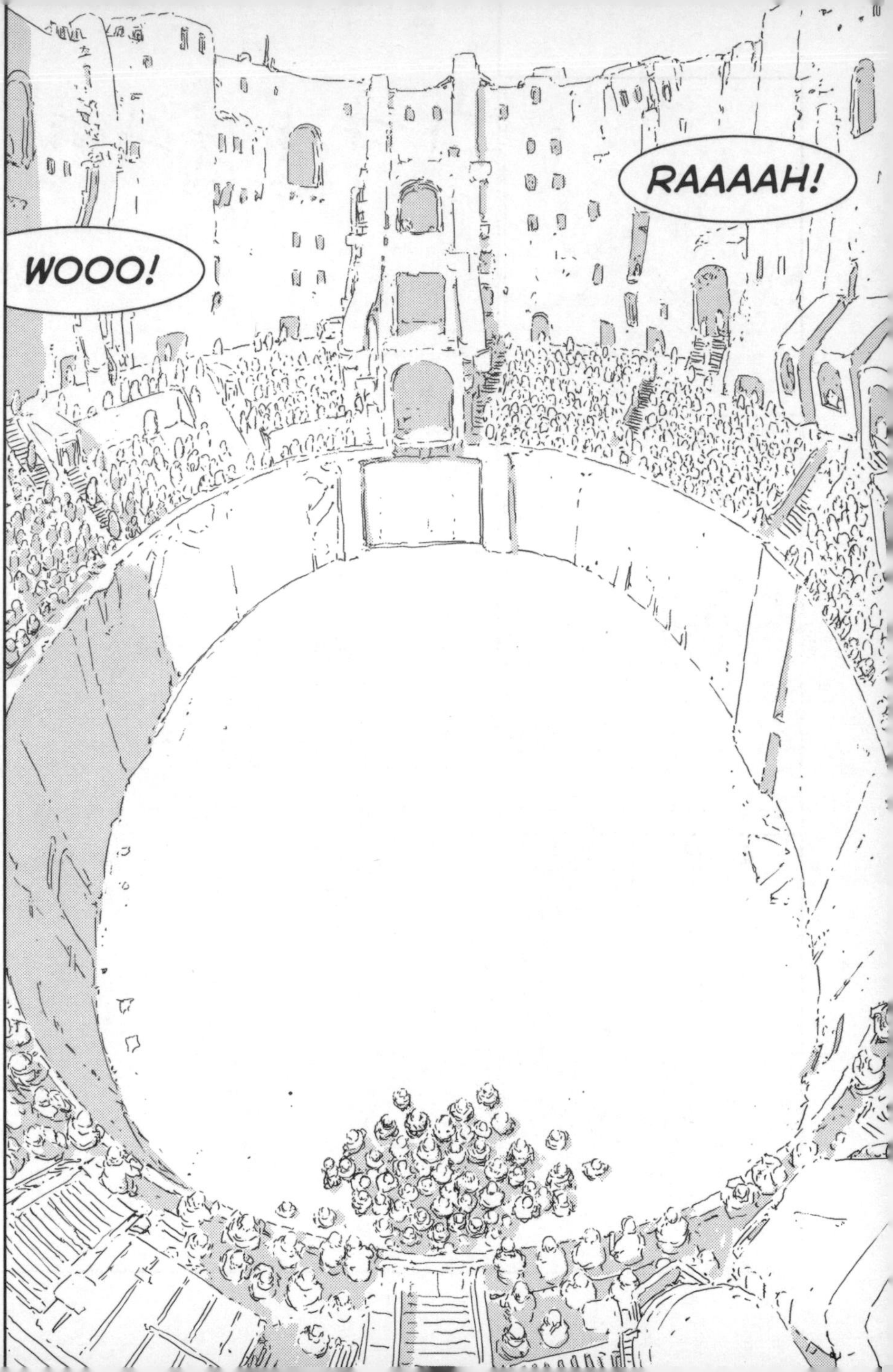
RAAAAH!
WOOO!

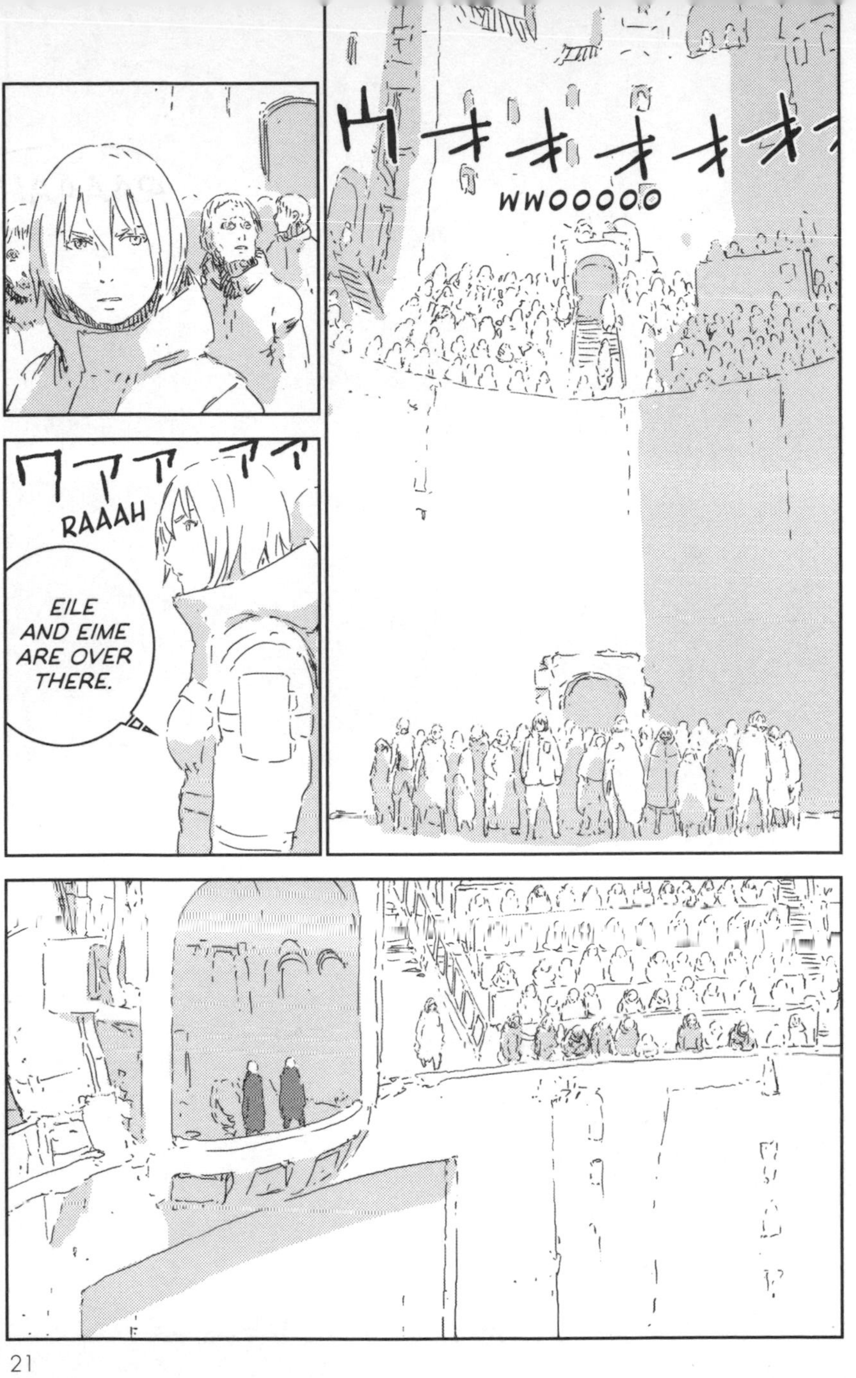
ウオオオオオ
WWOOOOO
ワアアアア
RAAAH
EILE AND EIME ARE OVER THERE.

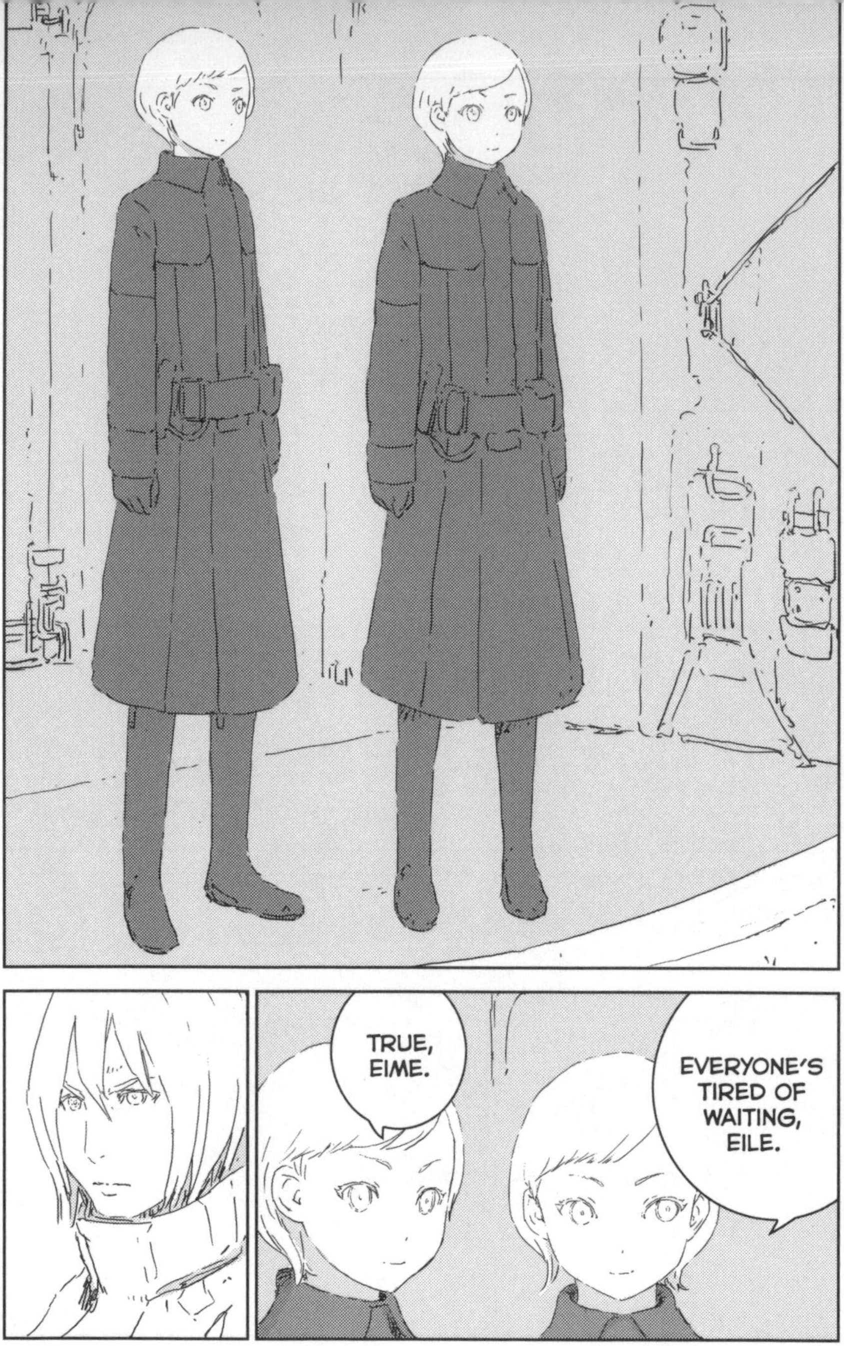
EVERYONE'S TIRED OF WAITING, EILE.
TRUE, EIME.

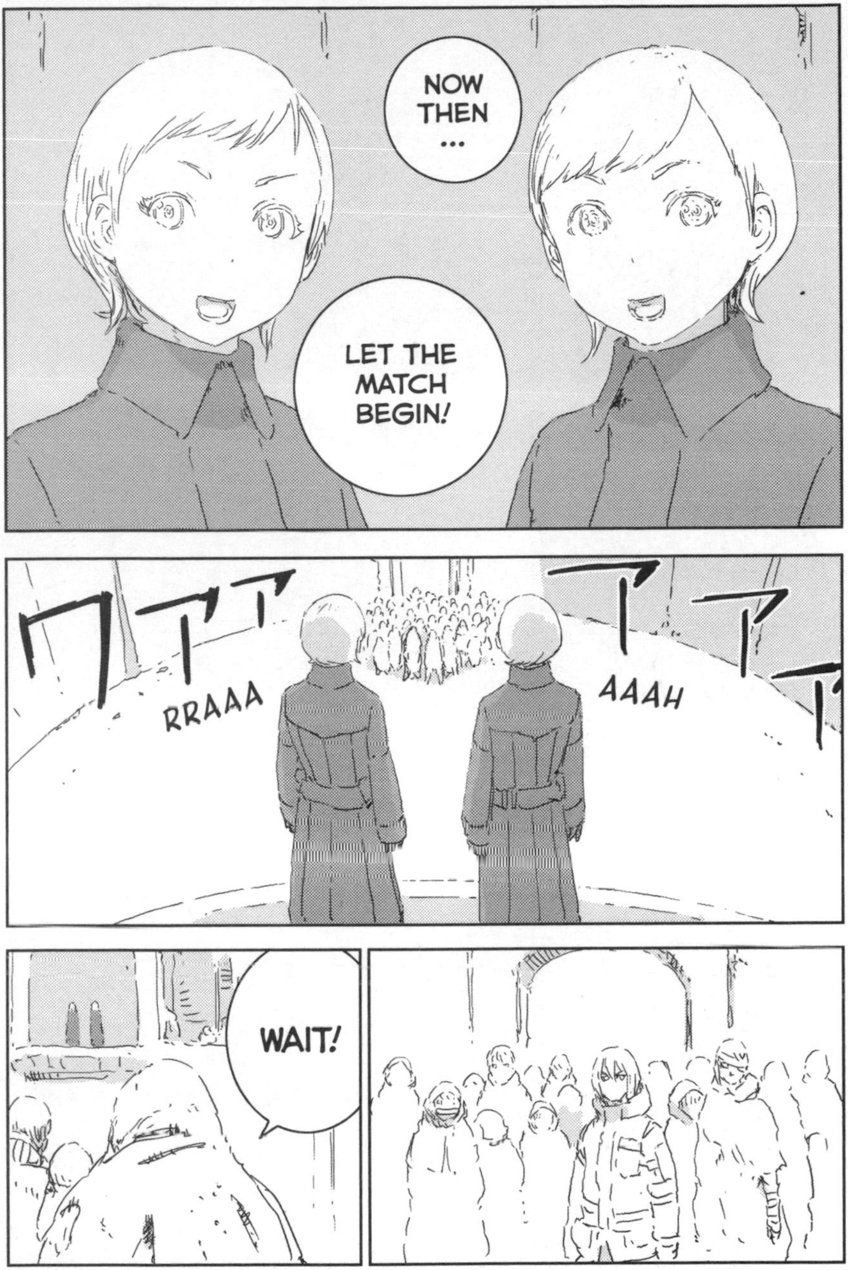
NOW THEN ...
LET THE MATCH BEGIN!
ワアア
RRAAA
アア
AAAH
WAIT!

THE FRAME DISEASE IS PUNISHMENT FOR MANKIND TURNING AGAINST THE CORE.

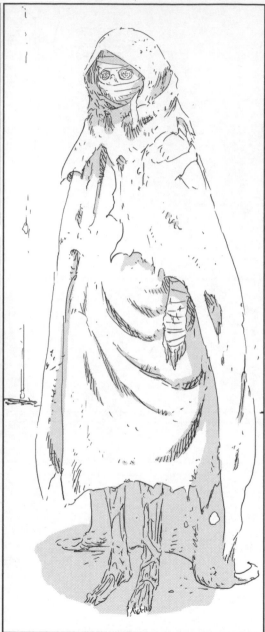

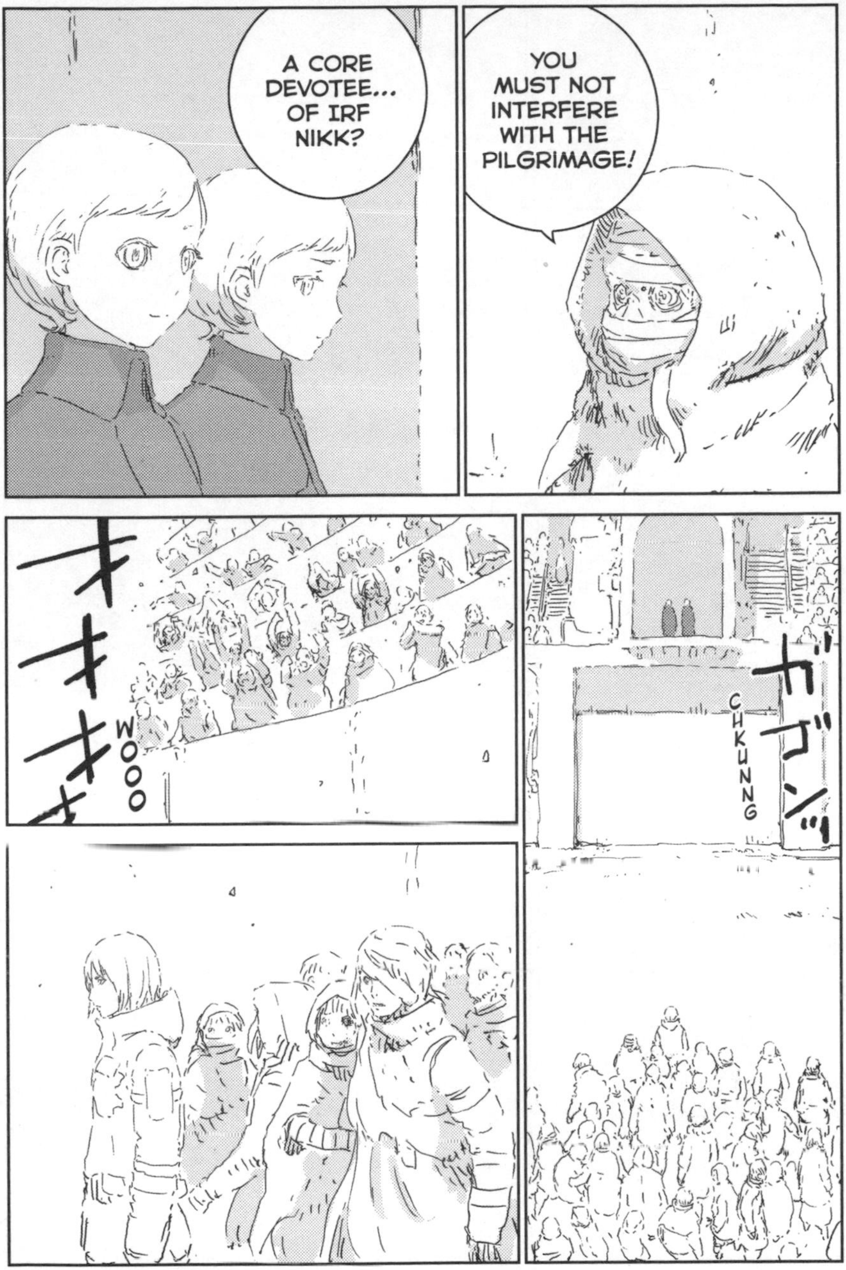
YOU MUST NOT INTERFERE WITH THE PILGRIMAGE!
A CORE DEVOTEE... OF IRF NIKK?
キキキキ
WOOO
ガゴンッ
CHKUNNG

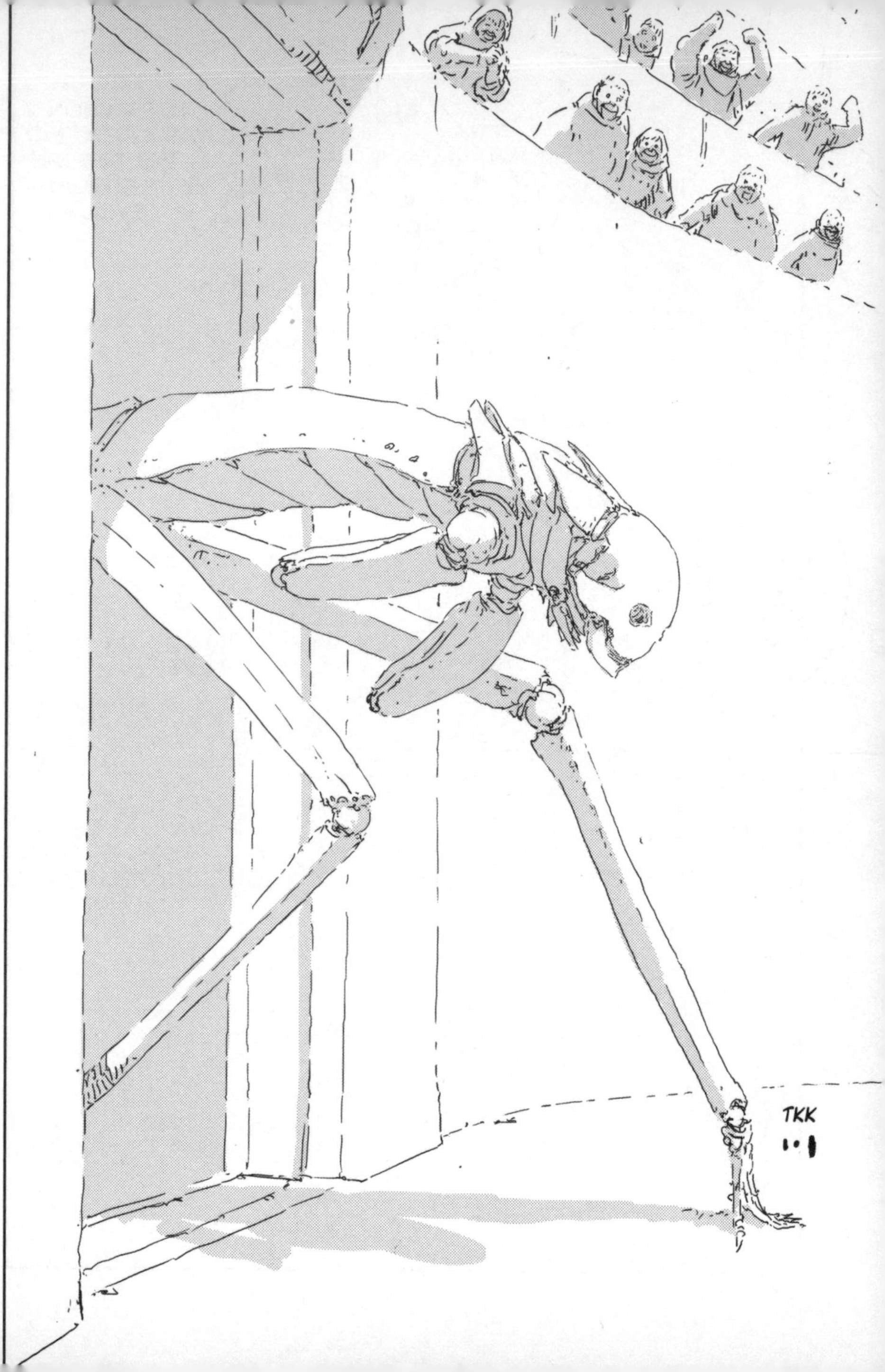
TKK

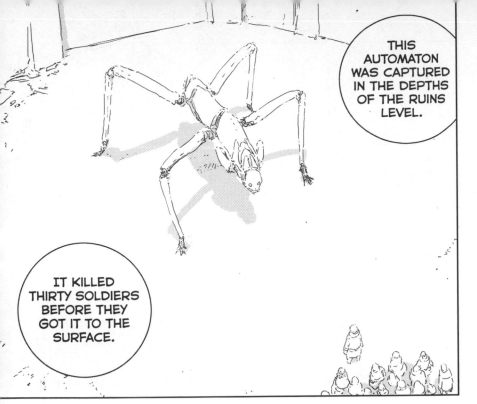

THIS AUTOMATON WAS CAPTURED IN THE DEPTHS OF THE RUINS LEVEL.

IT KILLED THIRTY SOLDIERS BEFORE THEY GOT IT TO THE SURFACE.

IF YOU BEAT IT, WE'LL GRANT ANY WISH YOU DESIRE.

GIMME A BREAK... HOW THE HELL IS THIS EVEN A CONTEST ...?

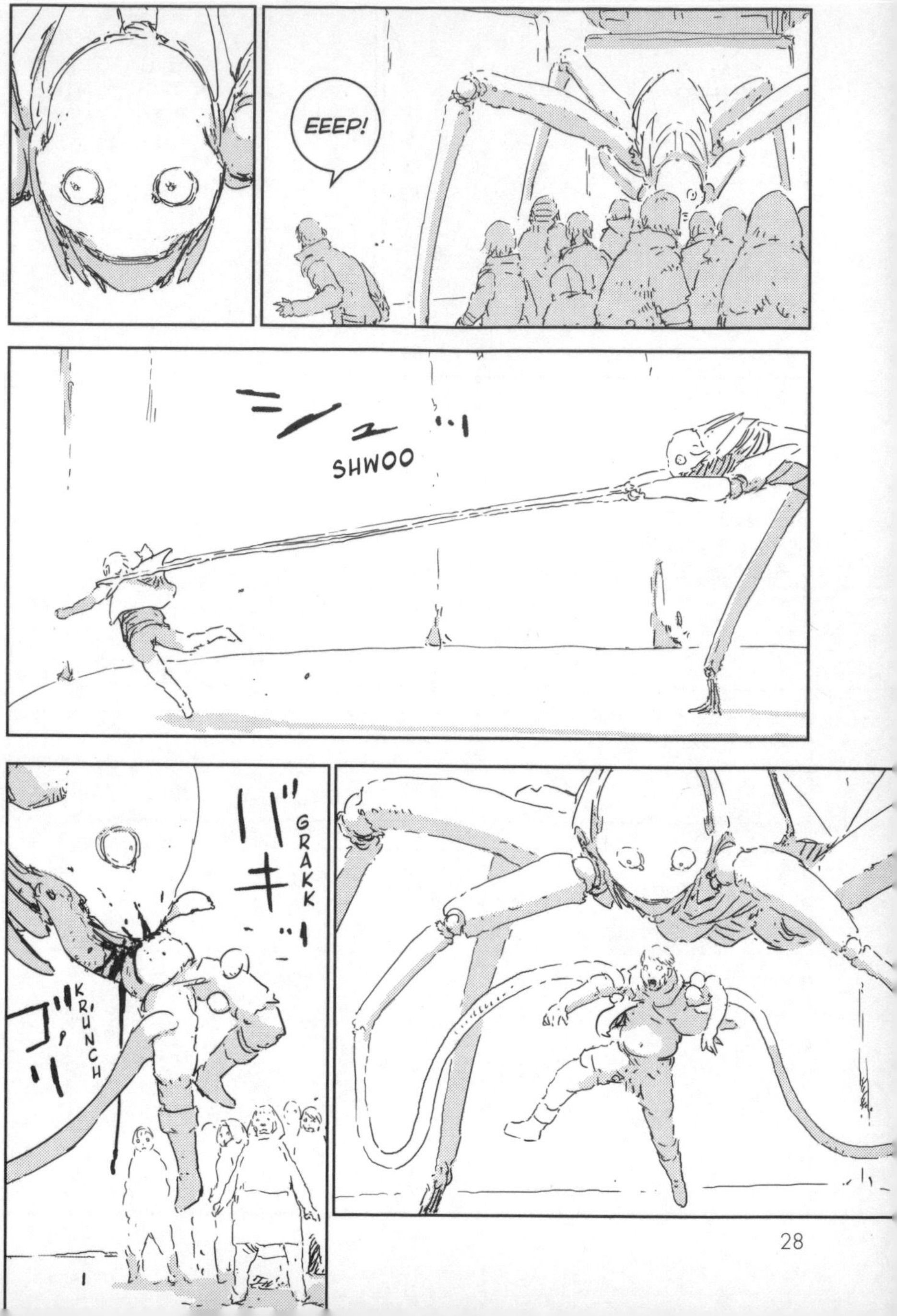
EEEP!
シュ…
SHWOO
バキ…
GRAKK
ゴリ
KRUNCH

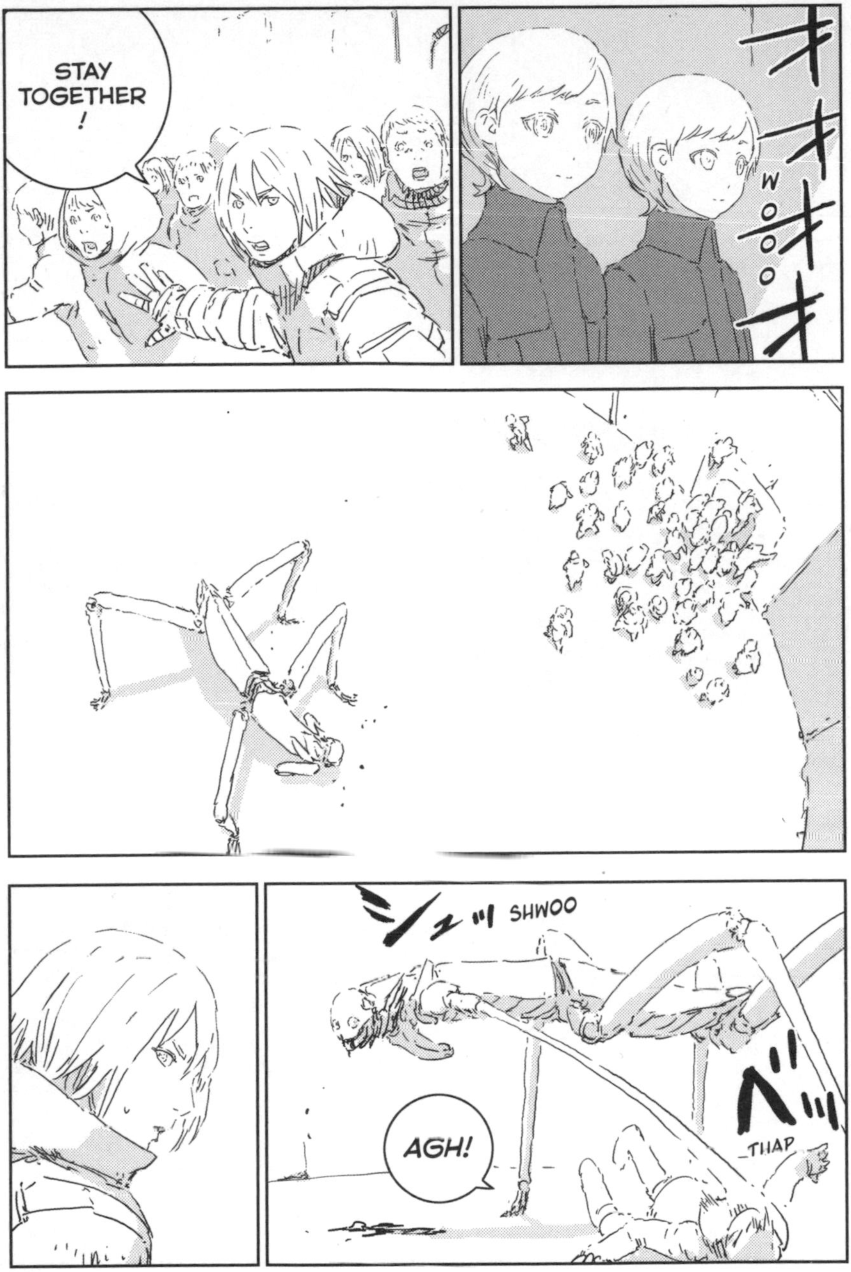

STAY TOGETHER!
オオオオオ
WOOOO
シュッ
SHWOO
ベッ
THAP
AGH!

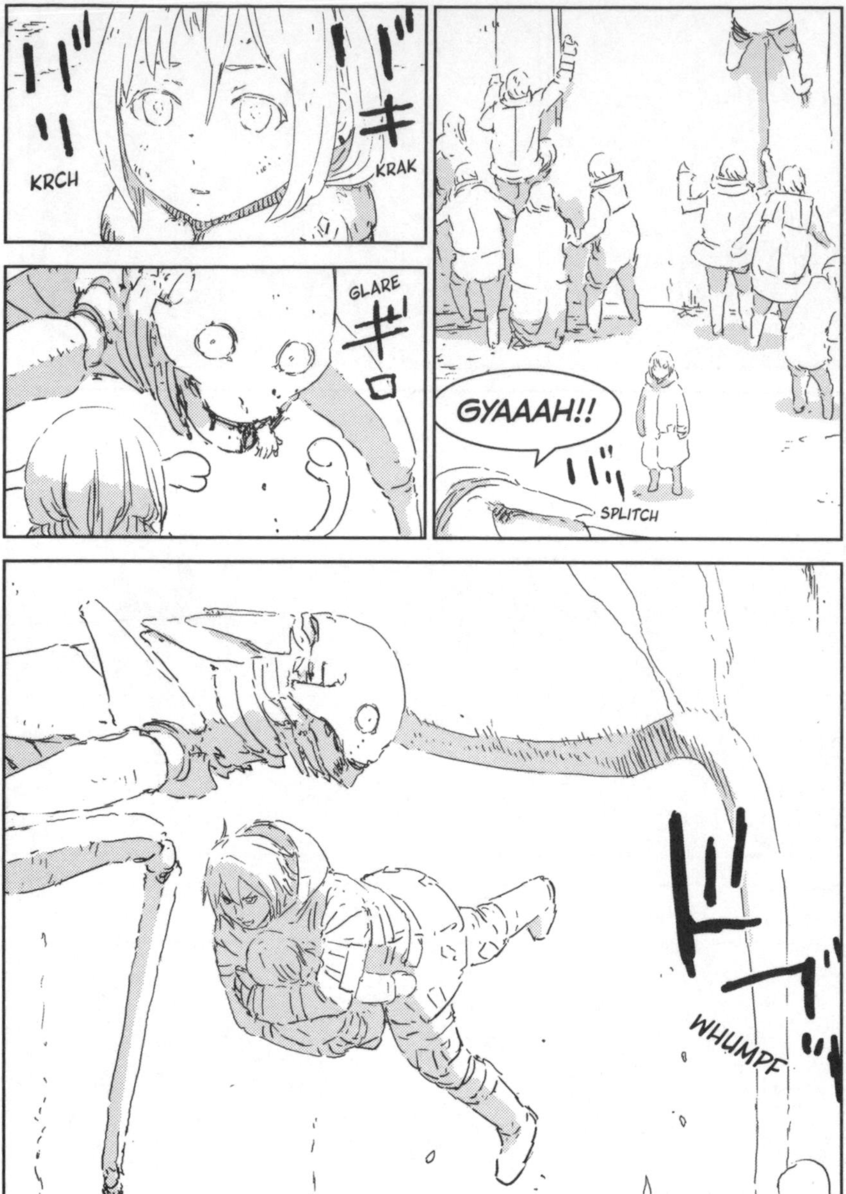

GYAAAH!!
SPLITCH
KRCH
KRAK
GLARE
WHUMPF

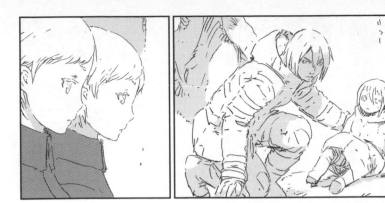

FWO

OMF

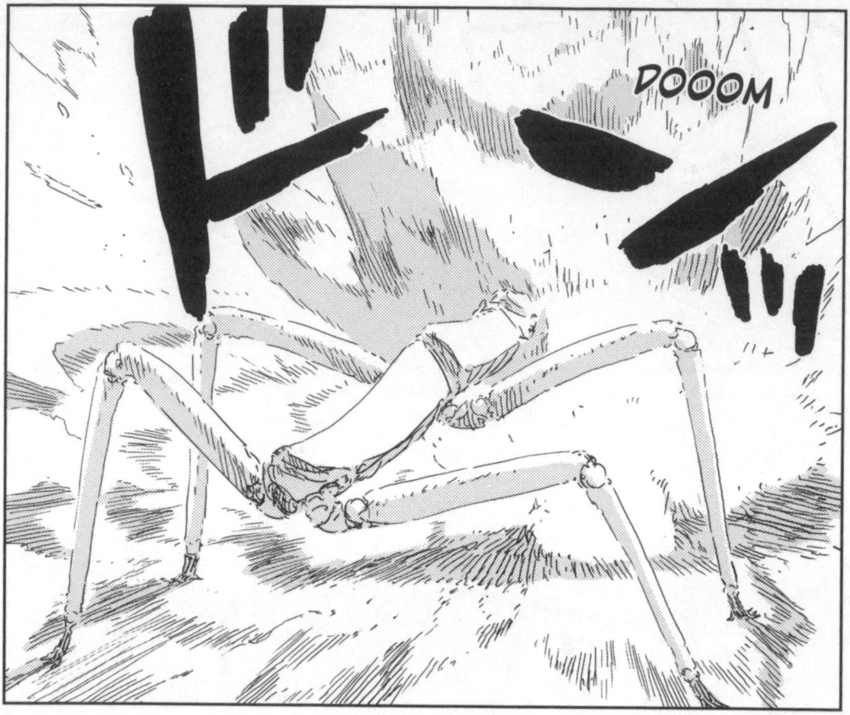
DOOOM

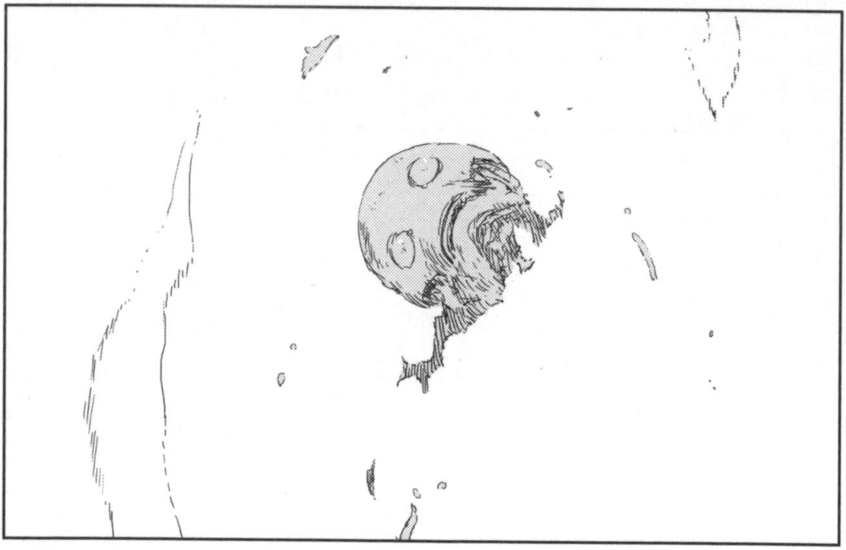

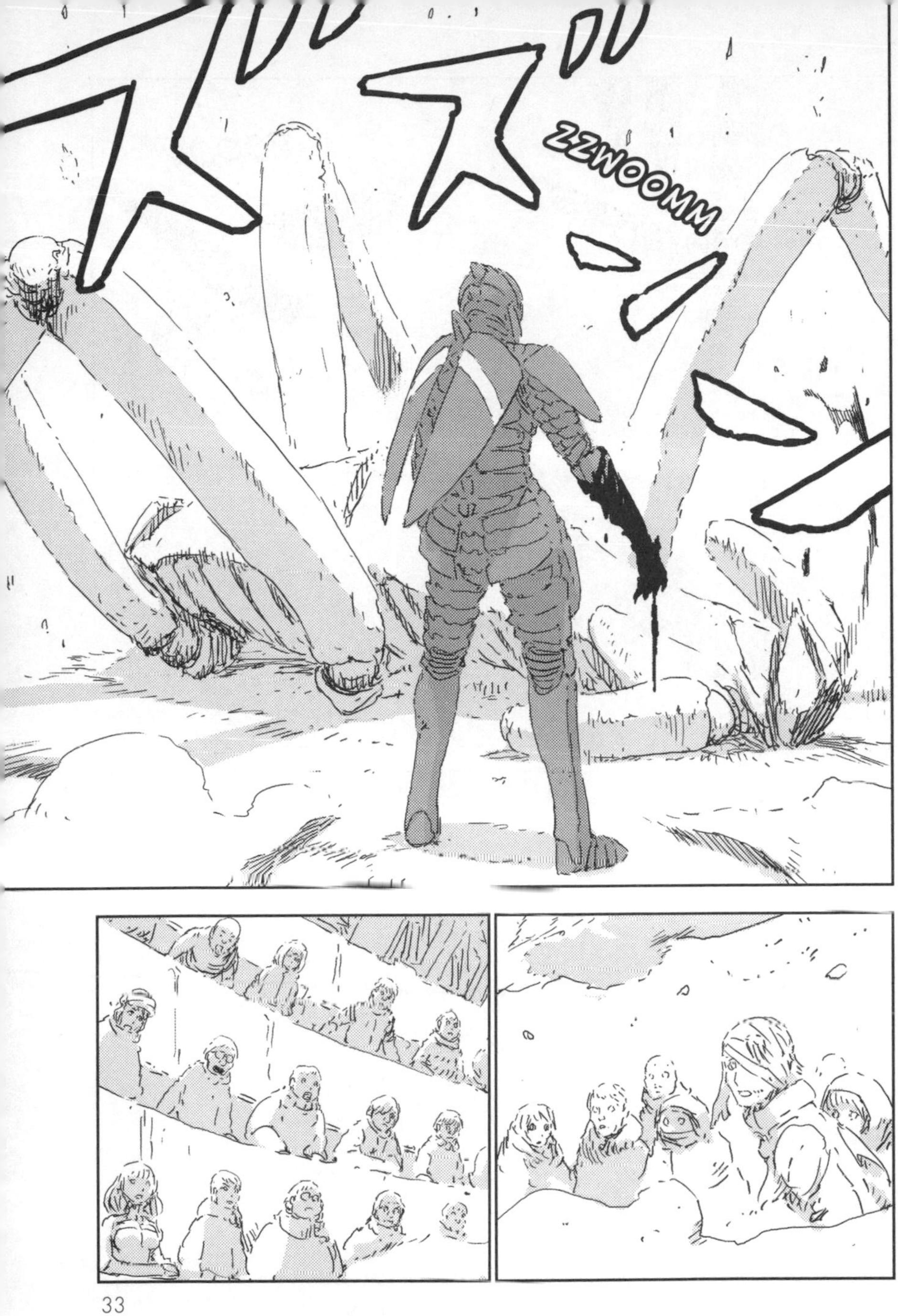
ZZWOOMM

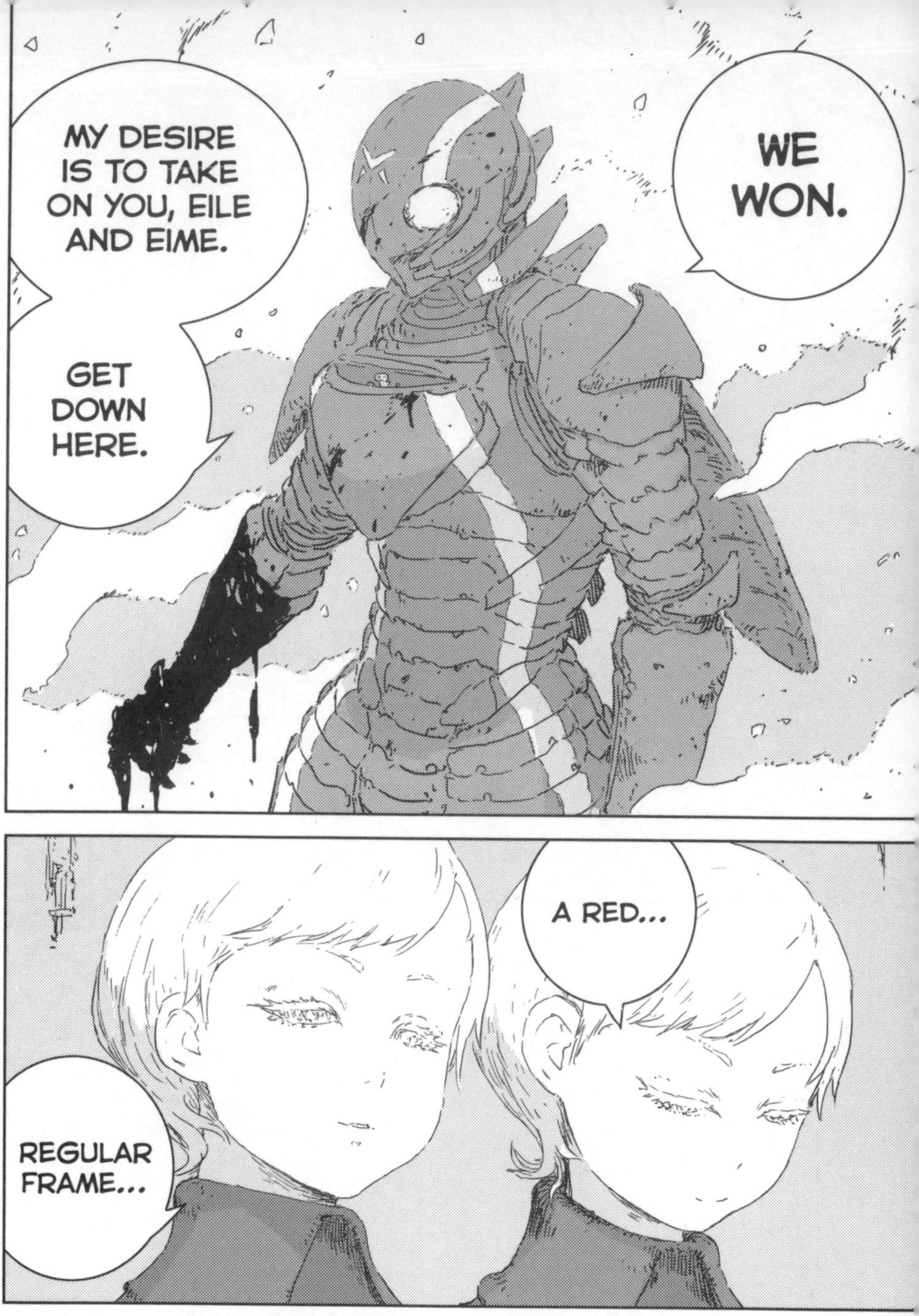
WE WON.
MY DESIRE IS TO TAKE ON YOU, EILE AND EIME.
GET DOWN HERE.
A RED...
REGULAR FRAME...

CHAPTER 04 END

APOSIMZ

CHAPTER 05

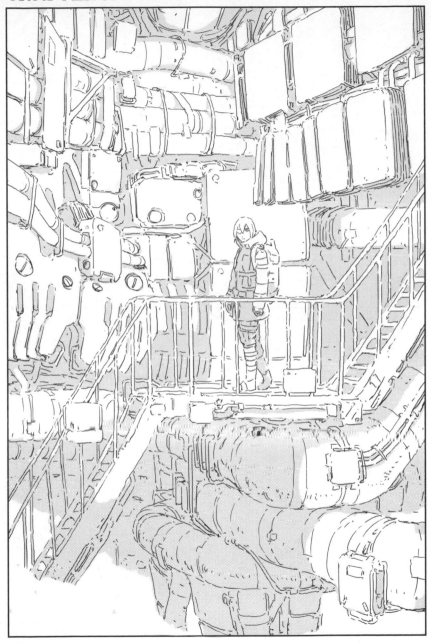

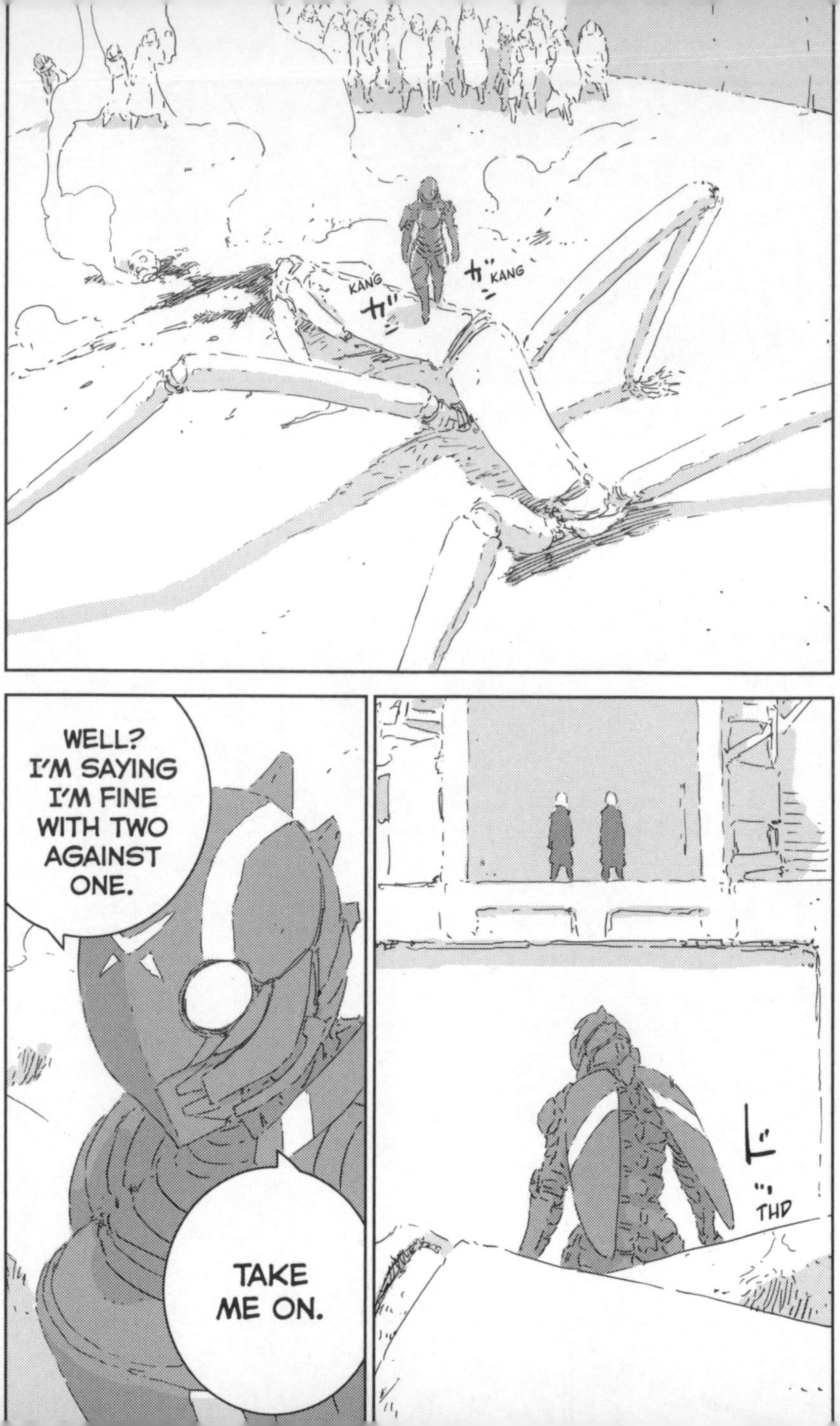
KANG
KANG
THD
WELL? I'M SAYING I'M FINE WITH TWO AGAINST ONE.
TAKE ME ON.

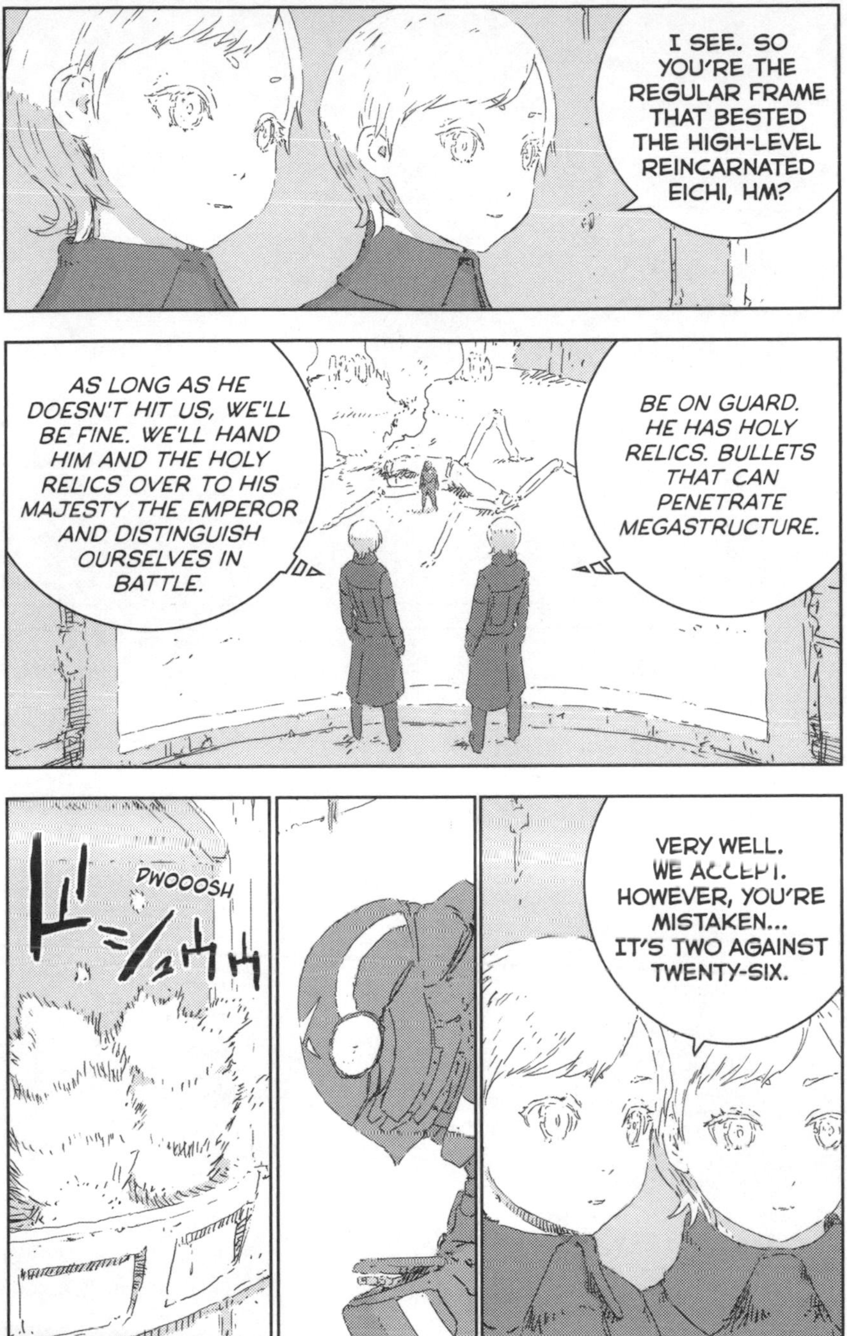
I SEE. SO YOU'RE THE REGULAR FRAME THAT BESTED THE HIGH-LEVEL REINCARNATED EICHI, HM?
BE ON GUARD. HE HAS HOLY RELICS. BULLETS THAT CAN PENETRATE MEGASTRUCTURE.
AS LONG AS HE DOESN'T HIT US, WE'LL BE FINE. WE'LL HAND HIM AND THE HOLY RELICS OVER TO HIS MAJESTY THE EMPEROR AND DISTINGUISH OURSELVES IN BATTLE.
VERY WELL. WE ACCEPT. HOWEVER, YOU'RE MISTAKEN... IT'S TWO AGAINST TWENTY-SIX.
DWOOOSH

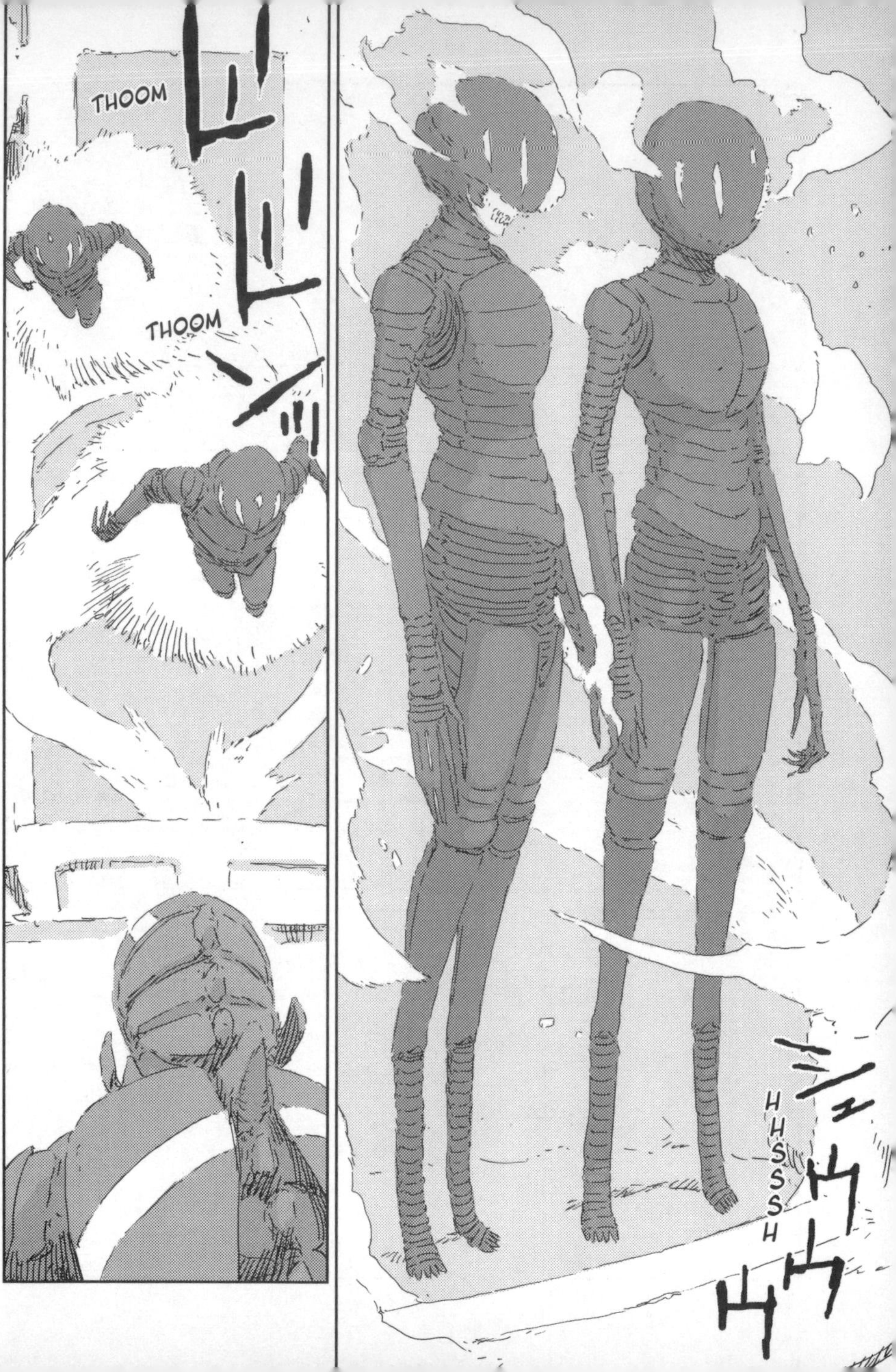
HHSSSH
THOOM
THOOM

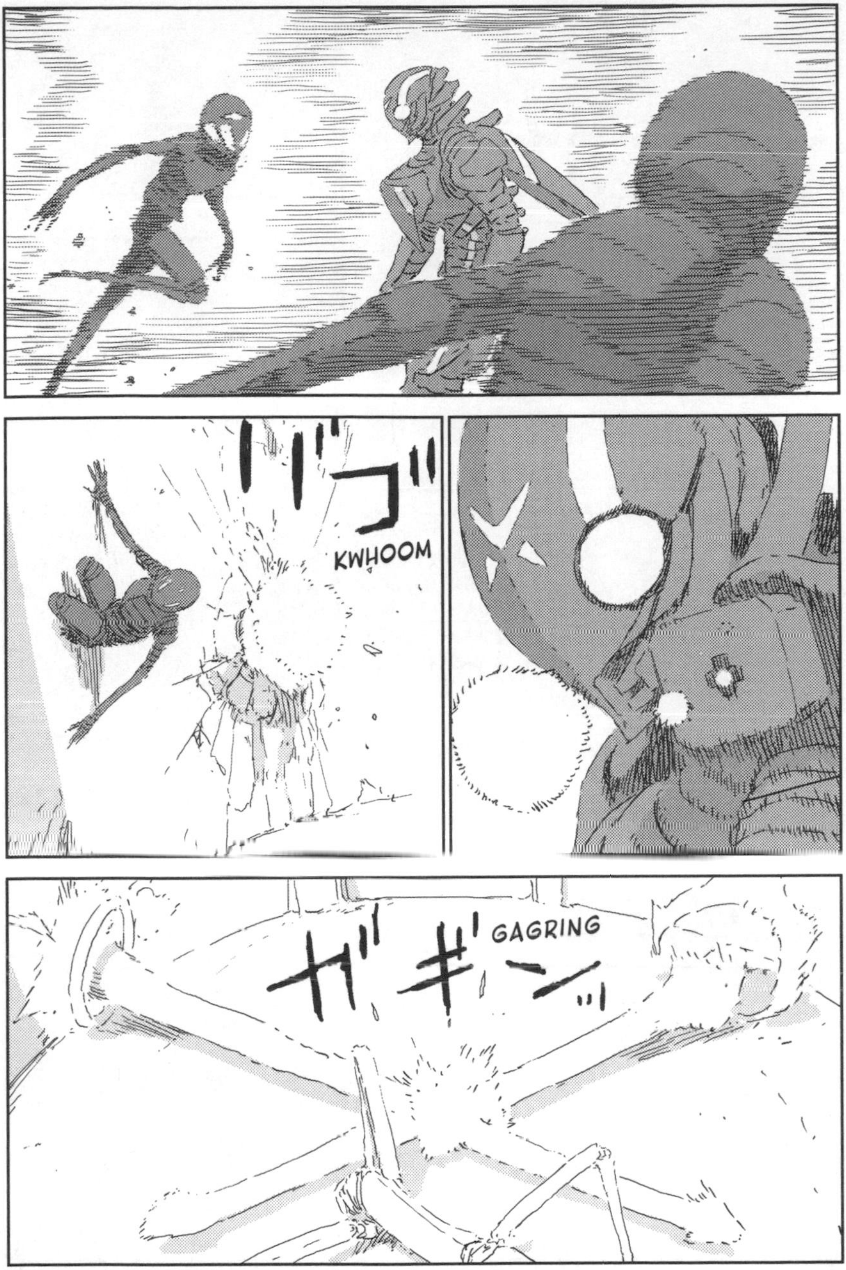
KWHOOM
ガギンッ
GAGRING

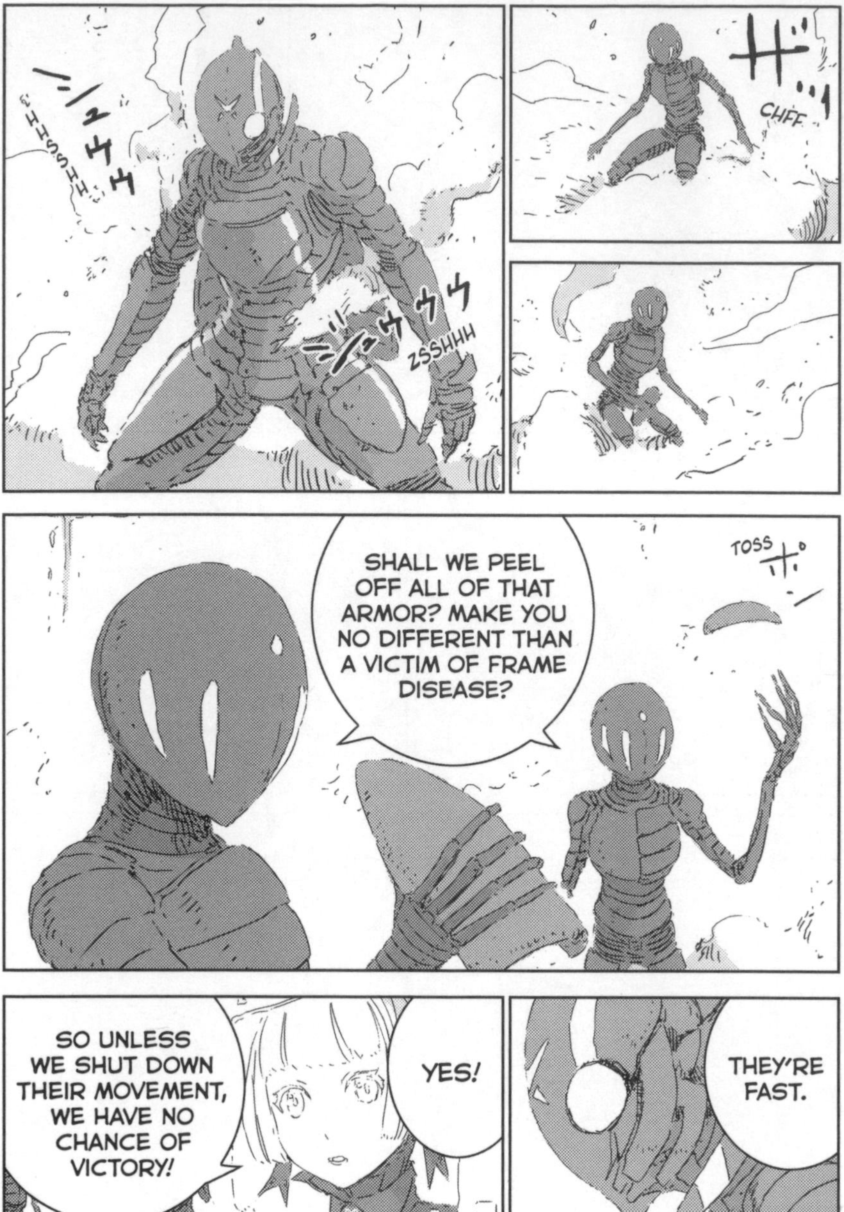
ザッ
CHFF
シュウウ
シュウウウ
ZSSHHH
TOSS
SHALL WE PEEL OFF ALL OF THAT ARMOR? MAKE YOU NO DIFFERENT THAN A VICTIM OF FRAME DISEASE?
THEY'RE FAST.
YES!
SO UNLESS WE SHUT DOWN THEIR MOVEMENT, WE HAVE NO CHANCE OF VICTORY!

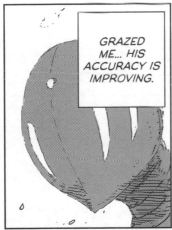

GRAZED
ME... HIS
ACCURACY IS
IMPROVING.

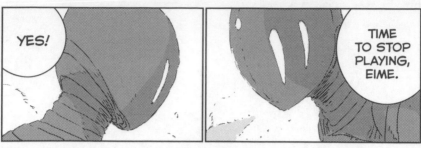

YES!

TIME TO STOP PLAYING, EIME.

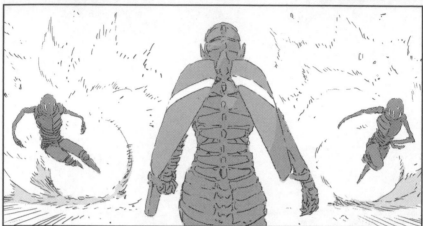

TITANIA! NOW!

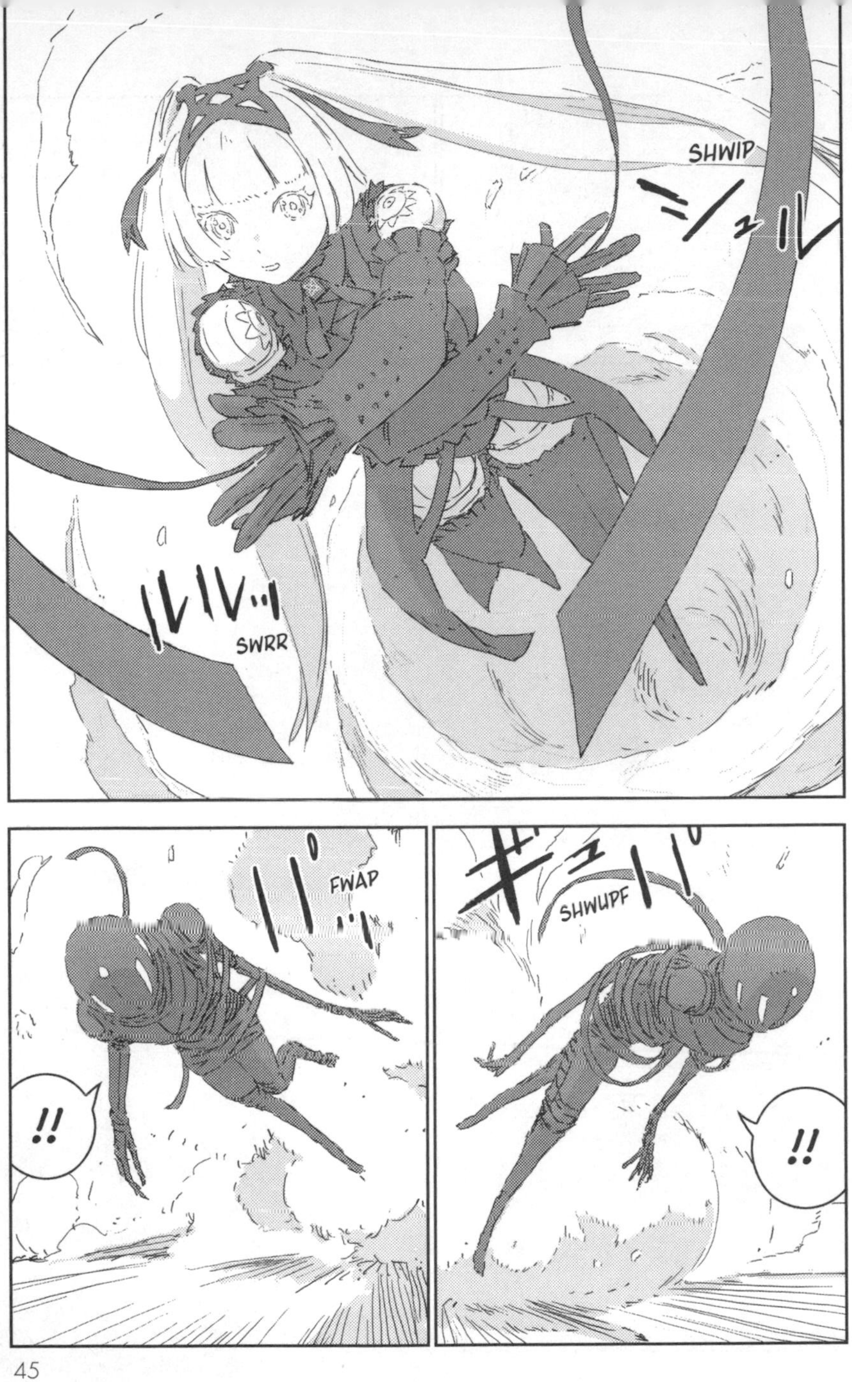
SHWIP
シュル
ルルルッ
SWRR
SHWUPF
!!
FWAP
!!

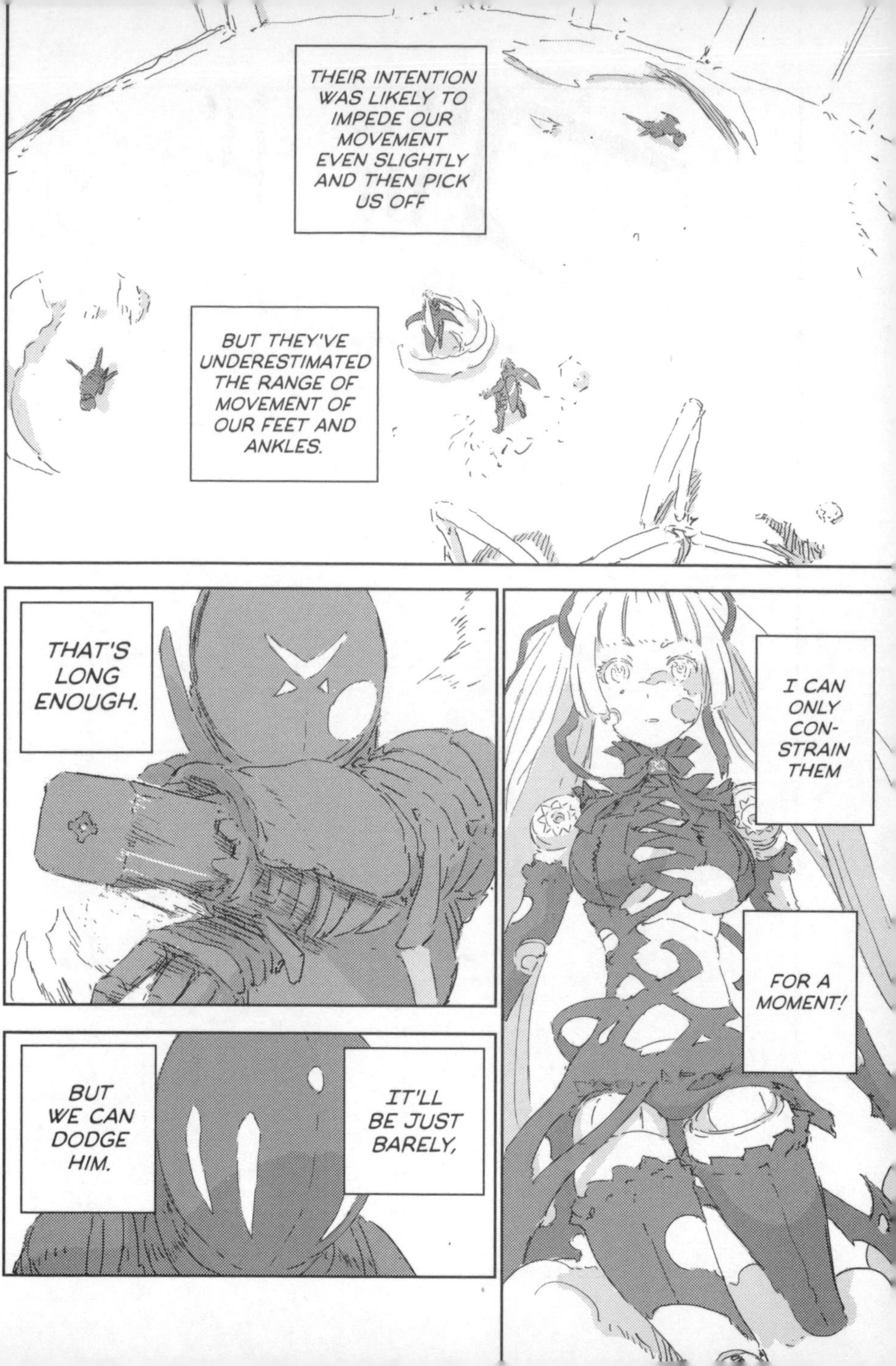
THEIR INTENTION WAS LIKELY TO IMPEDE OUR MOVEMENT EVEN SLIGHTLY AND THEN PICK US OFF
BUT THEY'VE UNDERESTIMATED THE RANGE OF MOVEMENT OF OUR FEET AND ANKLES.
I CAN ONLY CON-STRAIN THEM
FOR A MOMENT!
THAT'S LONG ENOUGH.
IT'LL BE JUST BARELY,
BUT WE CAN DODGE HIM.

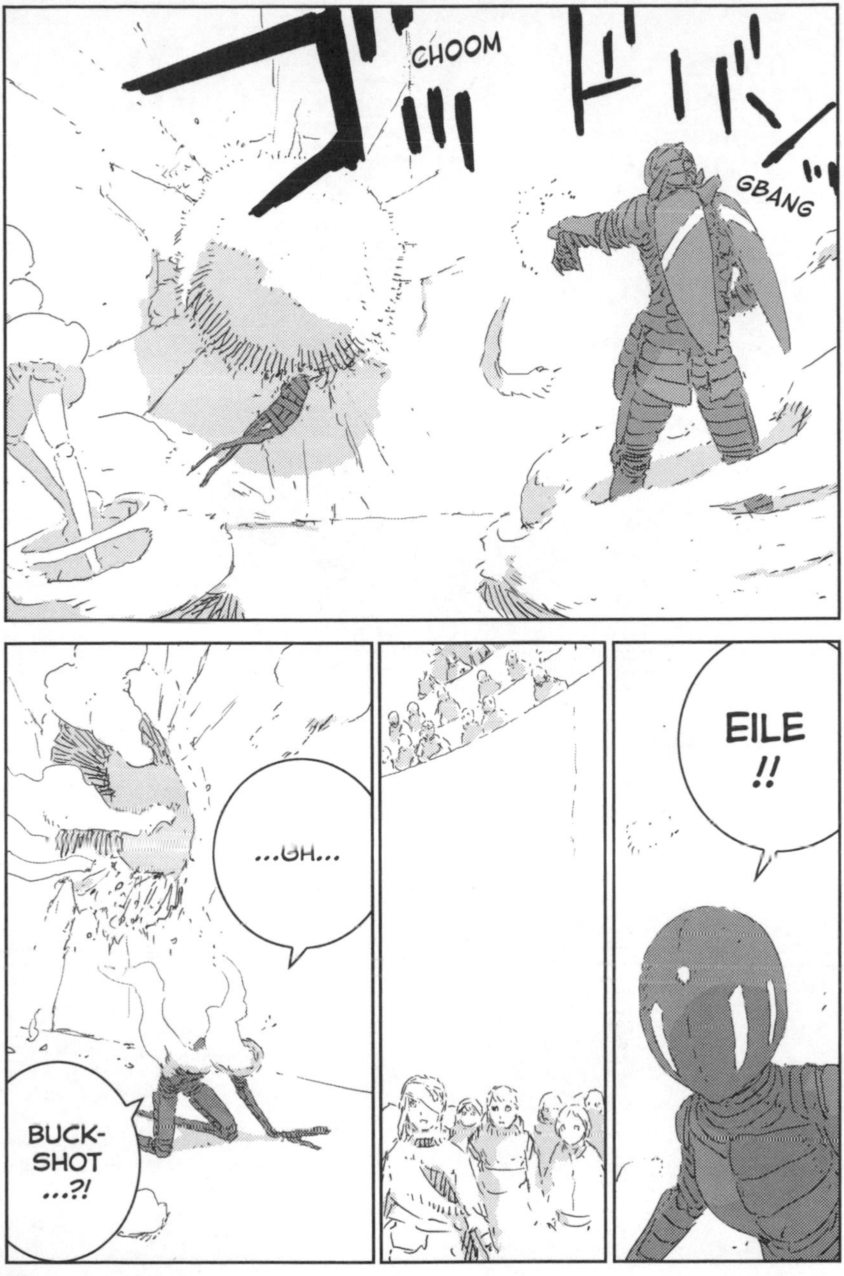
GBANG
CHOOM
EILE !!
...GH...
BUCK-SHOT ...?!

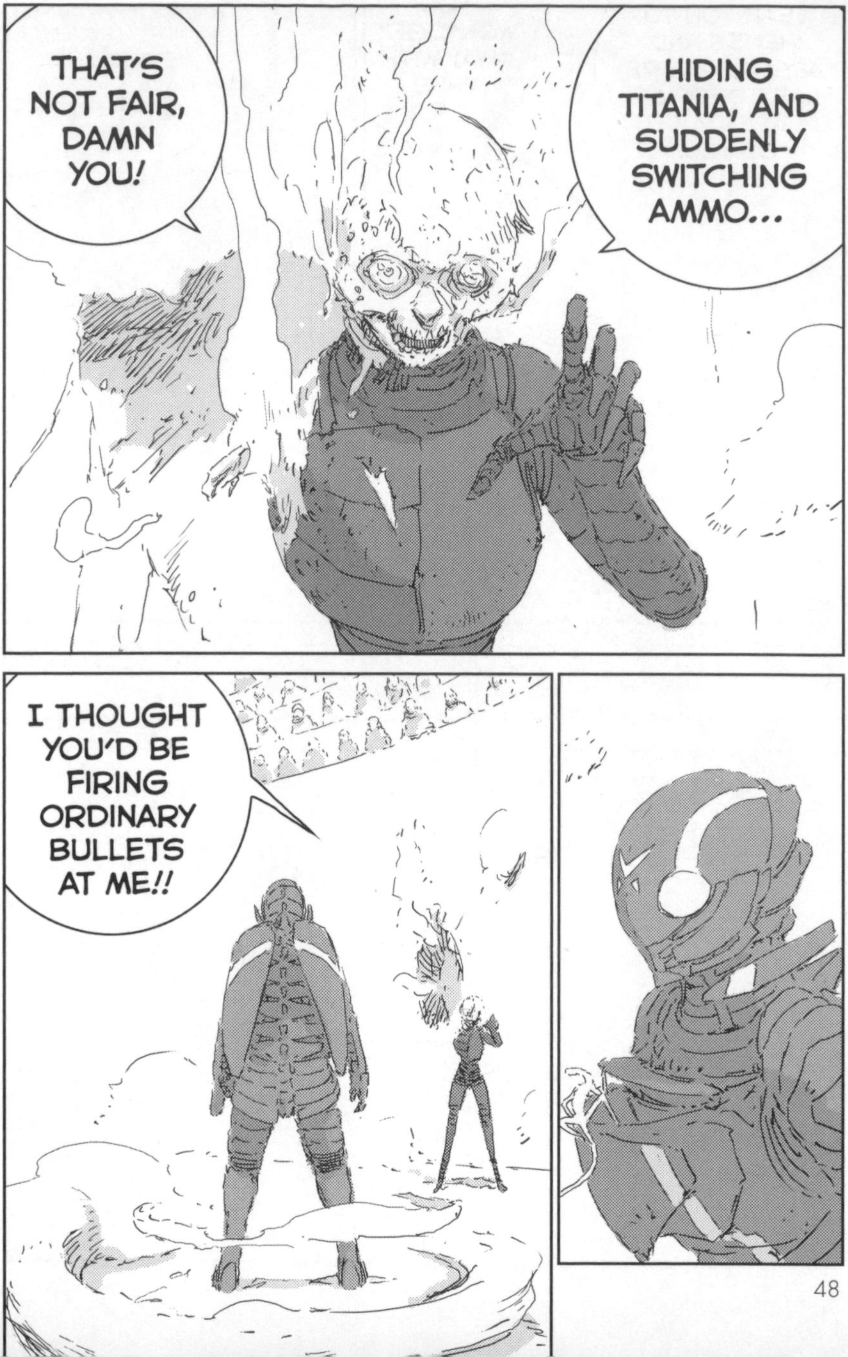
HIDING TITANIA, AND SUDDENLY SWITCHING AMMO...
THAT'S NOT FAIR, DAMN YOU!
I THOUGHT YOU'D BE FIRING ORDINARY BULLETS AT ME!!

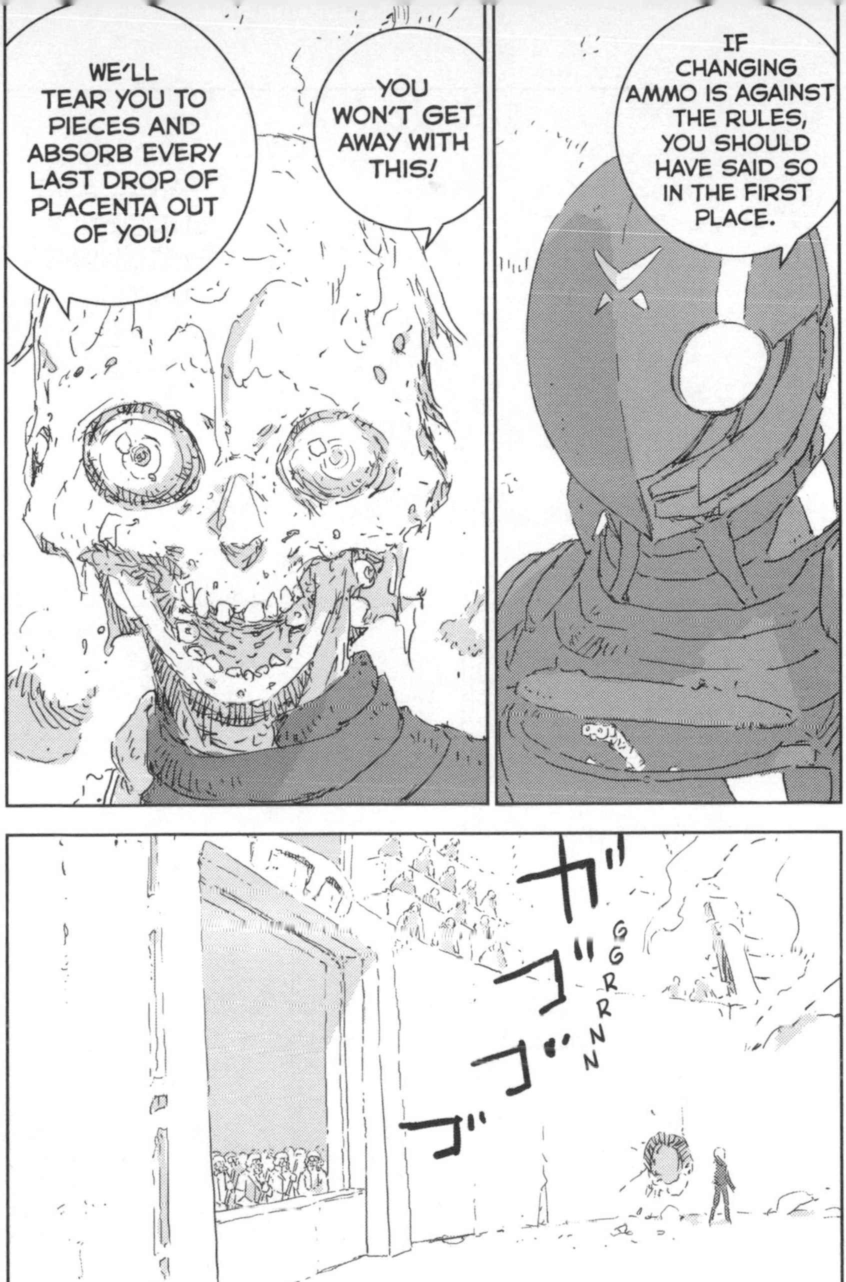
IF CHANGING AMMO IS AGAINST THE RULES, YOU SHOULD HAVE SAID SO IN THE FIRST PLACE.
YOU WON'T GET AWAY WITH THIS!
WE'LL TEAR YOU TO PIECES AND ABSORB EVERY LAST DROP OF PLACENTA OUT OF YOU!
ガゴゴゴ
GGRRNN

SEIZE HIM!!

THEY'RE ARMED WITH REINFORCED NETTING!

!

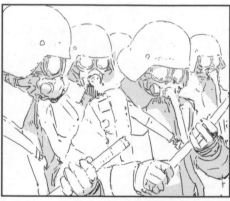

IT'S A WEAPON FOR SUPPRESSING PLACENTA ACTIVITY! BE CAREFUL!

RIGID FIBER CAPTURE NET ROD

SWITCHING LOADED ROUNDS

AIR

ピピピピ
BIP BIP BIP BIP

ガッチン
GCHAK

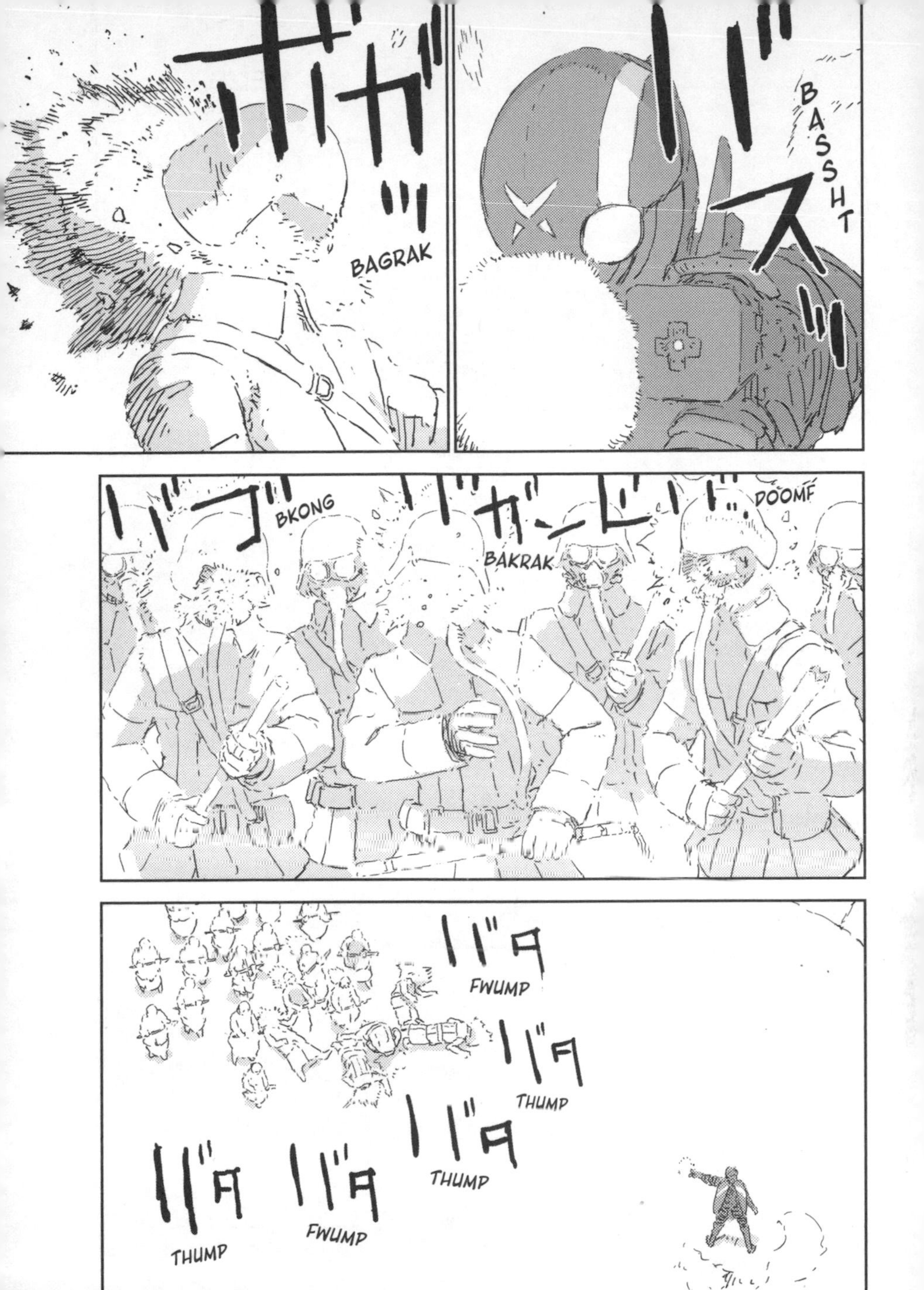

BASSHT
BAGRAK
DOOMF
BAKRAK
BKONG
バタ
FWUMP
バタ
THUMP
バタ
THUMP
バタ
FWUMP
バタ
THUMP

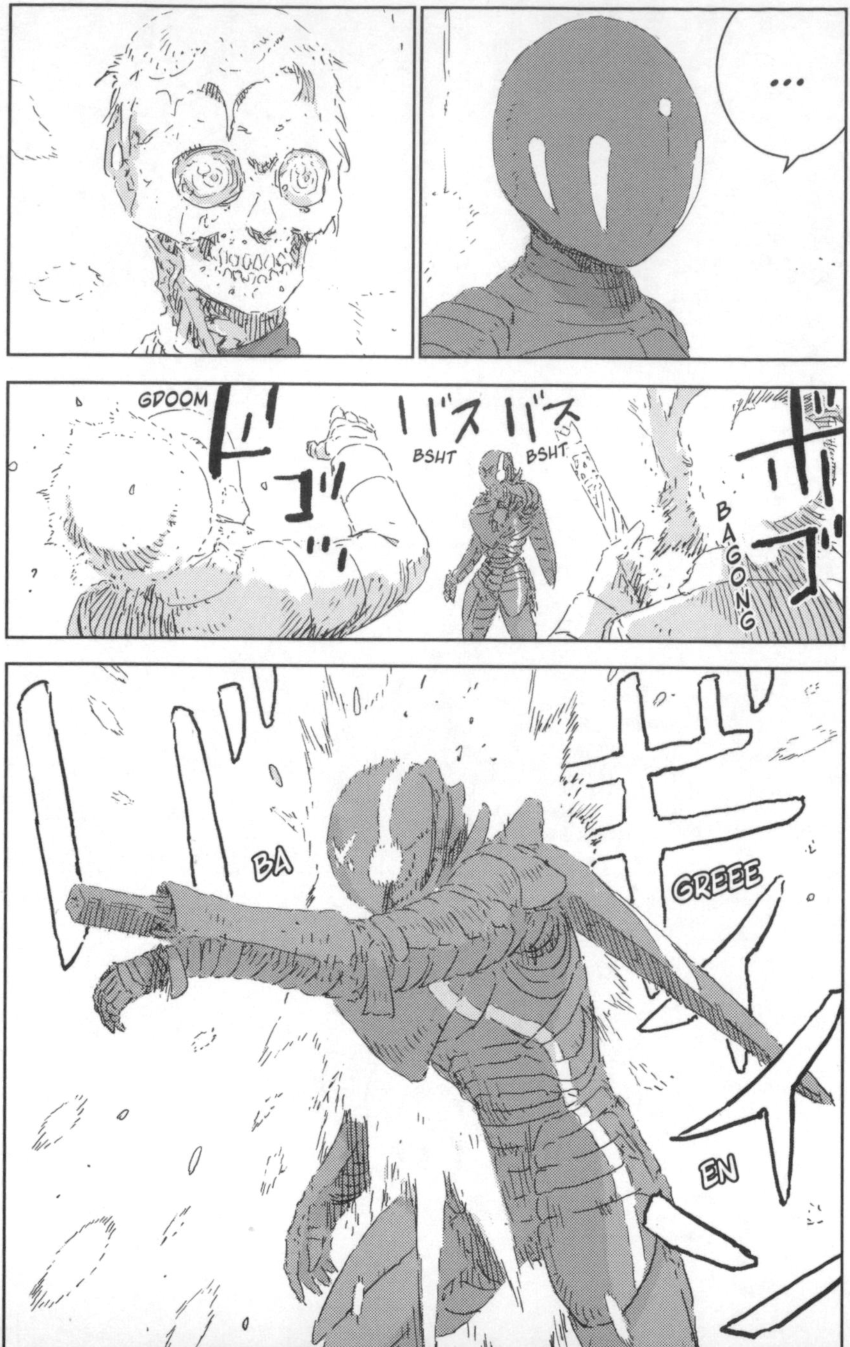
...
BAGONG
BSHT
BSHT
バスバス
GDOOM
GREEE
EN
BA

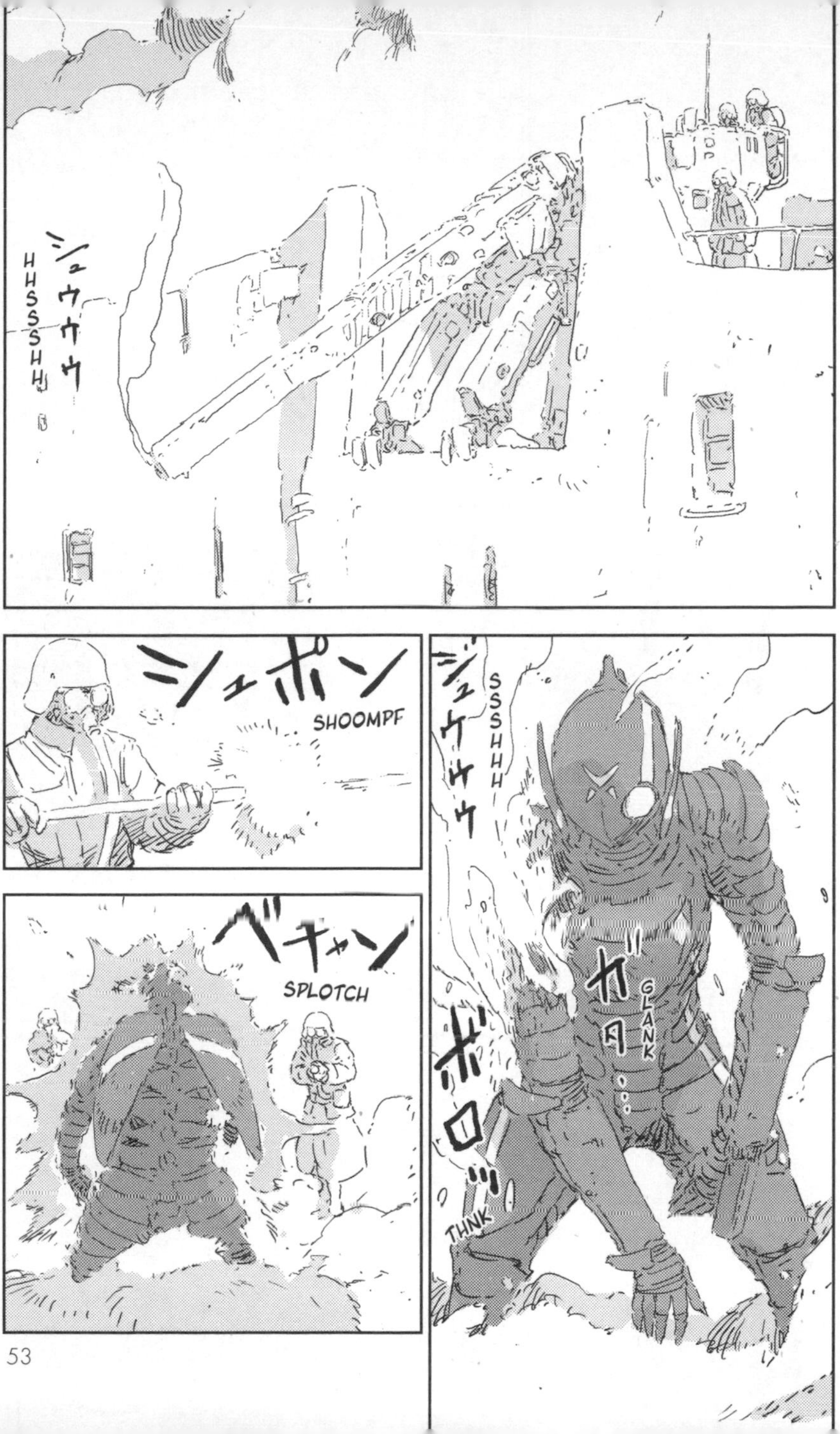
シュウウウ
HHSSSHH
シュポン
SHOOMPF
ジュウウウ
SSSHHH
ベキャン
SPLOTCH
ガク
GLANK
ボロ…
THNK

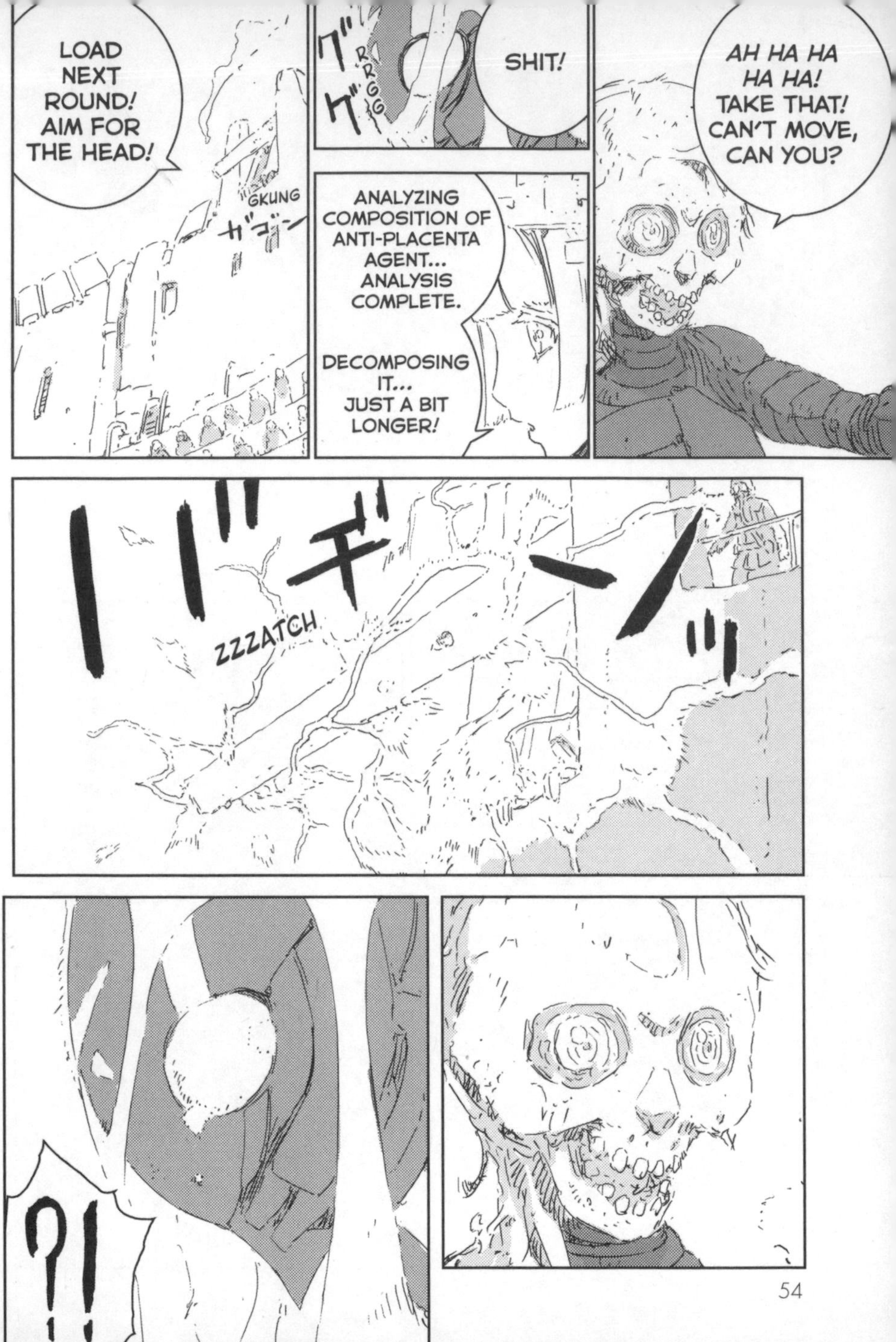
AH HA HA HA HA! TAKE THAT! CAN'T MOVE, CAN YOU?
SHIT!
RRGG
ANALYZING COMPOSITION OF ANTI-PLACENTA AGENT... ANALYSIS COMPLETE.
DECOMPOSING IT... JUST A BIT LONGER!
LOAD NEXT ROUND! AIM FOR THE HEAD!
GKUNG
バギーンッ
ZZZATCH
?!

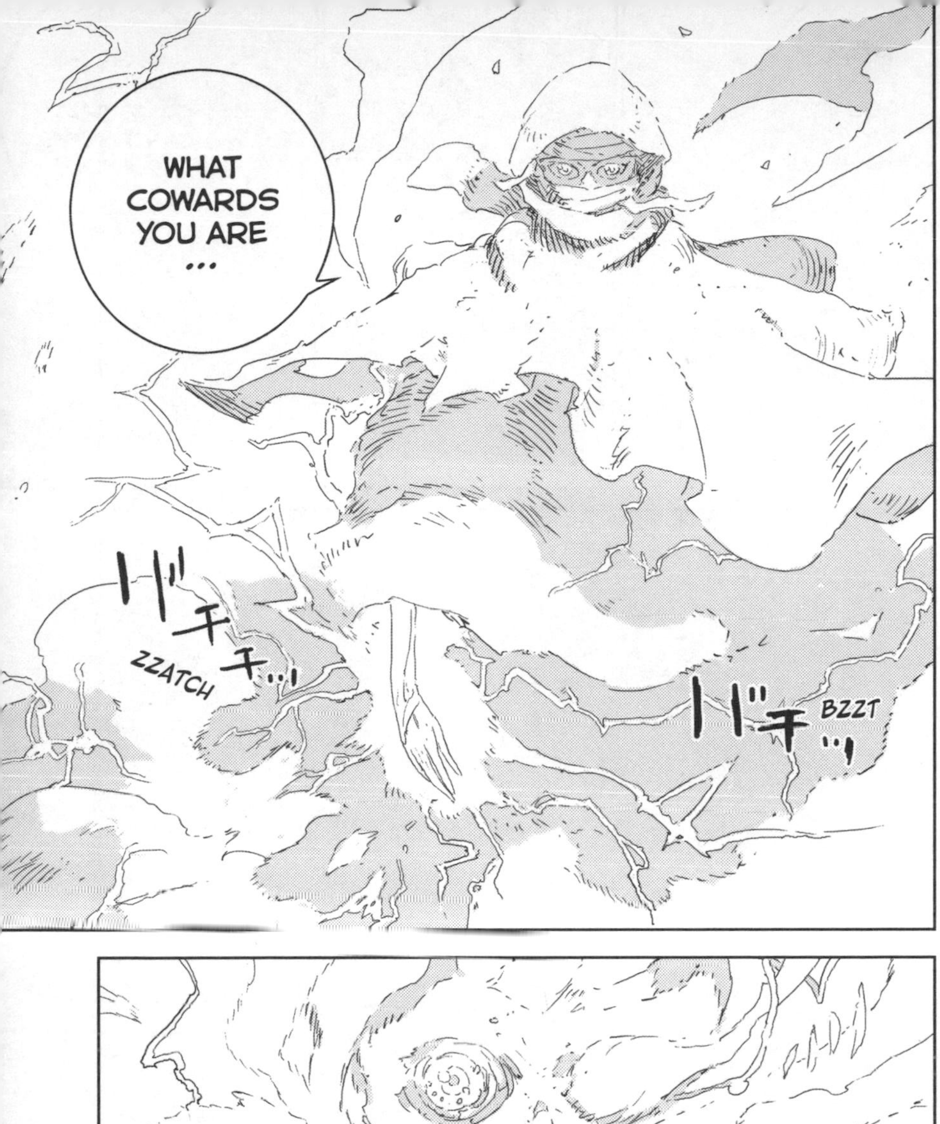
WHAT COWARDS YOU ARE ...
ZZATCH
BZZT

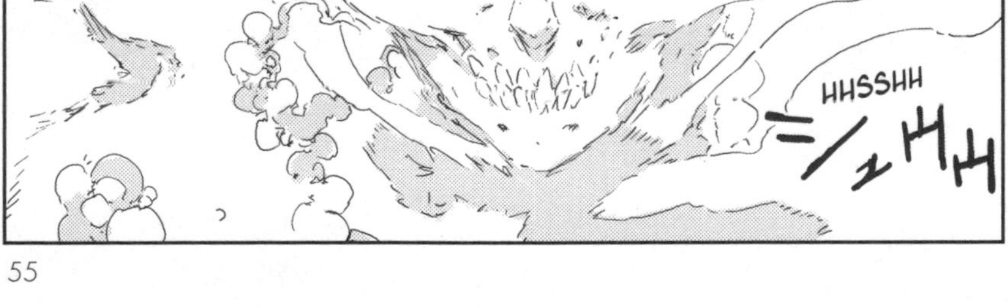
HHSSHH

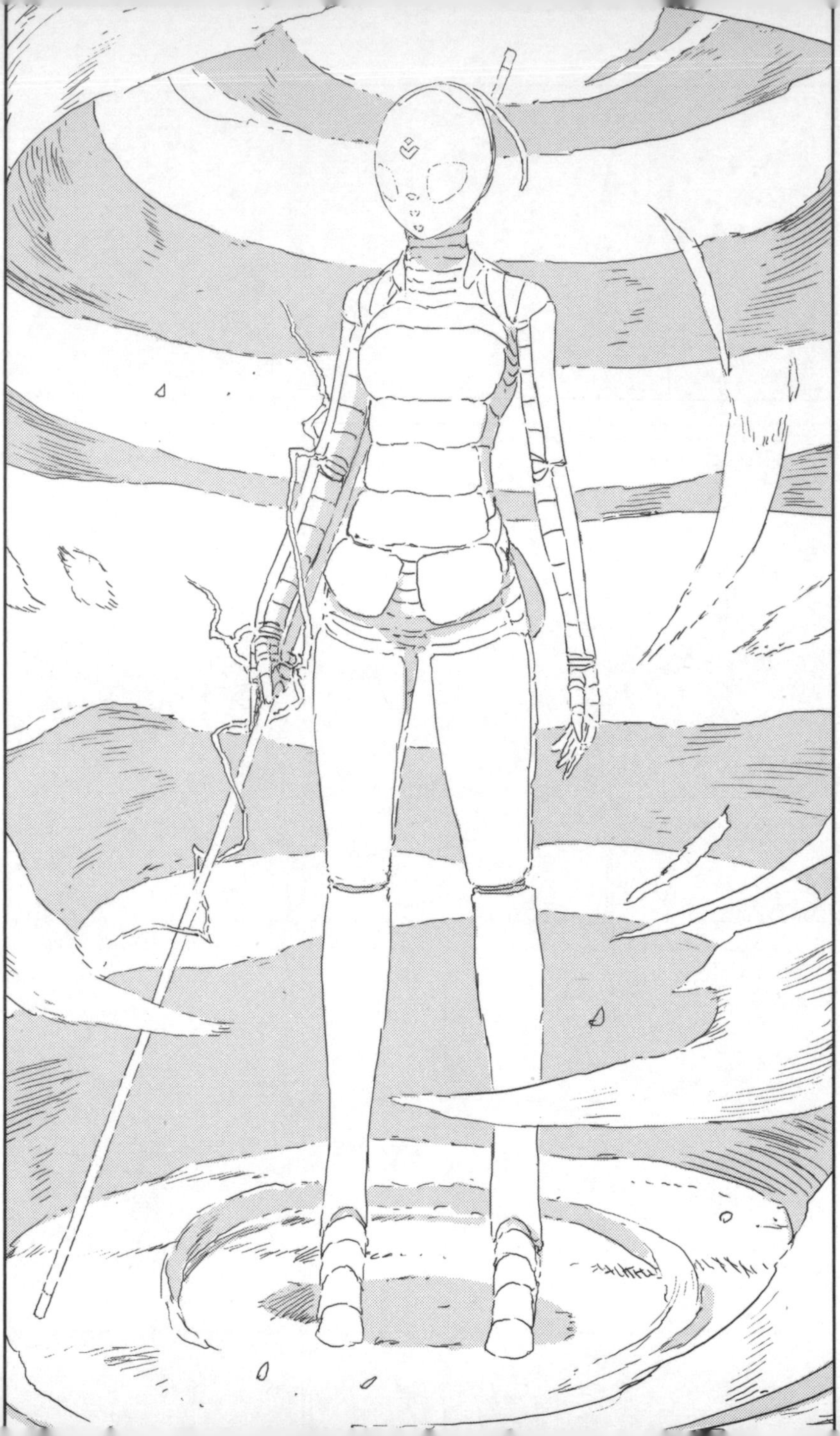

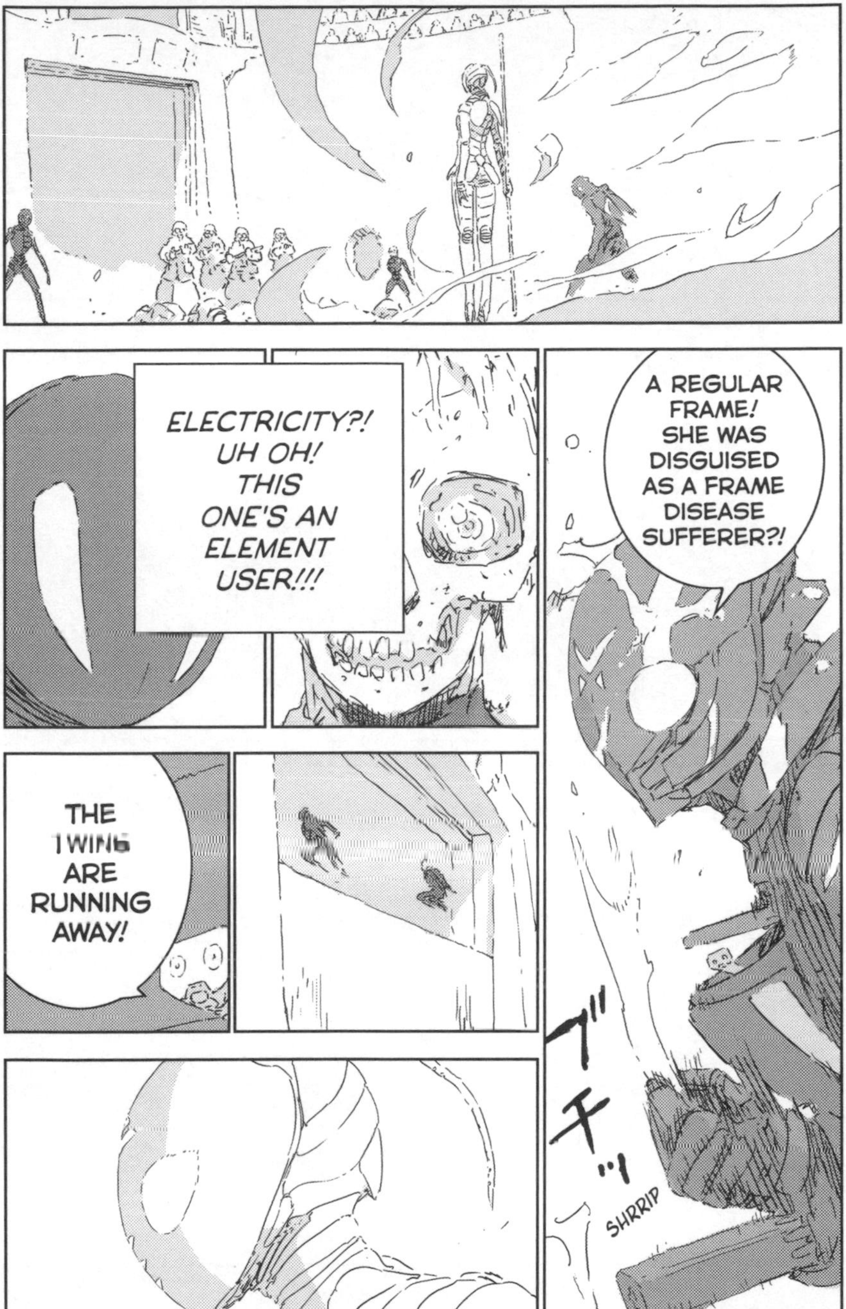
ELECTRICITY?! UH OH! THIS ONE'S AN ELEMENT USER!!!
A REGULAR FRAME! SHE WAS DISGUISED AS A FRAME DISEASE SUFFERER?!
THE TWINS ARE RUNNING AWAY!
ブチッ
SHRRIP

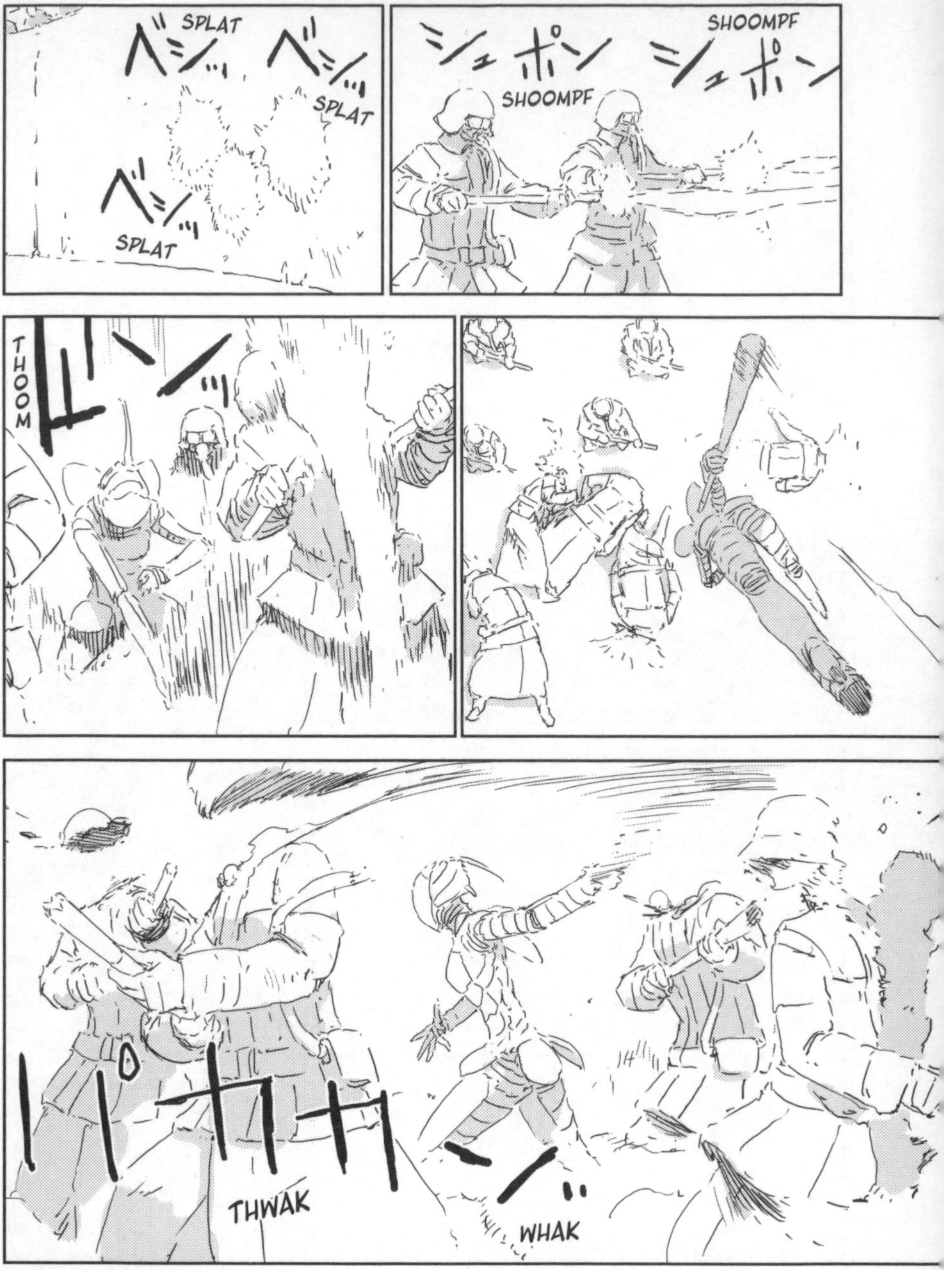

シュポン
SHOOMPF
シュポン
SHOOMPF
ベシッ
SPLAT
ベシッ
SPLAT
ベシッ
SPLAT
THOOM
THWAK
WHAK

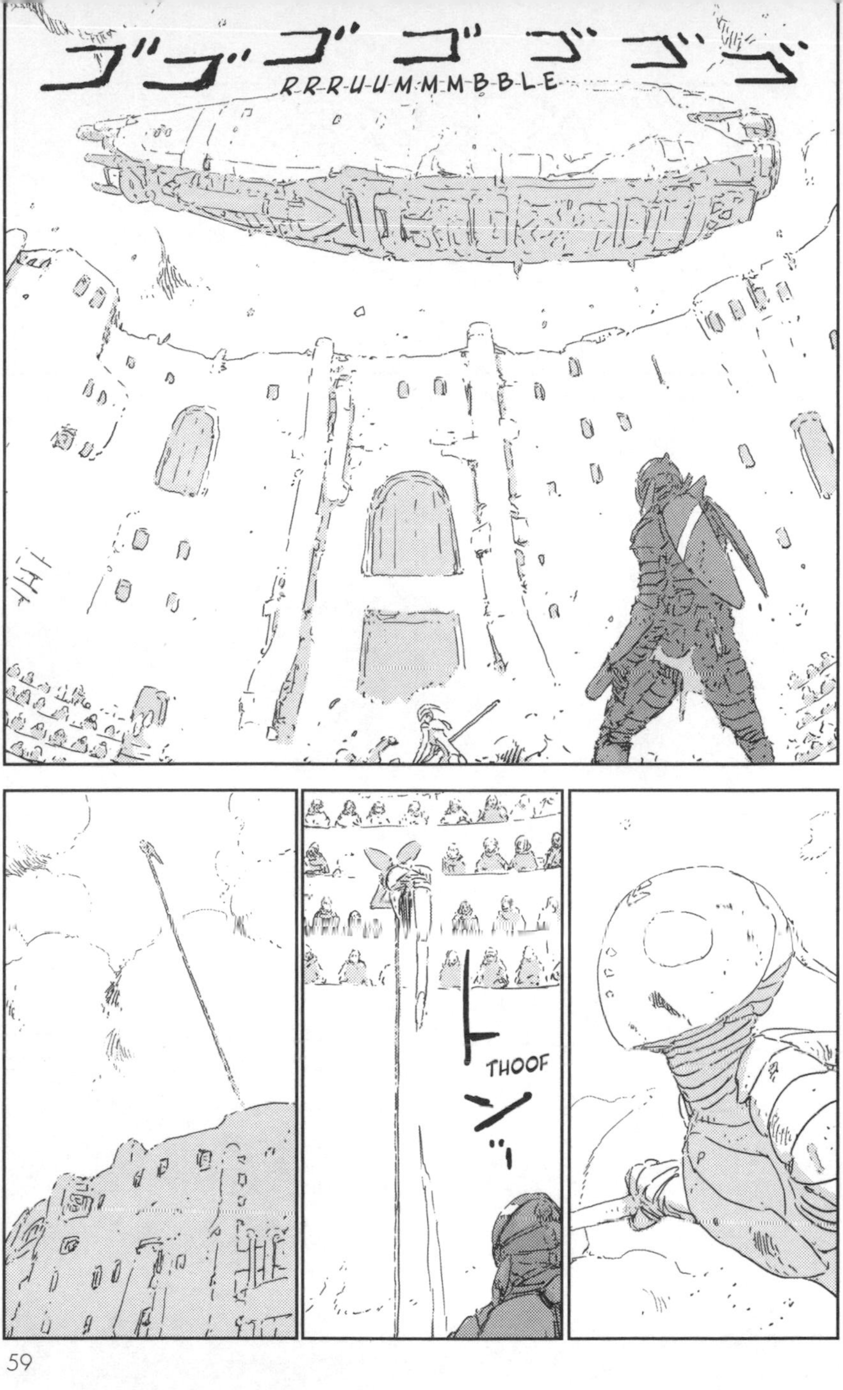
R-R-R-U-U-M-M-M-B-B-L-E
THOOF

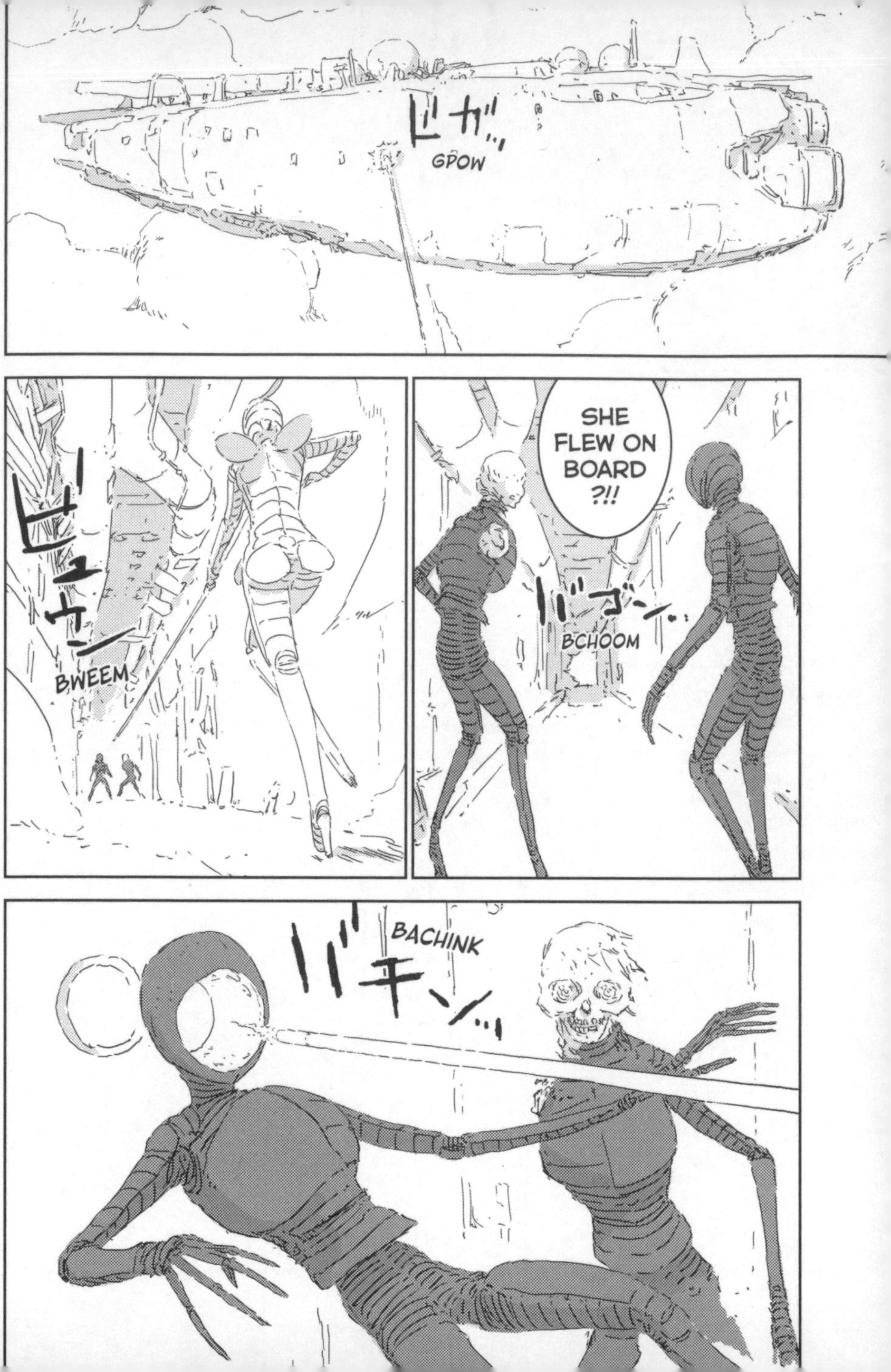
GPOW
SHE FLEW ON BOARD ?!!
BCHOOM
BWEEM
BACHINK

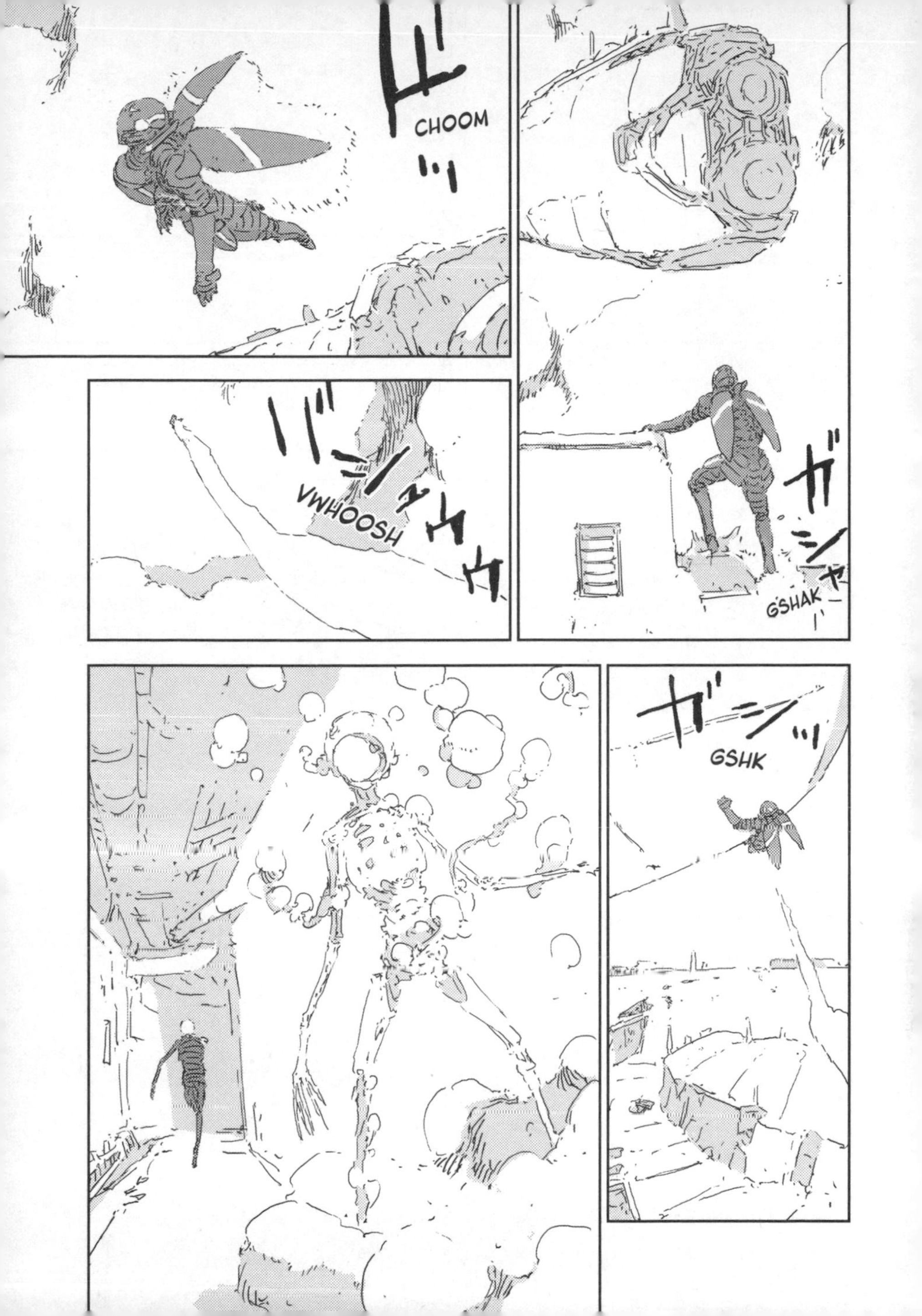
CHOOM
GSHAK
VWHOOSH
GSHK

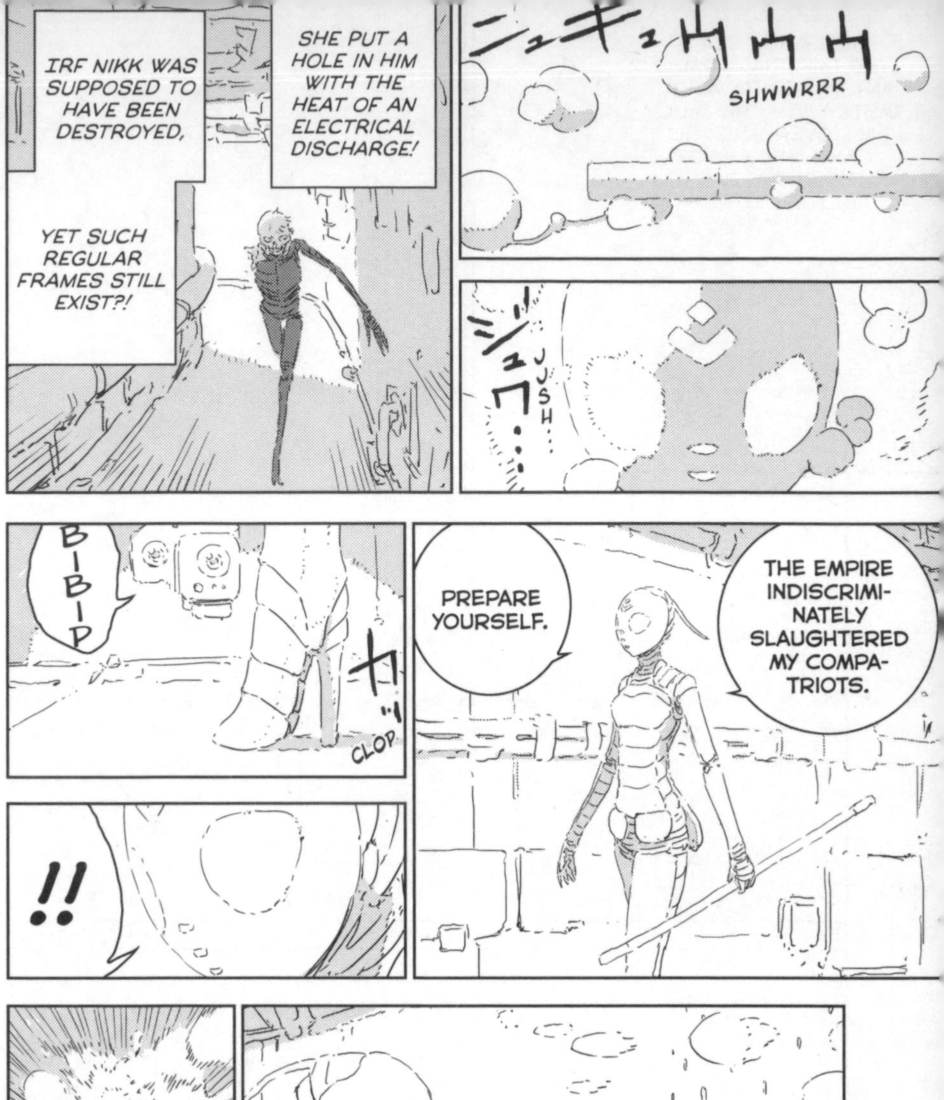
SHWWRRR
JUSH
SHE PUT A HOLE IN HIM WITH THE HEAT OF AN ELECTRICAL DISCHARGE!
IRF NIKK WAS SUPPOSED TO HAVE BEEN DESTROYED,
YET SUCH REGULAR FRAMES STILL EXIST?!
THE EMPIRE INDISCRIMINATELY SLAUGHTERED MY COMPATRIOTS.
PREPARE YOURSELF.
BIBIP
CLOP
!!
BWAMMF

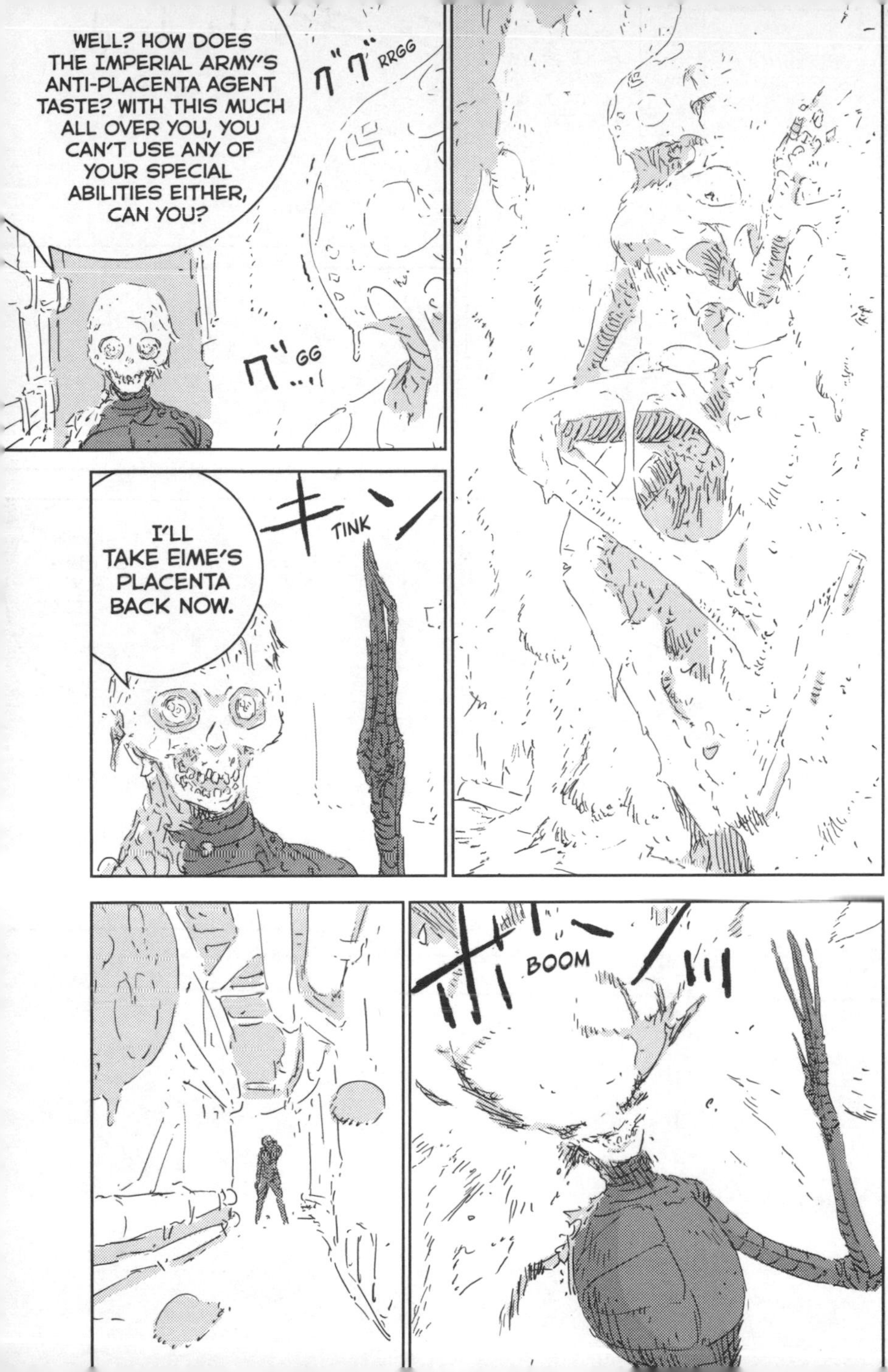
WELL? HOW DOES THE IMPERIAL ARMY'S ANTI-PLACENTA AGENT TASTE? WITH THIS MUCH ALL OVER YOU, YOU CAN'T USE ANY OF YOUR SPECIAL ABILITIES EITHER, CAN YOU?
RRGG
GG
I'LL TAKE EIME'S PLACENTA BACK NOW.
TINK
BOOM

ジュワァァ JUWWSSSSHH

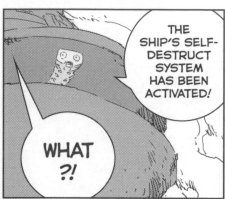

THE SHIP'S SELF-DESTRUCT SYSTEM HAS BEEN ACTIVATED!

WHAT ?!

HSSSHH

!!

KABOOOM

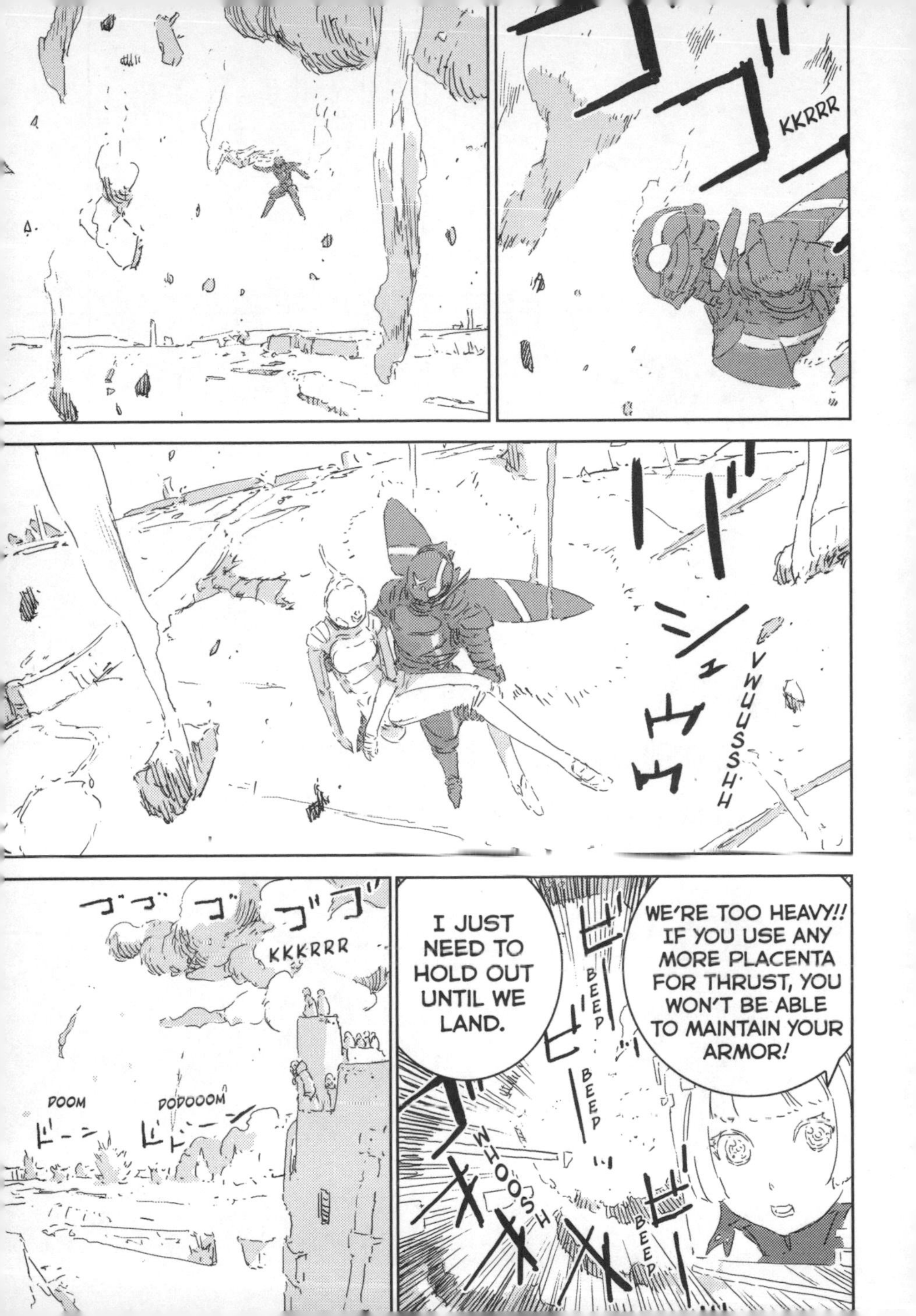
KKRRR
VWUUSSHH
WE'RE TOO HEAVY!! IF YOU USE ANY MORE PLACENTA FOR THRUST, YOU WON'T BE ABLE TO MAINTAIN YOUR ARMOR!
I JUST NEED TO HOLD OUT UNTIL WE LAND.
BEEP
BEEP
BEEP
BEEP
BEEP
WHOOOSH
KKKRRR
DOOM
DODOOOM

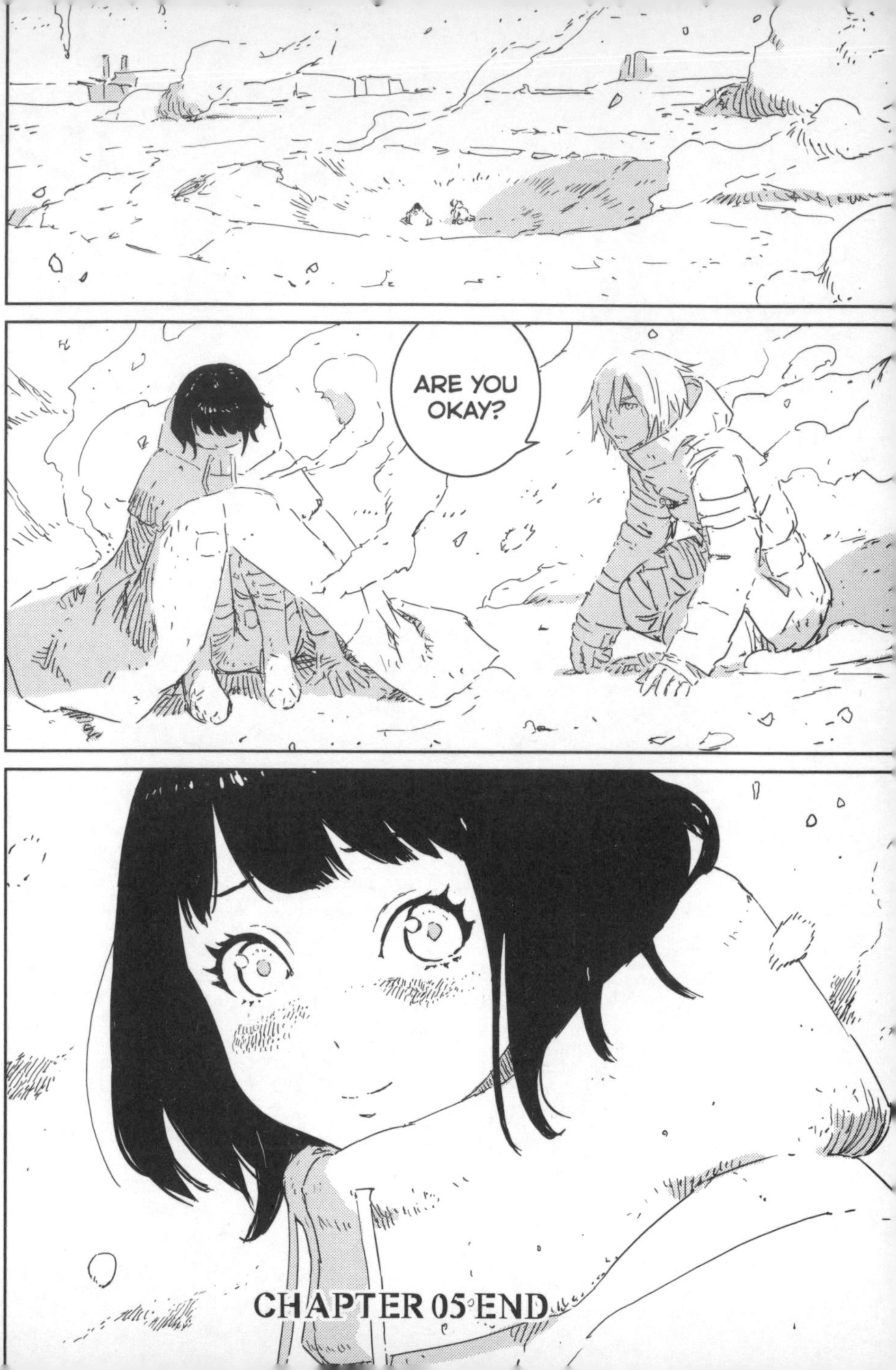
ARE YOU OKAY?
CHAPTER 05 END

APOSIMZ

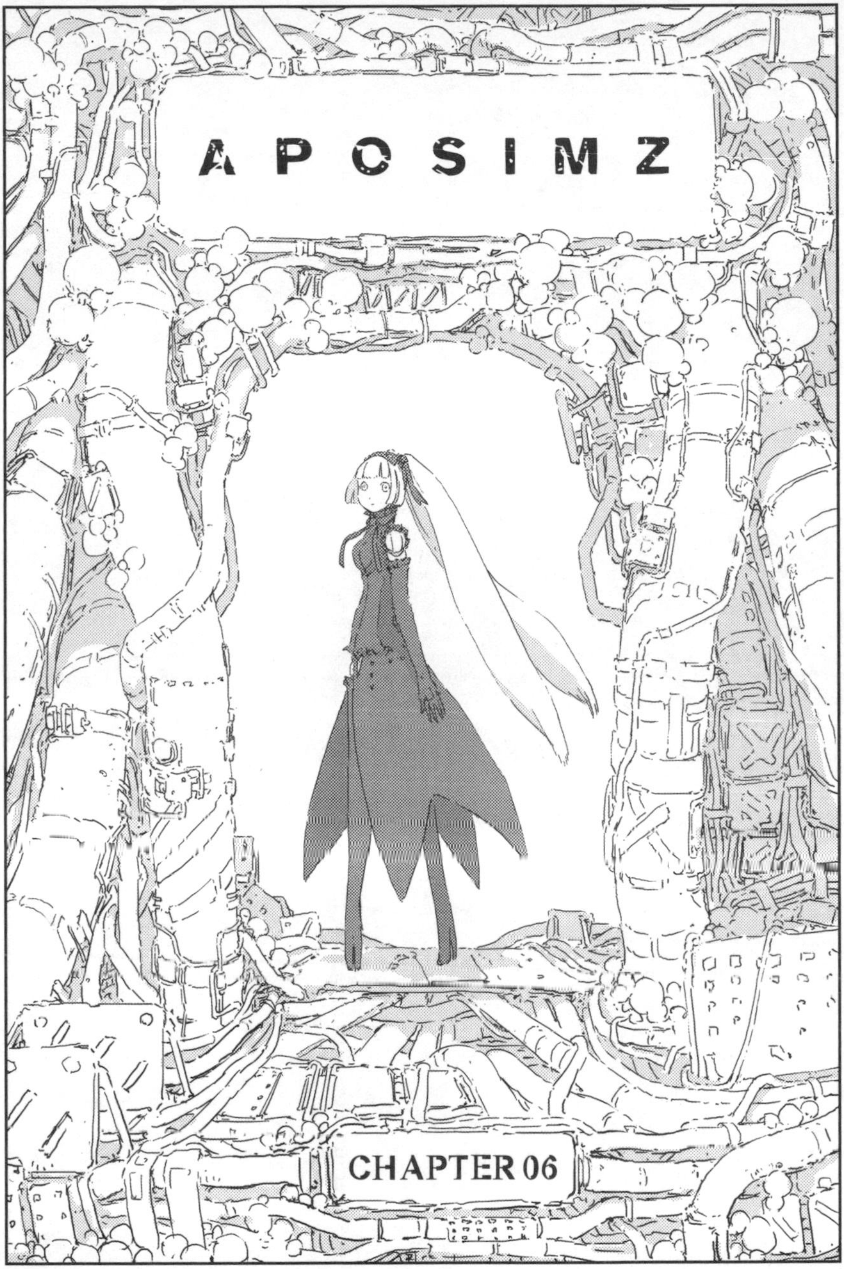
APOSIMZ
CHAPTER 06

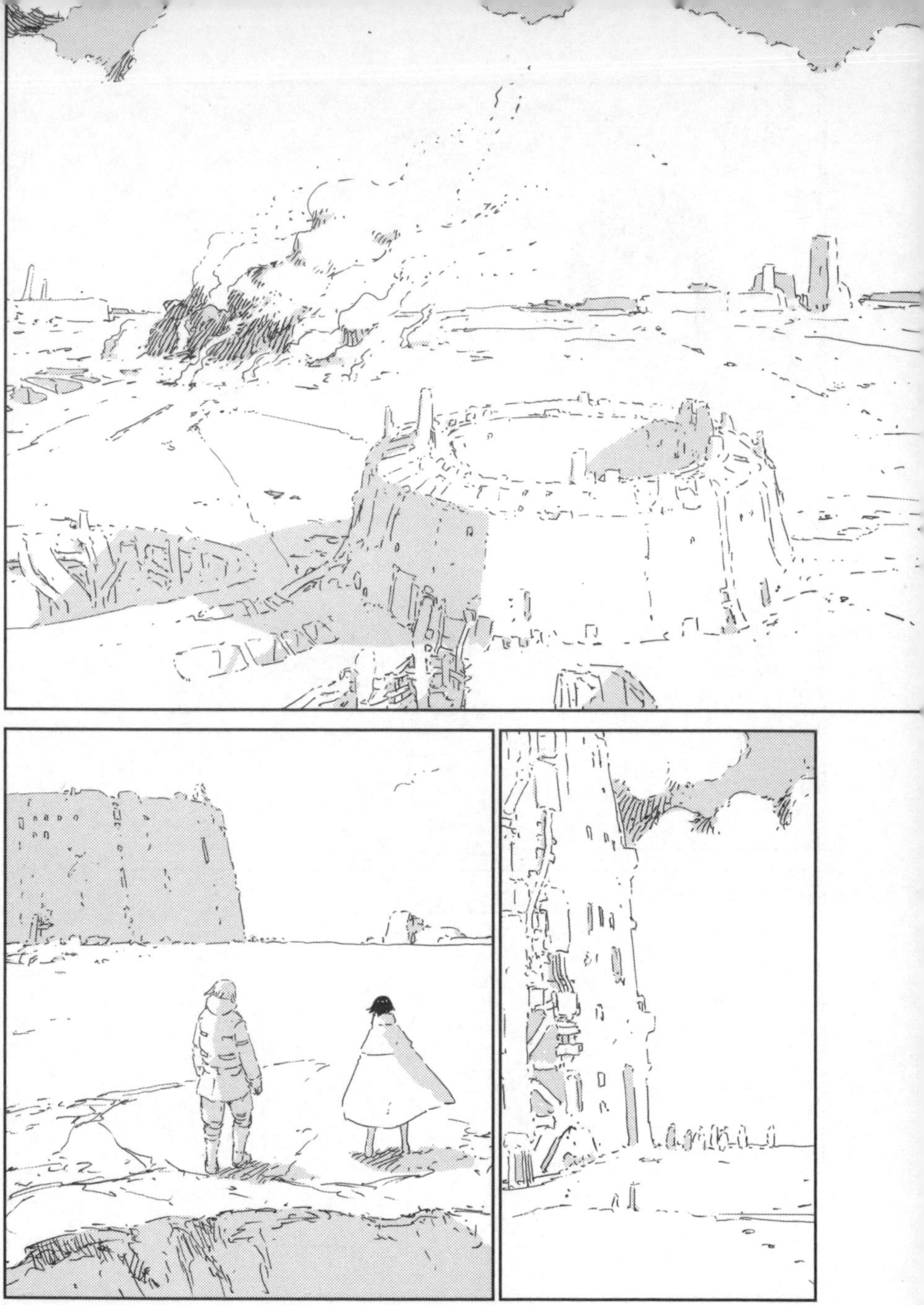

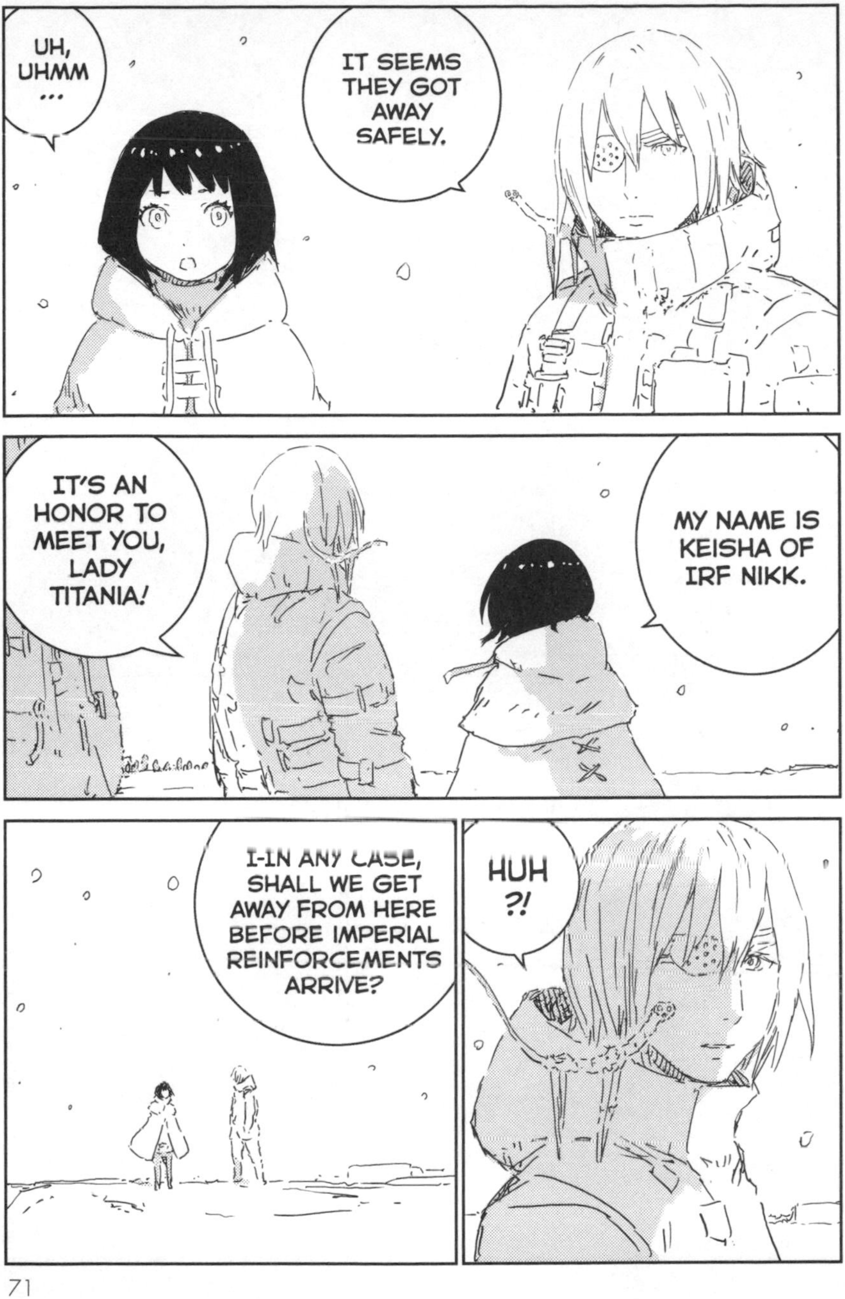
IT SEEMS THEY GOT AWAY SAFELY.
UH, UHMM ...
MY NAME IS KEISHA OF IRF NIKK.
IT'S AN HONOR TO MEET YOU, LADY TITANIA!
HUH ?!
I-IN ANY CASE, SHALL WE GET AWAY FROM HERE BEFORE IMPERIAL REINFORCEMENTS ARRIVE?

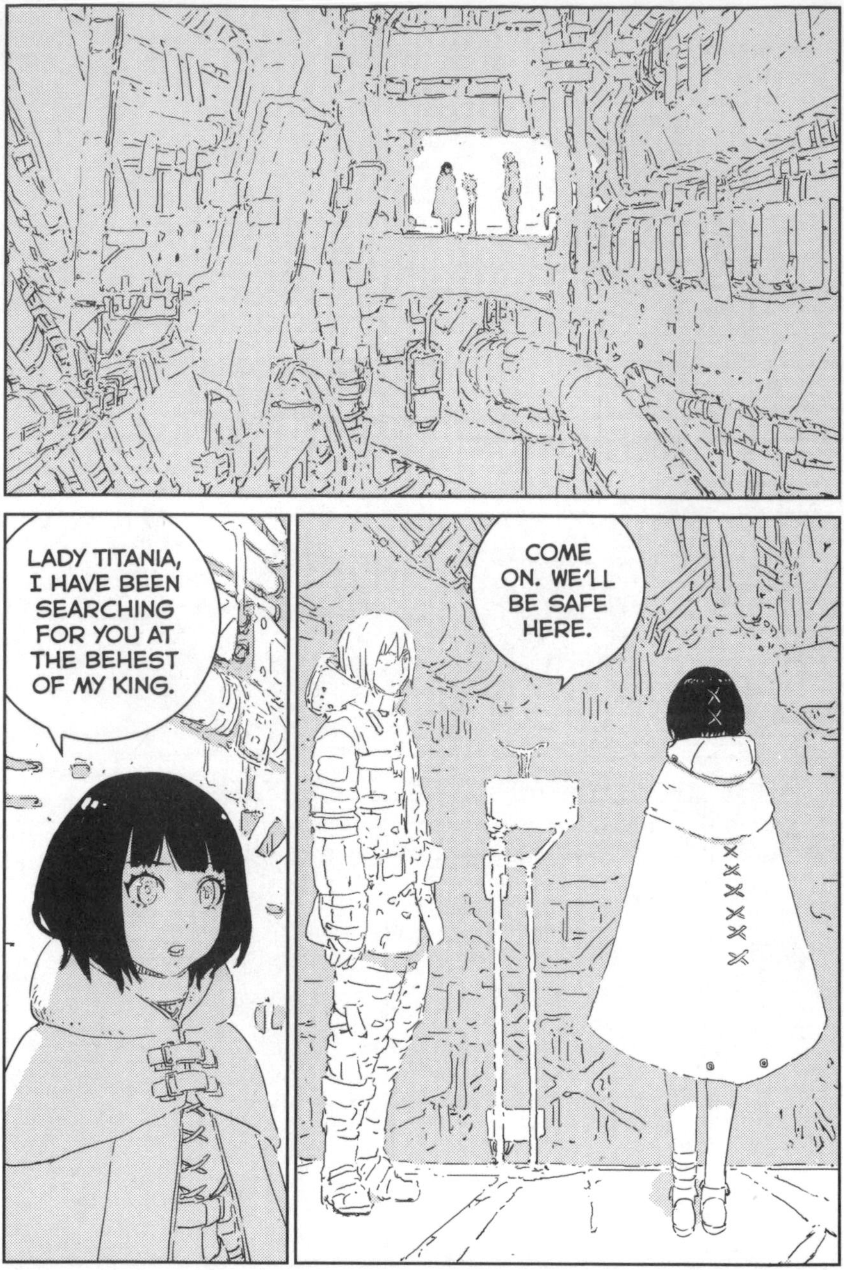
COME ON. WE'LL BE SAFE HERE.
LADY TITANIA, I HAVE BEEN SEARCHING FOR YOU AT THE BEHEST OF MY KING.

YOUR KING IS ALIVE?
I HEARD THAT IRF NIKK GOT WIPED OUT BY THE EMPIRE...
THAT IS A RUDE WAY TO PUT IT.
IRF NIKK HAS NOT BEEN WIPED OUT!
WE ONLY LOST OUR CAPITAL CITY FOR A TIME...
NEVER INSULT MY COUNTRY BY SPEAKING IN SUCH A WAY AGAIN.
NEXT TIME I WON'T LET YOU OFF SO EASILY.
O-OKAY ...
A-AHEM!

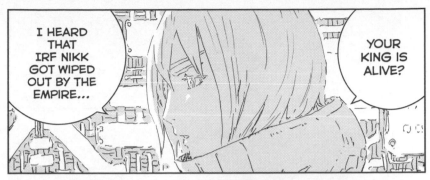

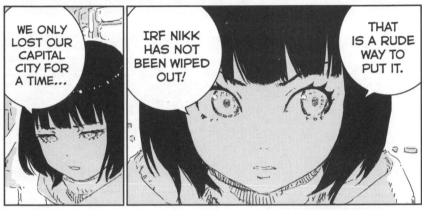

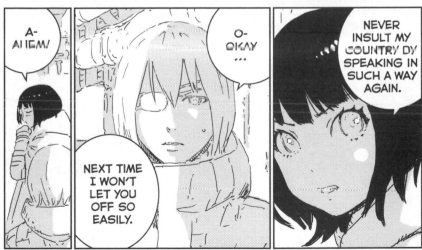

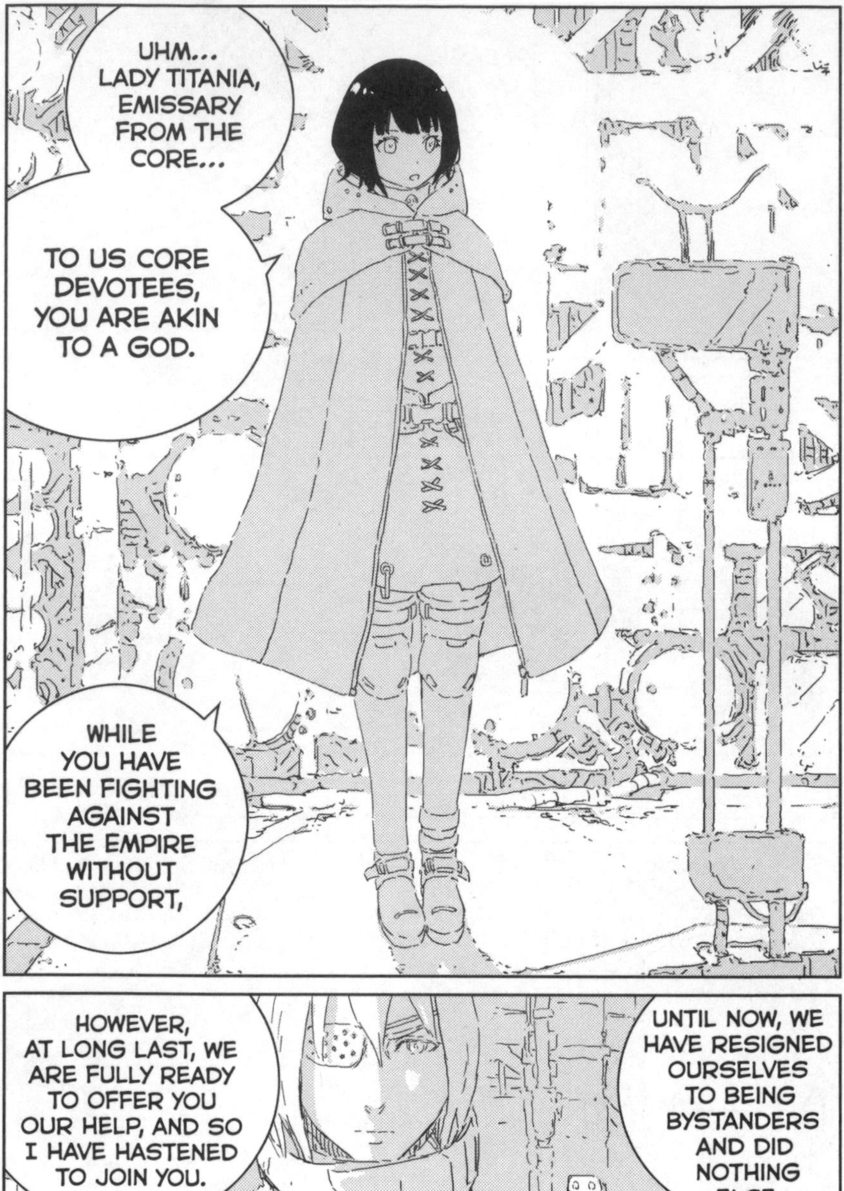
UHM... LADY TITANIA, EMISSARY FROM THE CORE...
TO US CORE DEVOTEES, YOU ARE AKIN TO A GOD.
WHILE YOU HAVE BEEN FIGHTING AGAINST THE EMPIRE WITHOUT SUPPORT,
UNTIL NOW, WE HAVE RESIGNED OURSELVES TO BEING BYSTANDERS AND DID NOTHING ELSE.
HOWEVER, AT LONG LAST, WE ARE FULLY READY TO OFFER YOU OUR HELP, AND SO I HAVE HASTENED TO JOIN YOU.

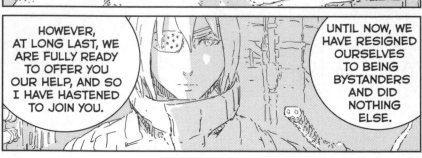

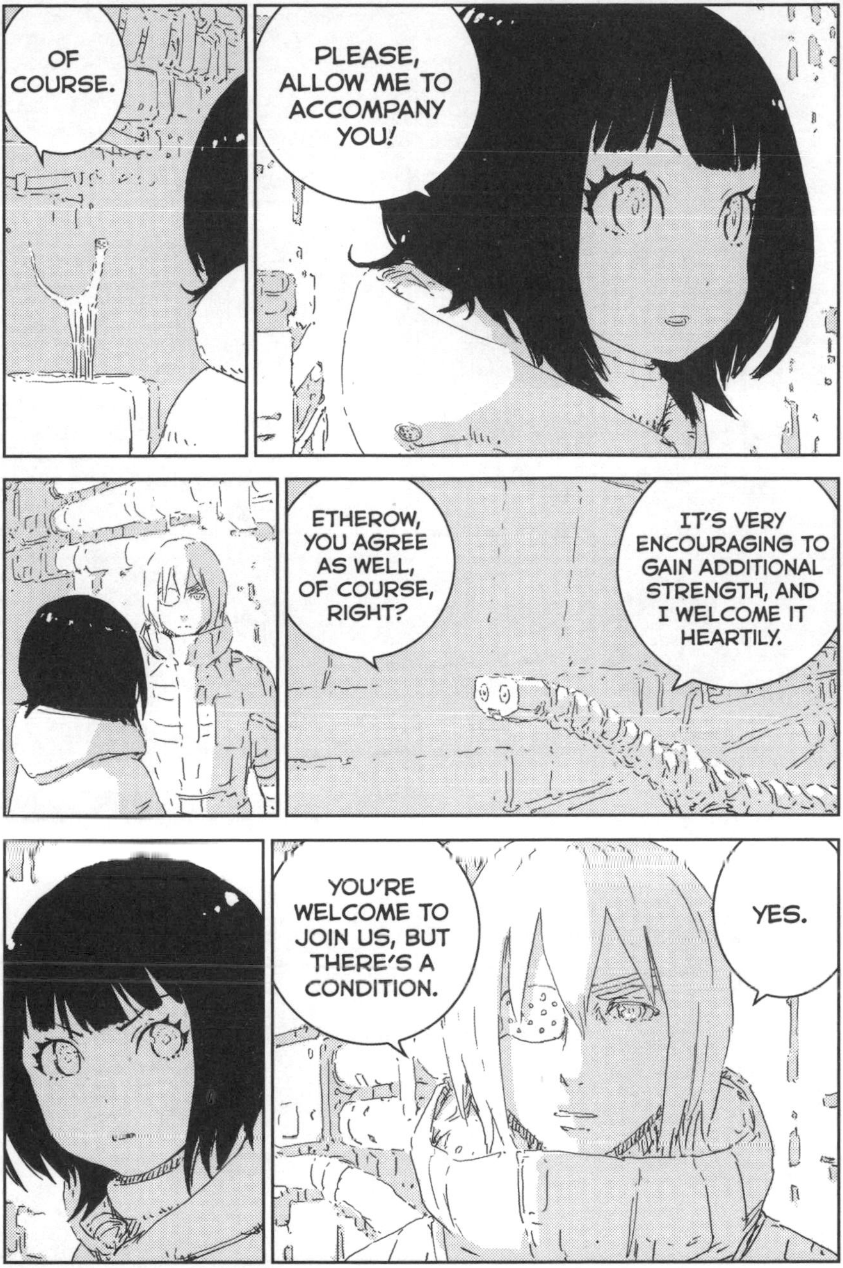
PLEASE, ALLOW ME TO ACCOMPANY YOU!
OF COURSE.
IT'S VERY ENCOURAGING TO GAIN ADDITIONAL STRENGTH, AND I WELCOME IT HEARTILY.
ETHEROW, YOU AGREE AS WELL, OF COURSE, RIGHT?
YES.
YOU'RE WELCOME TO JOIN US, BUT THERE'S A CONDITION.

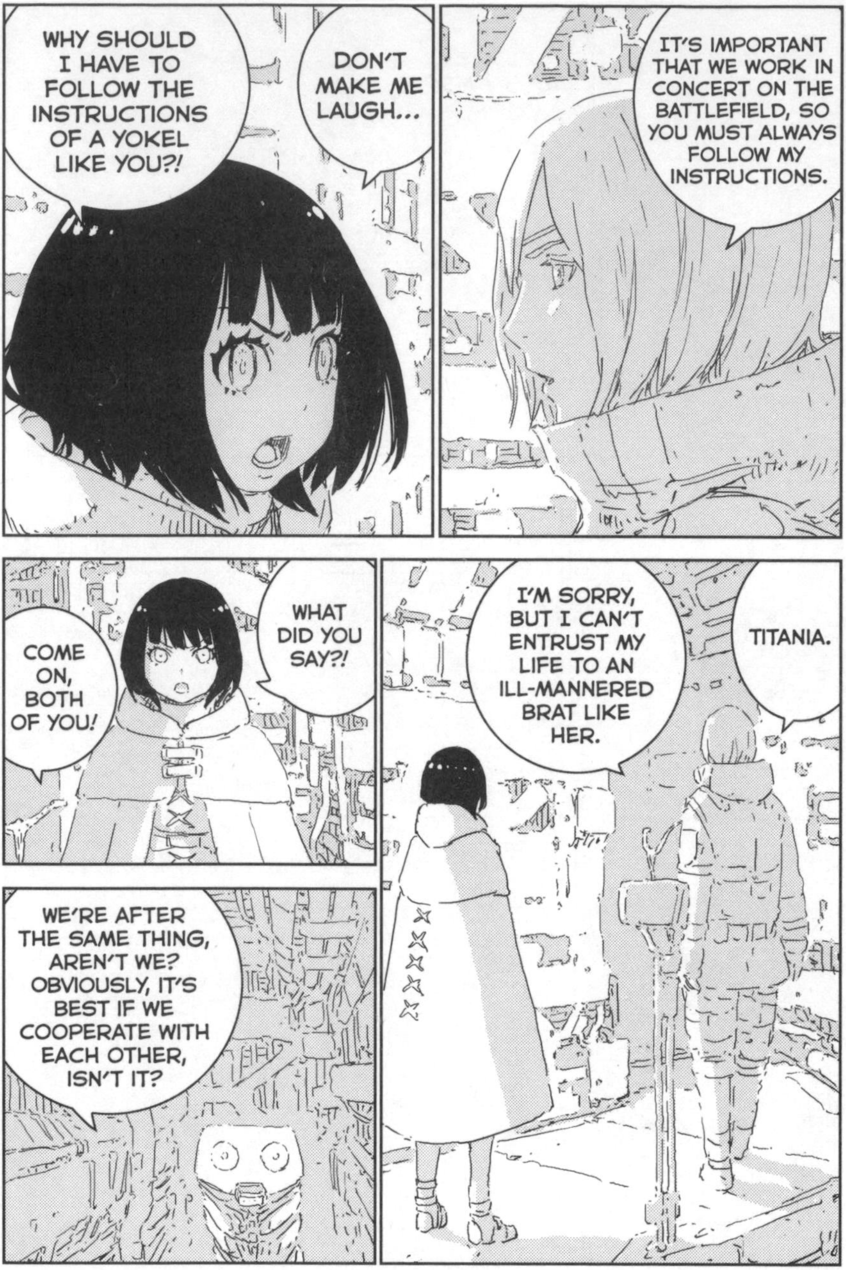
IT'S IMPORTANT THAT WE WORK IN CONCERT ON THE BATTLEFIELD, SO YOU MUST ALWAYS FOLLOW MY INSTRUCTIONS.
DON'T MAKE ME LAUGH...
WHY SHOULD I HAVE TO FOLLOW THE INSTRUCTIONS OF A YOKEL LIKE YOU?!
TITANIA.
I'M SORRY, BUT I CAN'T ENTRUST MY LIFE TO AN ILL-MANNERED BRAT LIKE HER.
WHAT DID YOU SAY?!
COME ON, BOTH OF YOU!
WE'RE AFTER THE SAME THING, AREN'T WE? OBVIOUSLY, IT'S BEST IF WE COOPERATE WITH EACH OTHER, ISN'T IT?

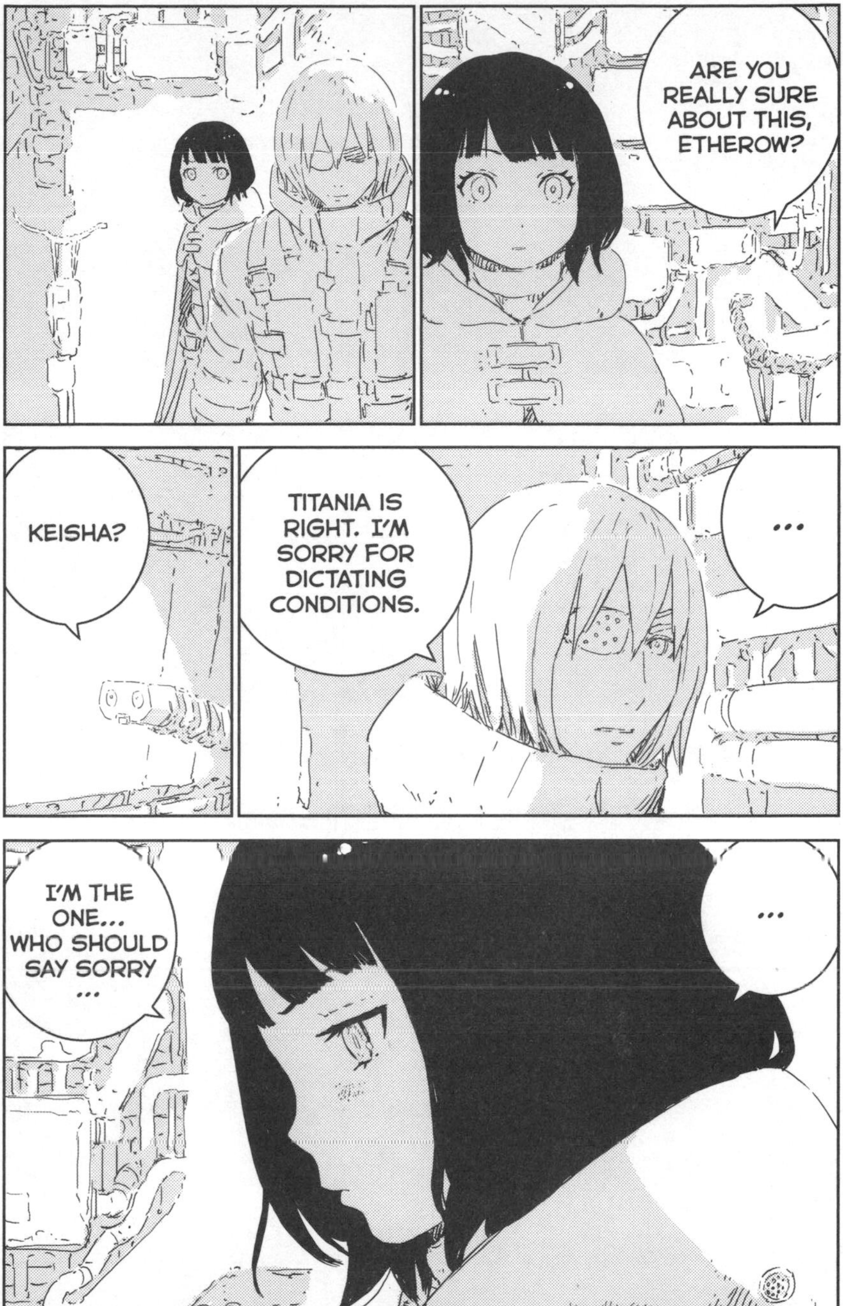
ARE YOU REALLY SURE ABOUT THIS, ETHEROW?
KEISHA?
TITANIA IS RIGHT. I'M SORRY FOR DICTATING CONDITIONS.
...
I'M THE ONE... WHO SHOULD SAY SORRY ...
...

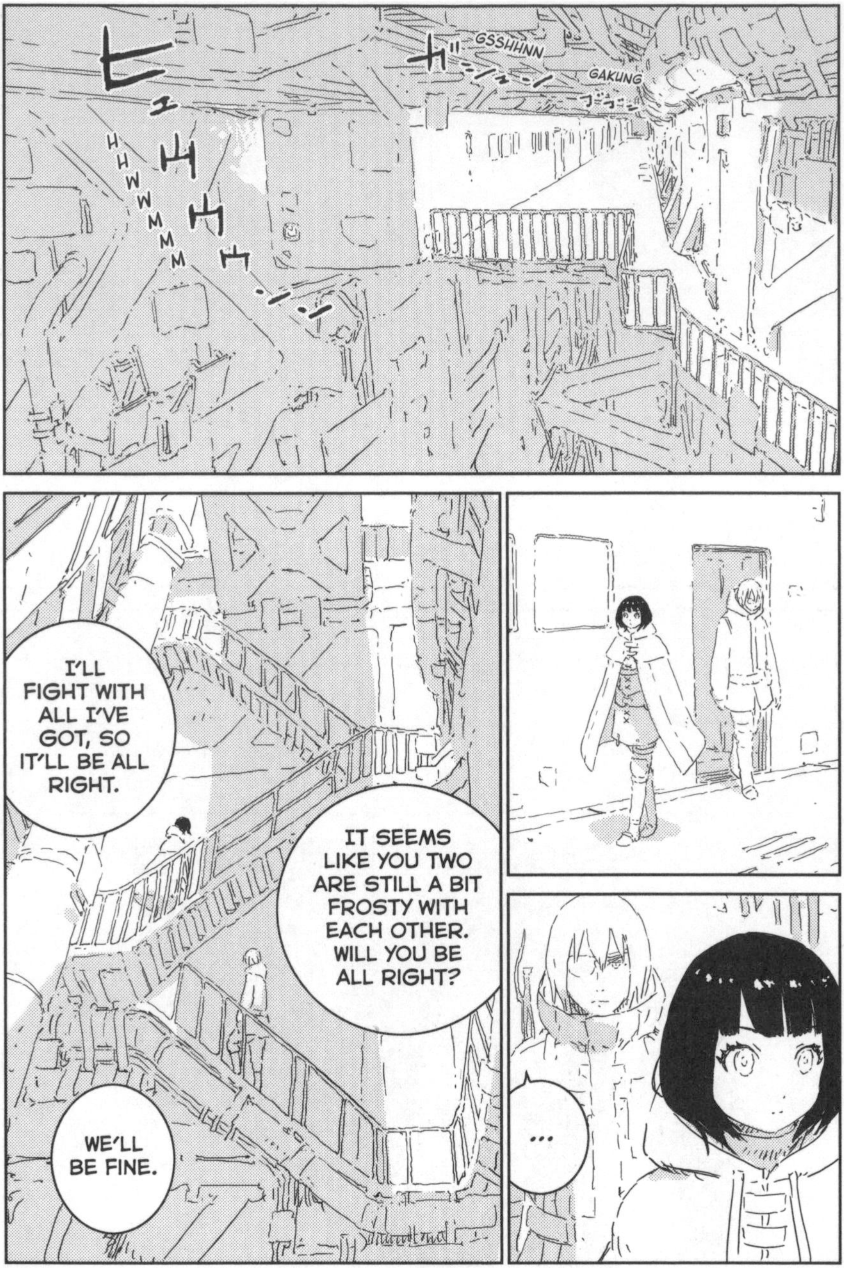
GAKUNG
GSSHHNN
HHWWMMMM
...
IT SEEMS LIKE YOU TWO ARE STILL A BIT FROSTY WITH EACH OTHER. WILL YOU BE ALL RIGHT?
I'LL FIGHT WITH ALL I'VE GOT, SO IT'LL BE ALL RIGHT.
WE'LL BE FINE.

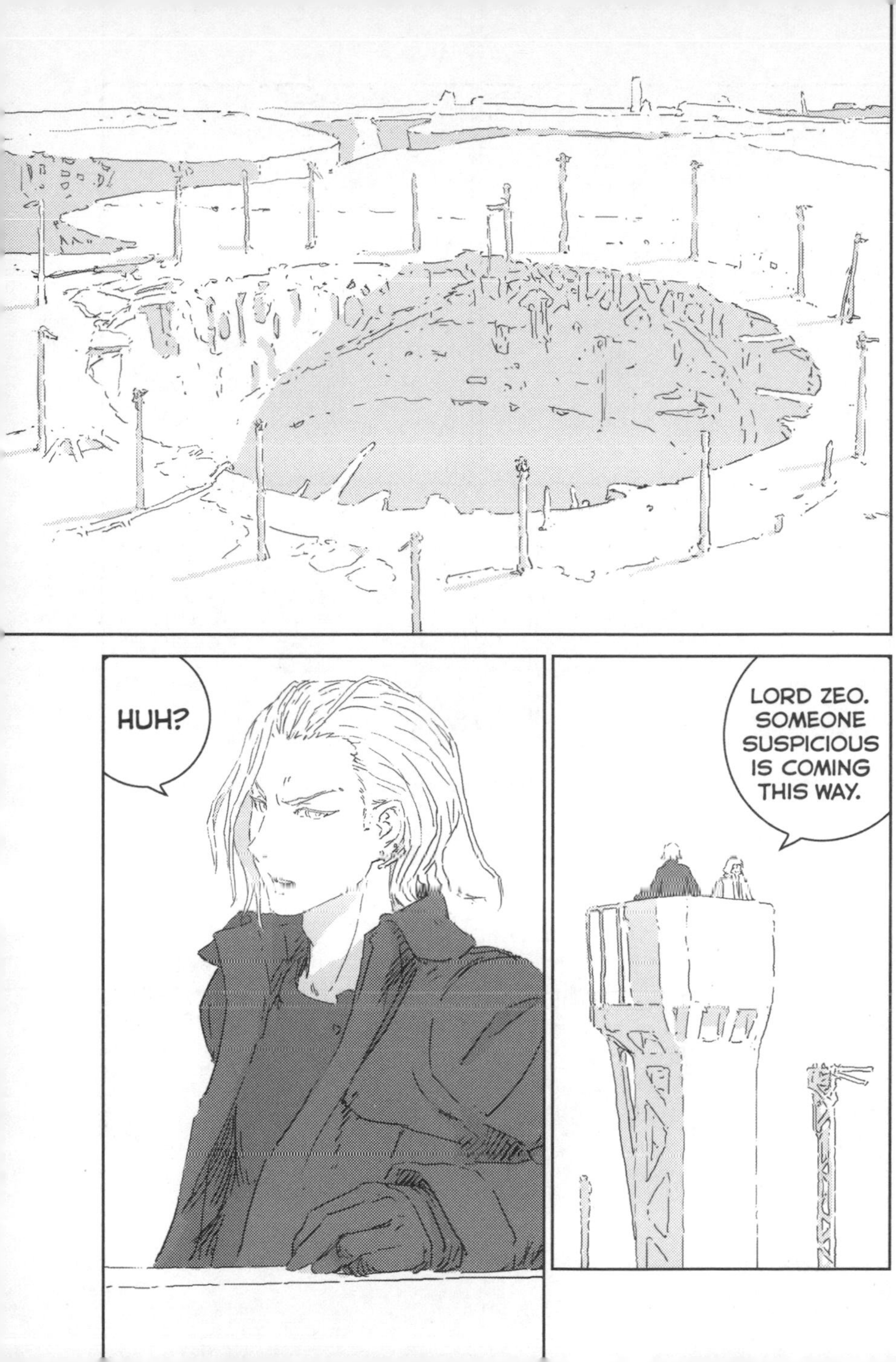
LORD ZEO. SOMEONE SUSPICIOUS IS COMING THIS WAY.
HUH?

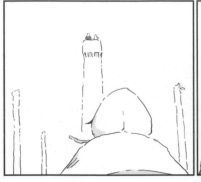

DON'T COME ANY CLOSER! LEAVE NOW!

THIS IS AN IMPERIAL MINING COMPLEX.

I'M HERE FOR YOUR HEAD.

REINCARNATED ZEO, YES?

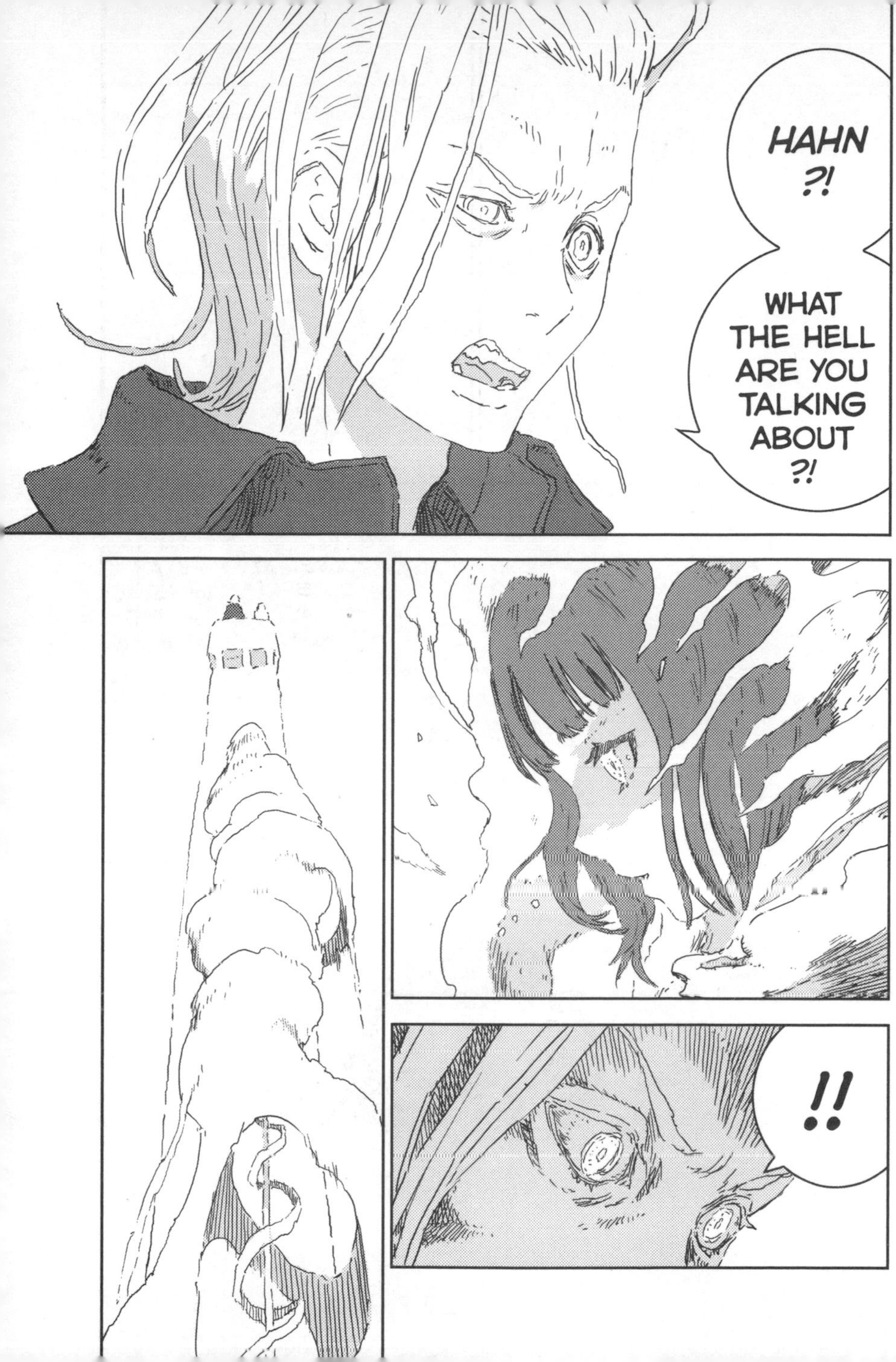
HAHN ?!
WHAT THE HELL ARE YOU TALKING ABOUT ?!
!!

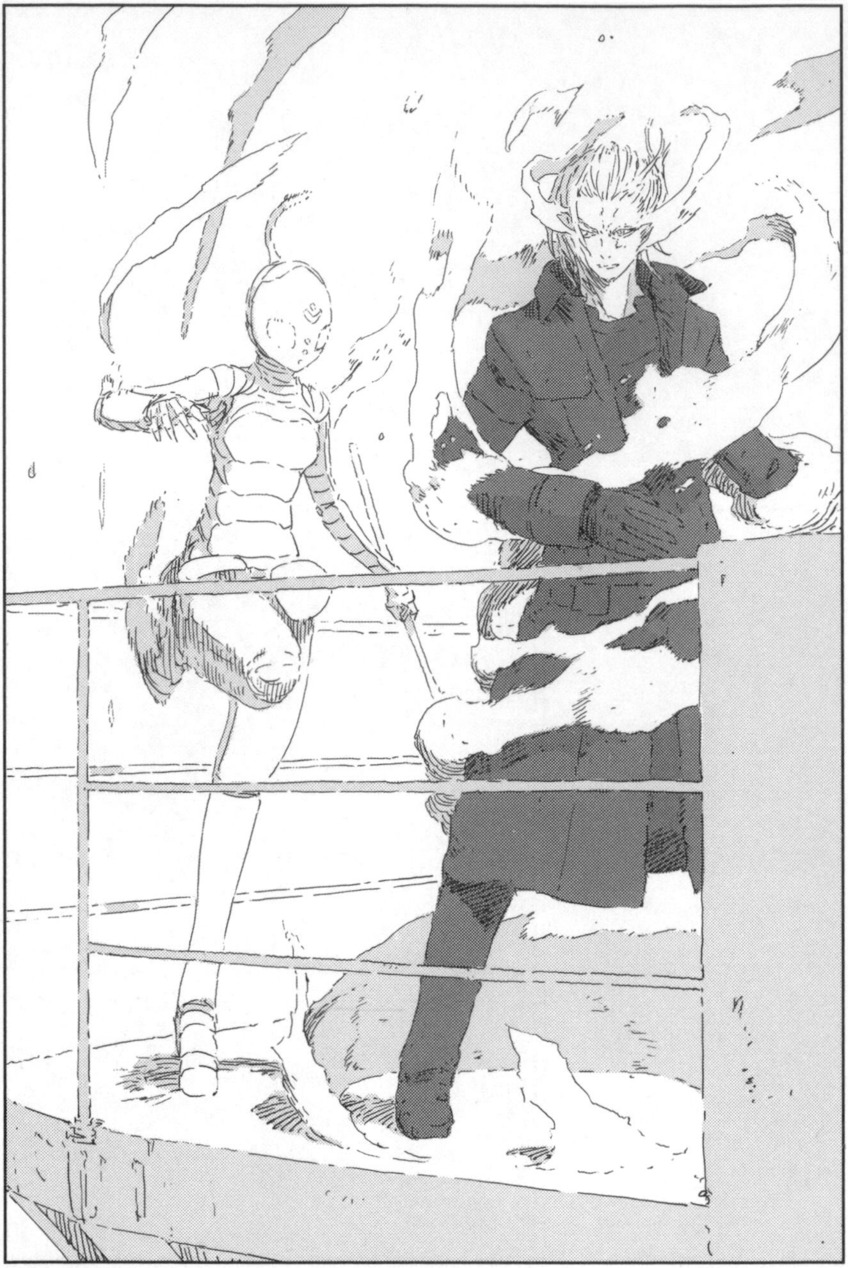

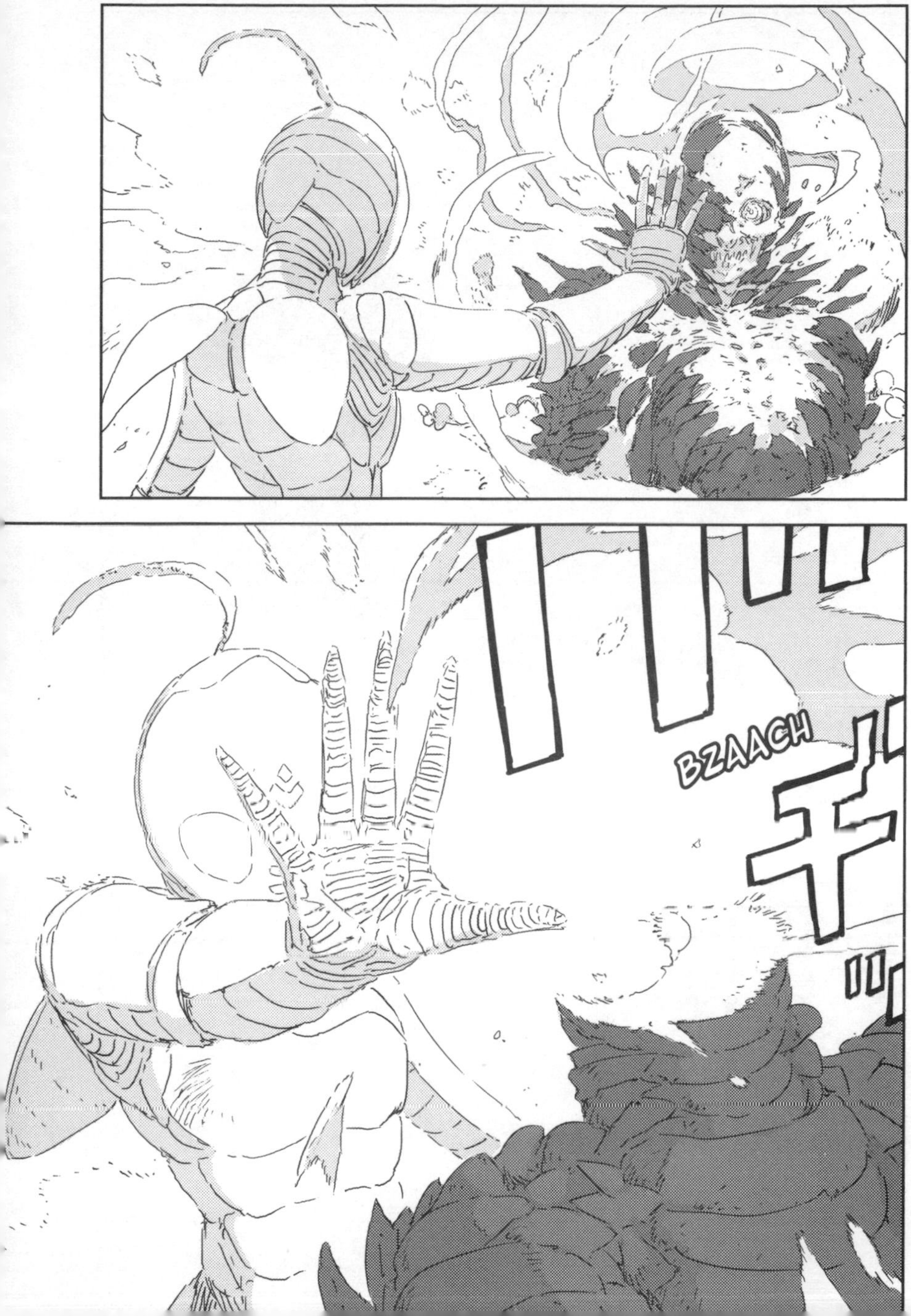
BZAACH

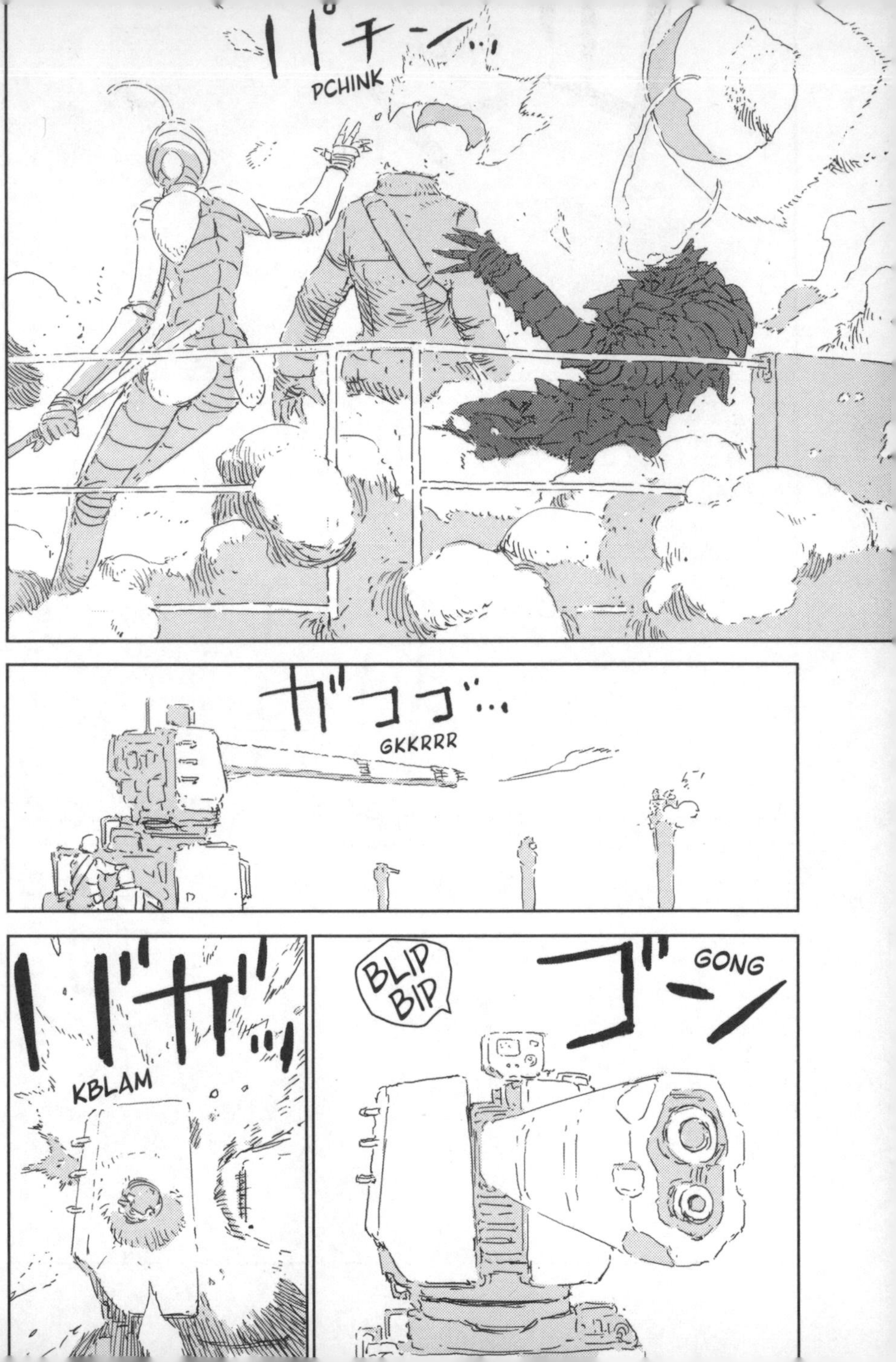
パチーン…
PCHINK
ガコゴ…
GKKRRR
BLIP BIP
ゴーン
GONG
ドガッ
KBLAM

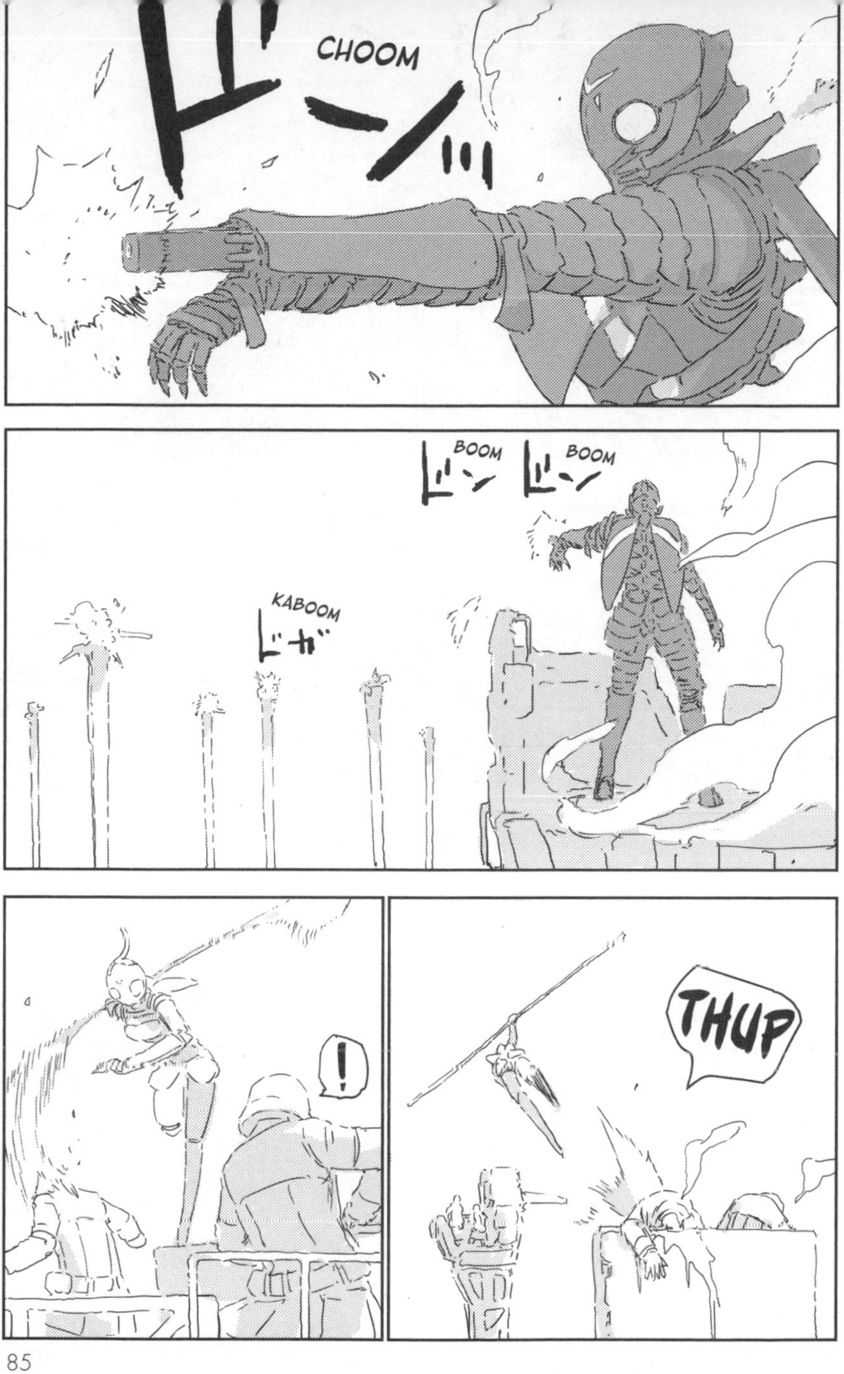
CHOOM
BOOM
BOOM
KABOOM
!
THUP

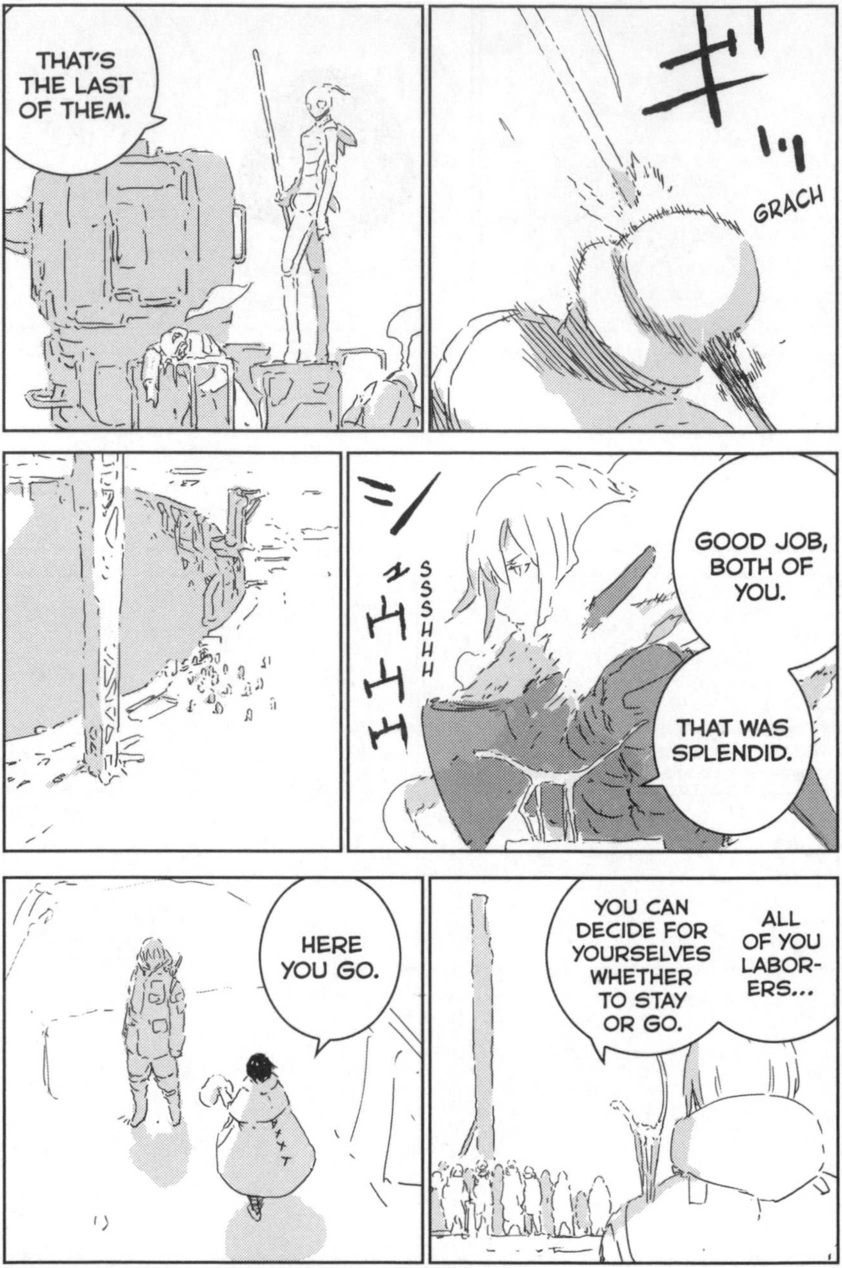
THAT'S THE LAST OF THEM.
GRACH
SSSHHH
GOOD JOB, BOTH OF YOU.
THAT WAS SPLENDID.
HERE YOU GO.
ALL OF YOU LABOR-ERS...
YOU CAN DECIDE FOR YOURSELVES WHETHER TO STAY OR GO.

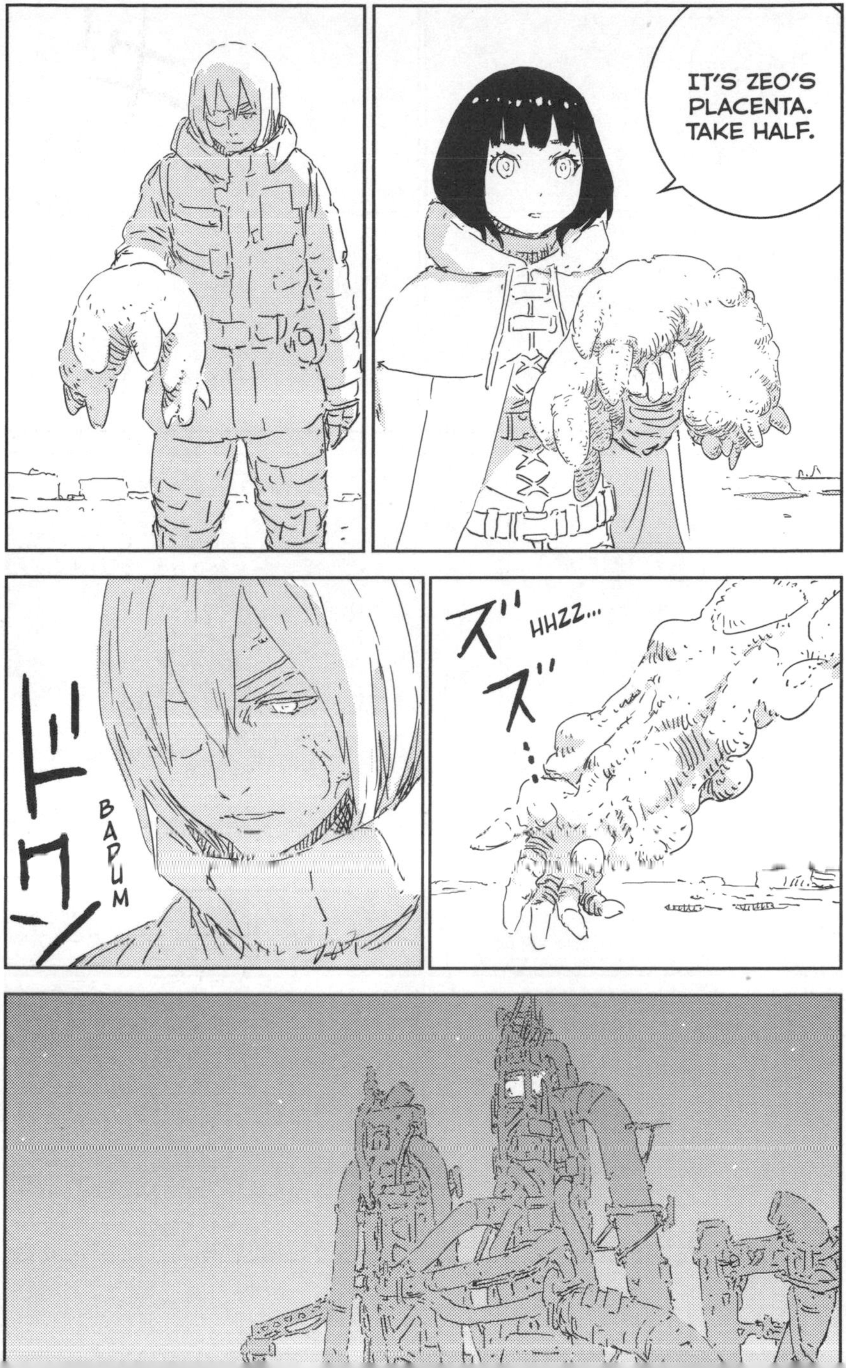
IT'S ZEO'S PLACENTA. TAKE HALF.
ドクン
BADUM
ズズ…
HHZZ...

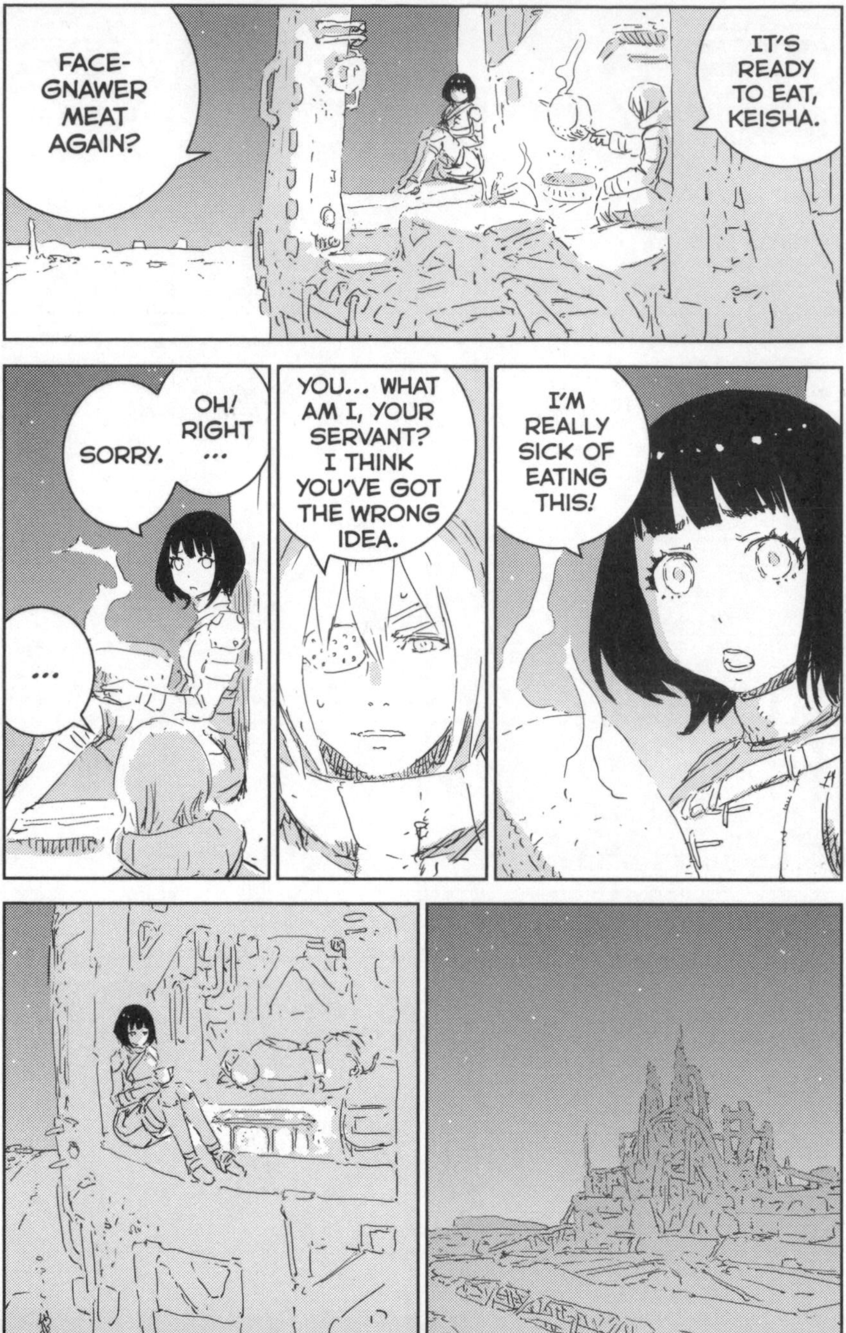
IT'S READY TO EAT, KEISHA.
FACE-GNAWER MEAT AGAIN?
I'M REALLY SICK OF EATING THIS!
YOU... WHAT AM I, YOUR SERVANT? I THINK YOU'VE GOT THE WRONG IDEA.
OH! RIGHT ...
SORRY.
...

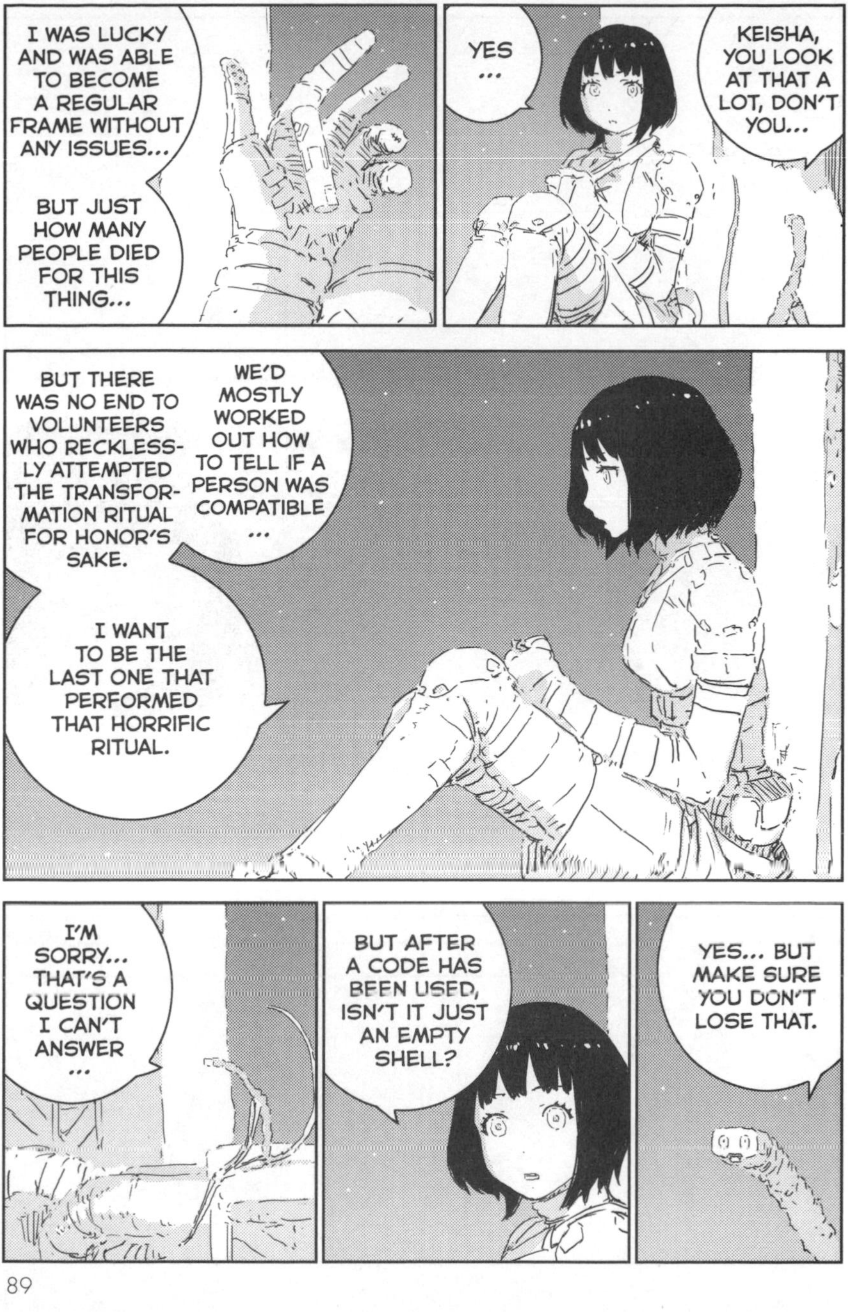
KEISHA, YOU LOOK AT THAT A LOT, DON'T YOU...
YES ...
I WAS LUCKY AND WAS ABLE TO BECOME A REGULAR FRAME WITHOUT ANY ISSUES...
BUT JUST HOW MANY PEOPLE DIED FOR THIS THING...
WE'D MOSTLY WORKED OUT HOW TO TELL IF A PERSON WAS COMPATIBLE ...
BUT THERE WAS NO END TO VOLUNTEERS WHO RECKLESS-LY ATTEMPTED THE TRANSFOR-MATION RITUAL FOR HONOR'S SAKE.
I WANT TO BE THE LAST ONE THAT PERFORMED THAT HORRIFIC RITUAL.
YES... BUT MAKE SURE YOU DON'T LOSE THAT.
BUT AFTER A CODE HAS BEEN USED, ISN'T IT JUST AN EMPTY SHELL?
I'M SORRY... THAT'S A QUESTION I CAN'T ANSWER ...

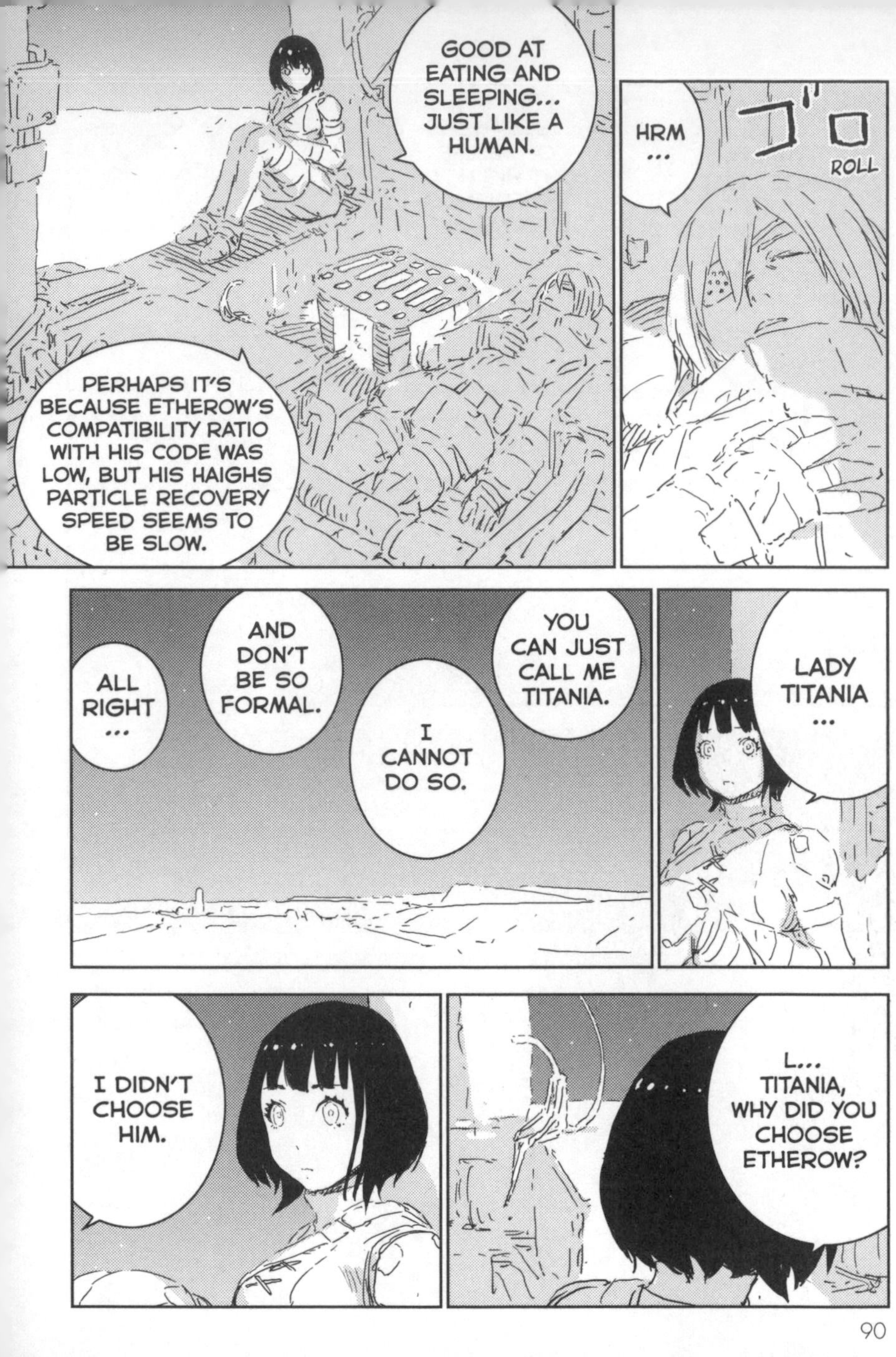

HRM ...
ゴロ
ROLL
GOOD AT EATING AND SLEEPING... JUST LIKE A HUMAN.
PERHAPS IT'S BECAUSE ETHEROW'S COMPATIBILITY RATIO WITH HIS CODE WAS LOW, BUT HIS HAIGHS PARTICLE RECOVERY SPEED SEEMS TO BE SLOW.
LADY TITANIA ...
YOU CAN JUST CALL ME TITANIA.
I CANNOT DO SO.
AND DON'T BE SO FORMAL.
ALL RIGHT ...
L... TITANIA, WHY DID YOU CHOOSE ETHEROW?
I DIDN'T CHOOSE HIM.

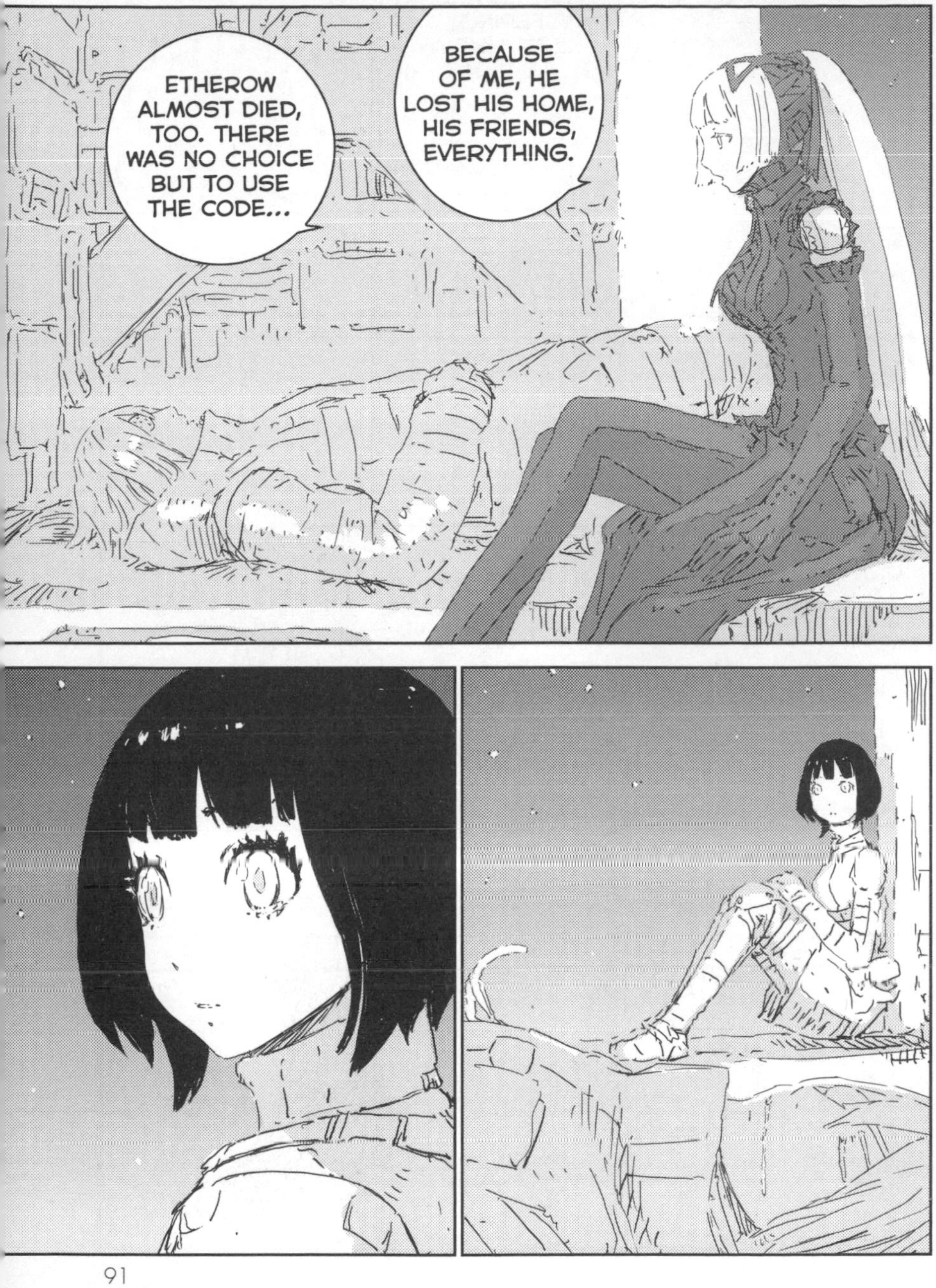
BECAUSE OF ME, HE LOST HIS HOME, HIS FRIENDS, EVERYTHING.
ETHEROW ALMOST DIED, TOO. THERE WAS NO CHOICE BUT TO USE THE CODE...

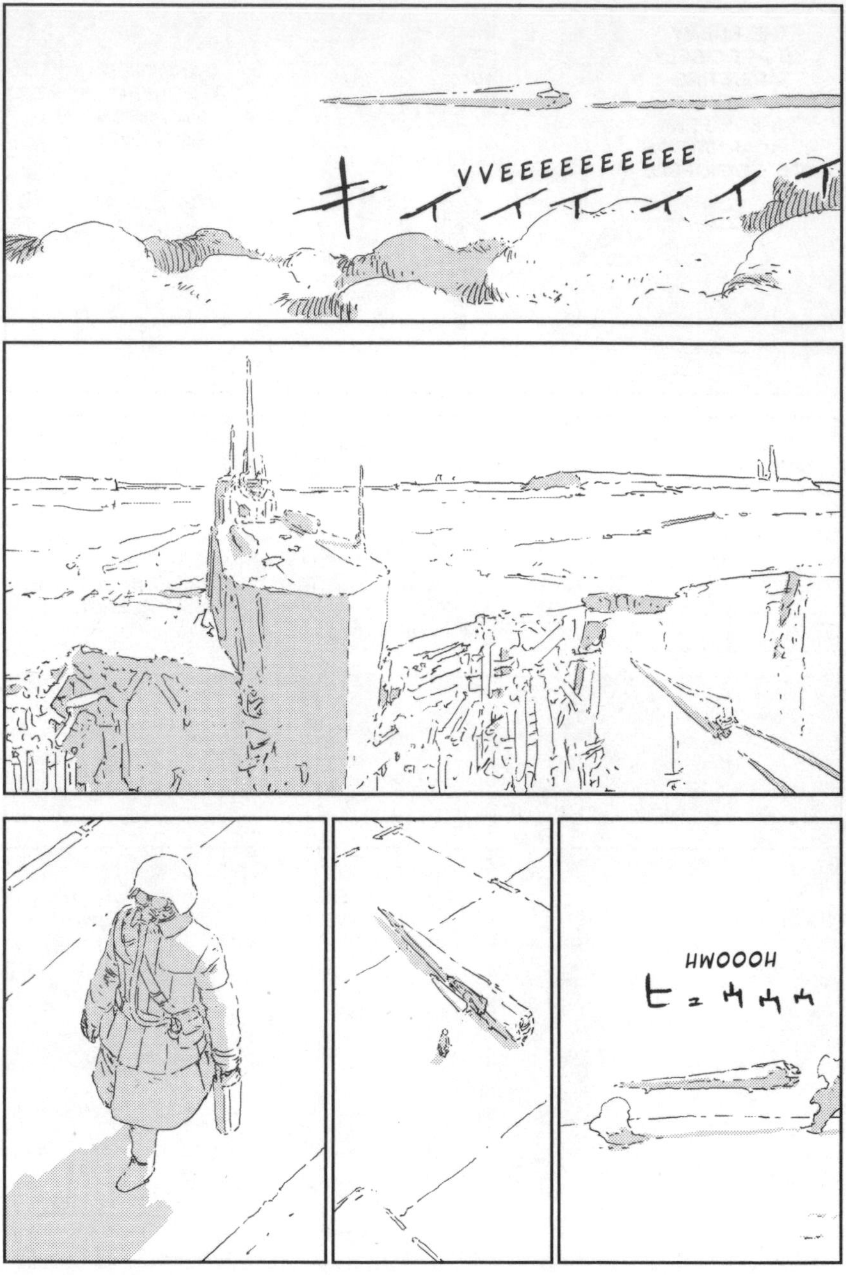
VVEEEEEEEEEE
HWOOOH

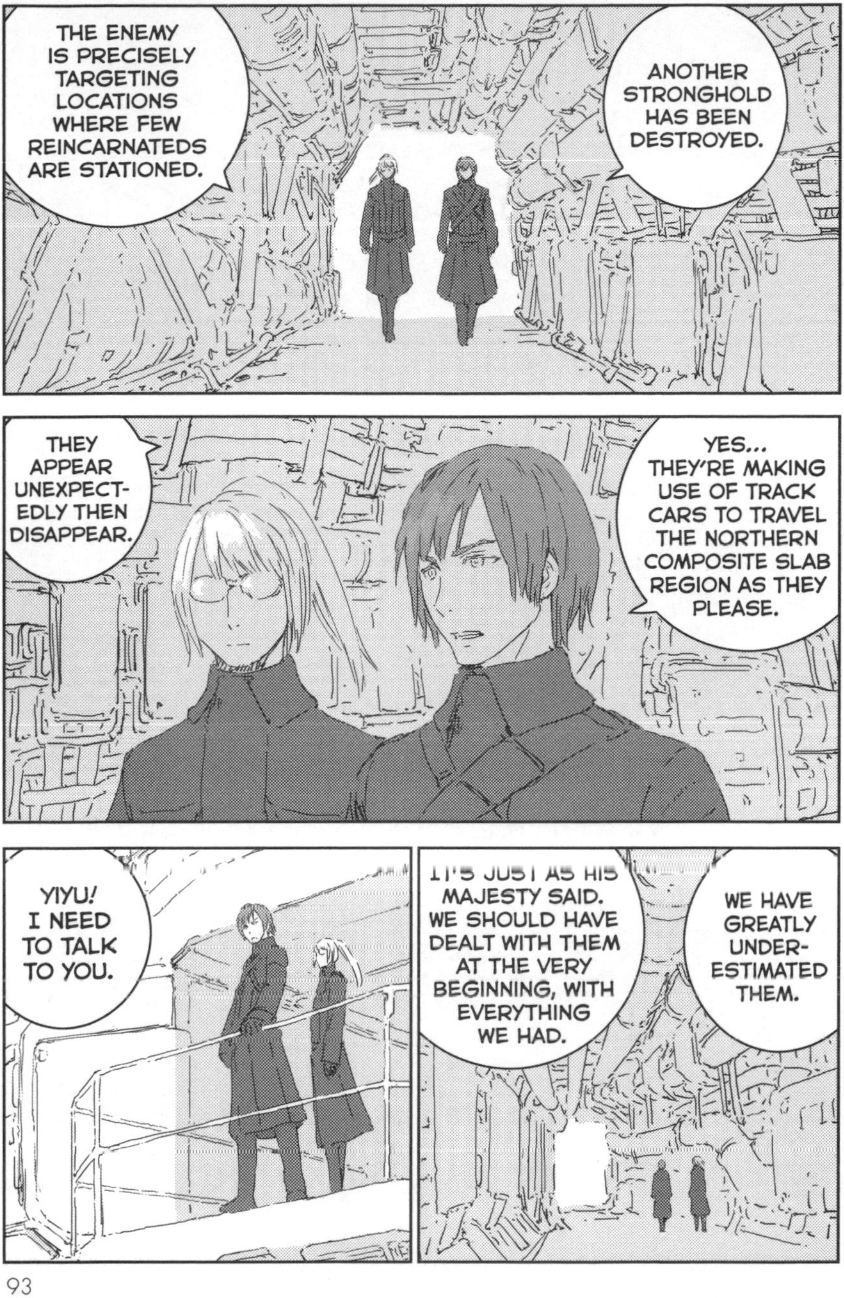
THE ENEMY IS PRECISELY TARGETING LOCATIONS WHERE FEW REINCARNATEDS ARE STATIONED.
ANOTHER STRONGHOLD HAS BEEN DESTROYED.
THEY APPEAR UNEXPECTEDLY THEN DISAPPEAR.
YES... THEY'RE MAKING USE OF TRACK CARS TO TRAVEL THE NORTHERN COMPOSITE SLAB REGION AS THEY PLEASE.
YIYU! I NEED TO TALK TO YOU.
IT'S JUST AS HIS MAJESTY SAID. WE SHOULD HAVE DEALT WITH THEM AT THE VERY BEGINNING, WITH EVERYTHING WE HAD.
WE HAVE GREATLY UNDERESTIMATED THEM.

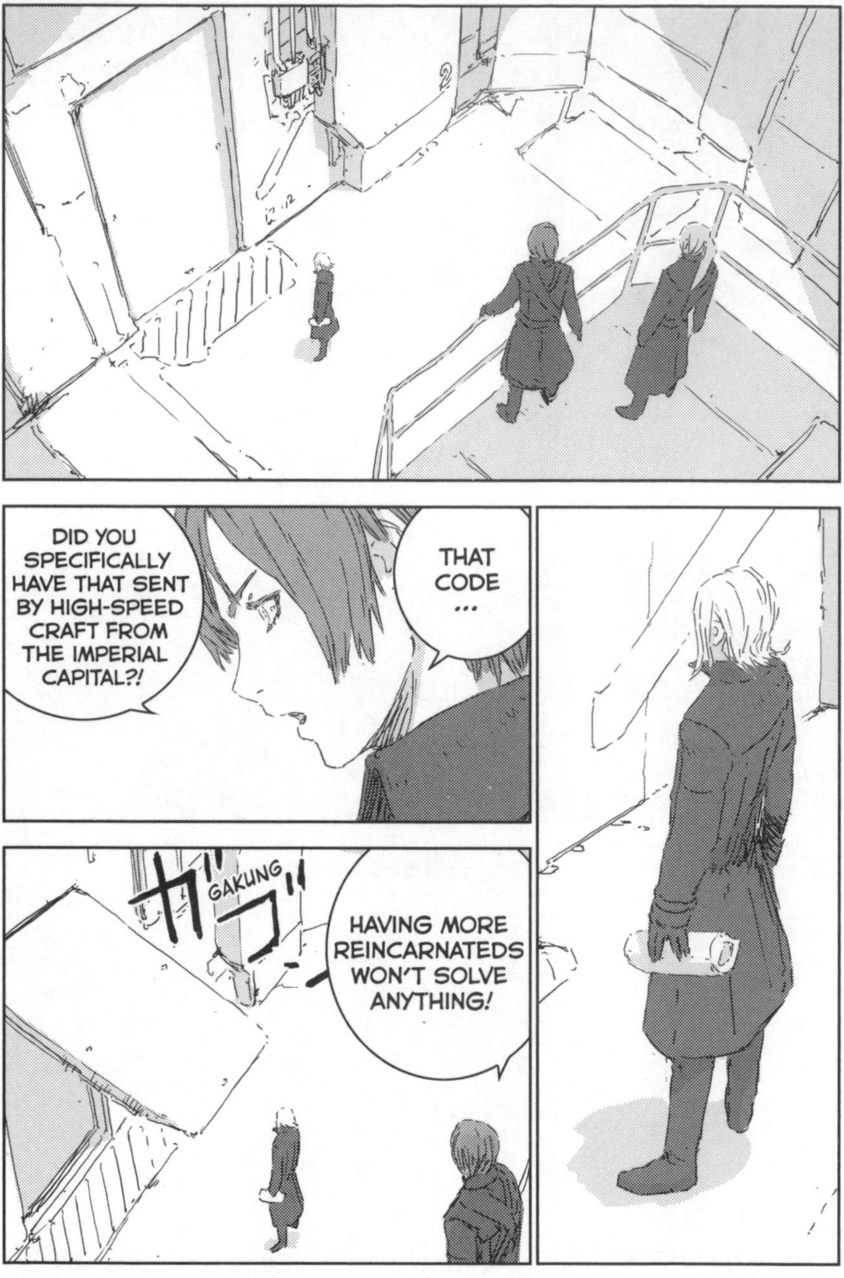
THAT CODE...
DID YOU SPECIFICALLY HAVE THAT SENT BY HIGH-SPEED CRAFT FROM THE IMPERIAL CAPITAL?!
GAKUNG
HAVING MORE REINCARNATEDS WON'T SOLVE ANYTHING!

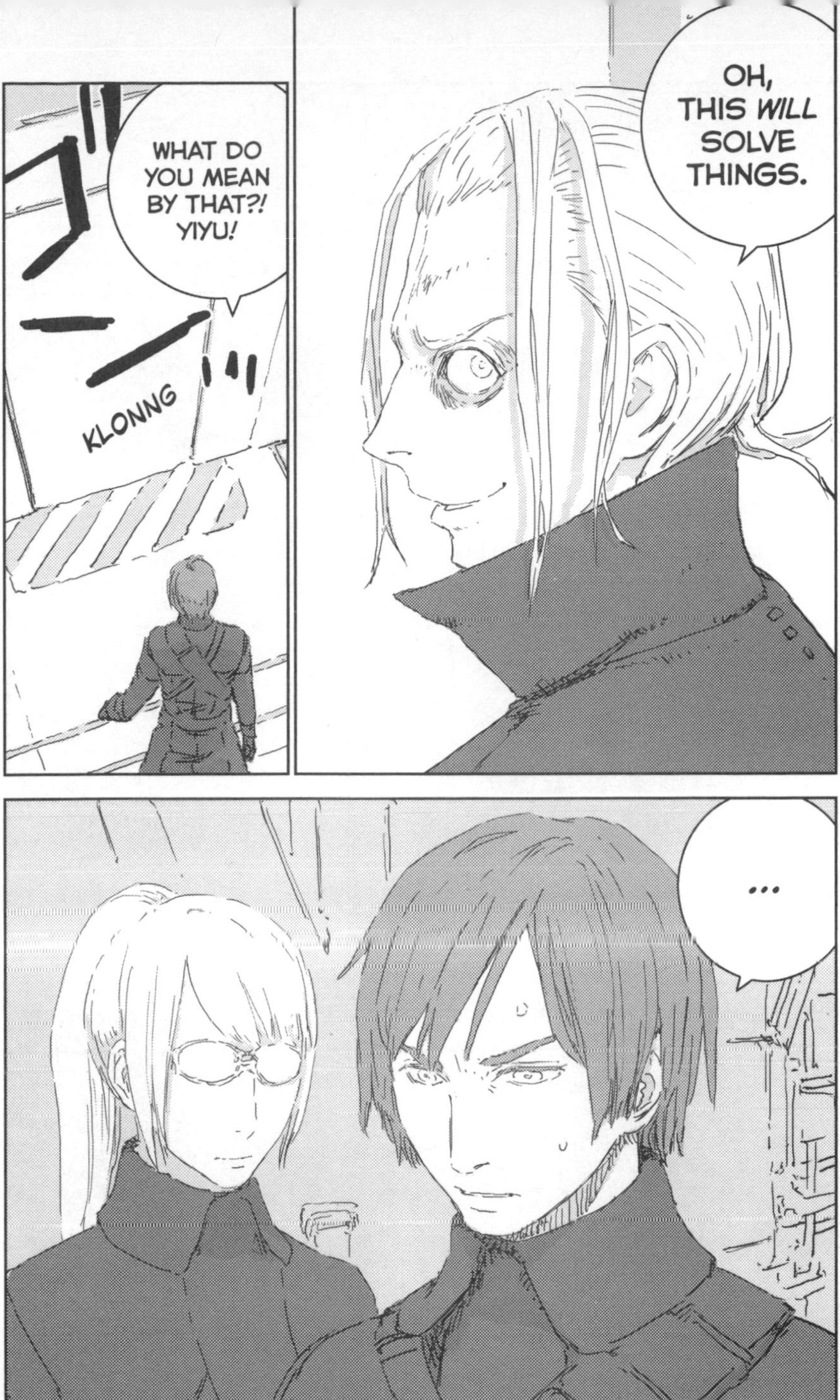
OH, THIS WILL SOLVE THINGS.
WHAT DO YOU MEAN BY THAT?! YIYU!
KLONNG
...

ZEO
...

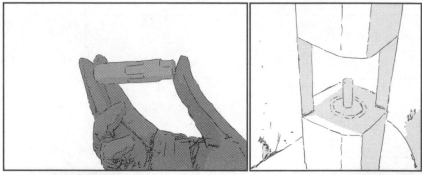

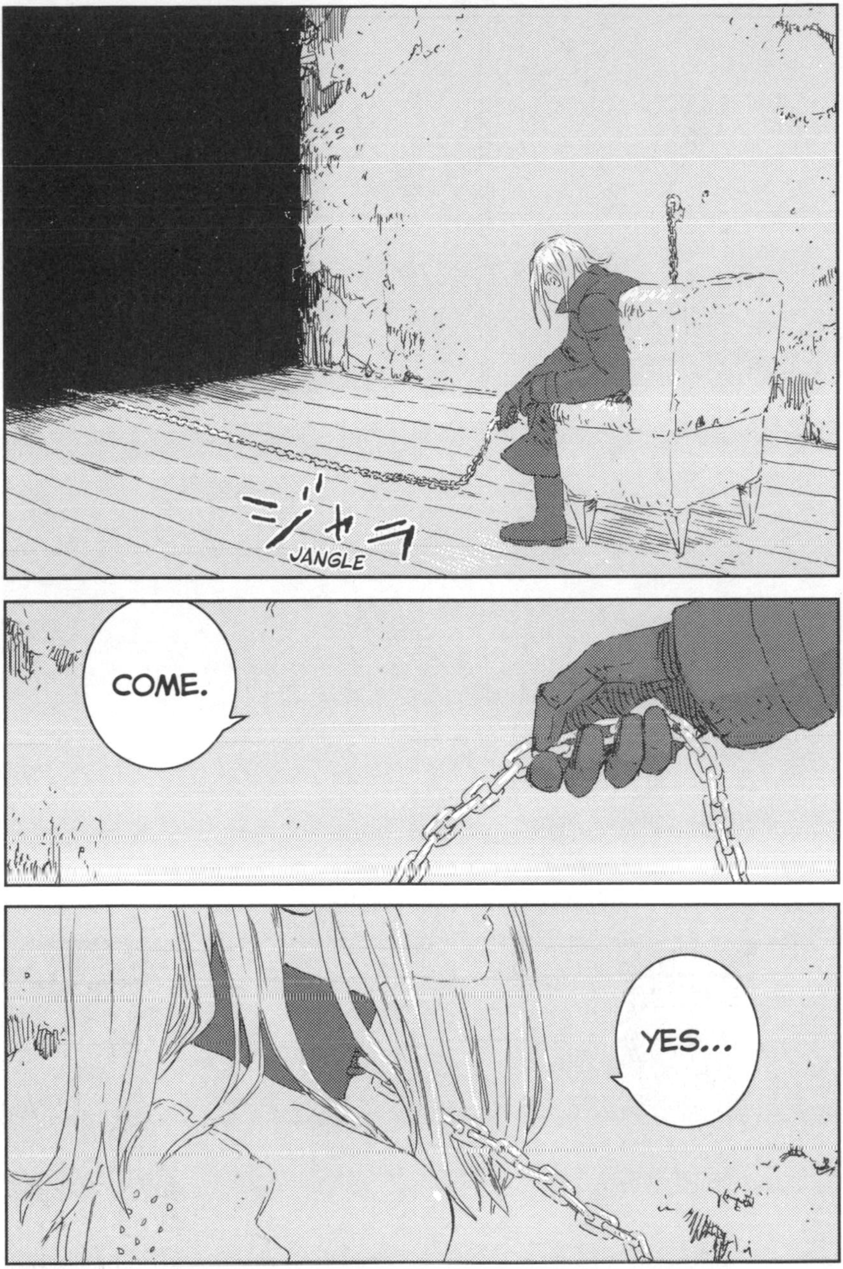
ジャラ
JANGLE
COME.
YES...

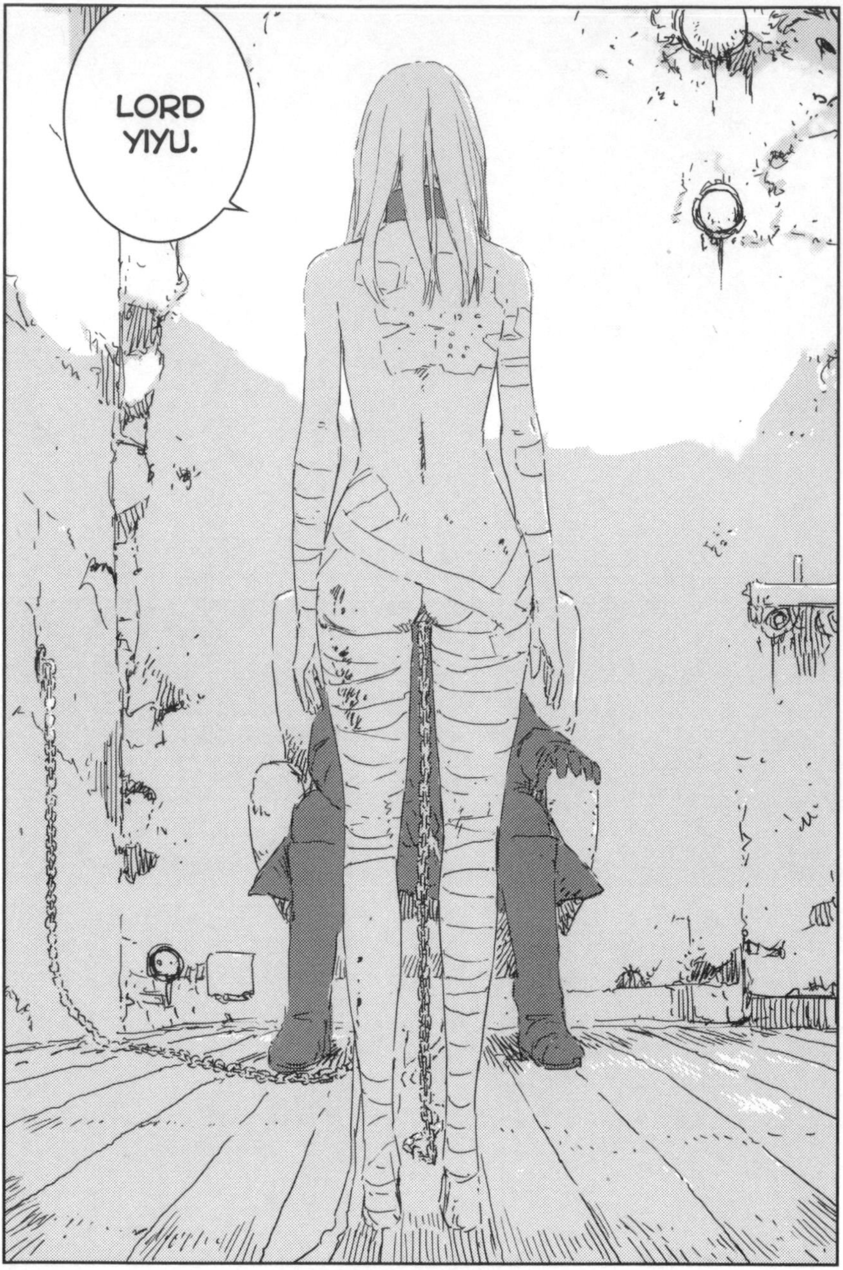
LORD YIYU.

CHAPTER 06 END

APOSIMZ

CHAPTER 07

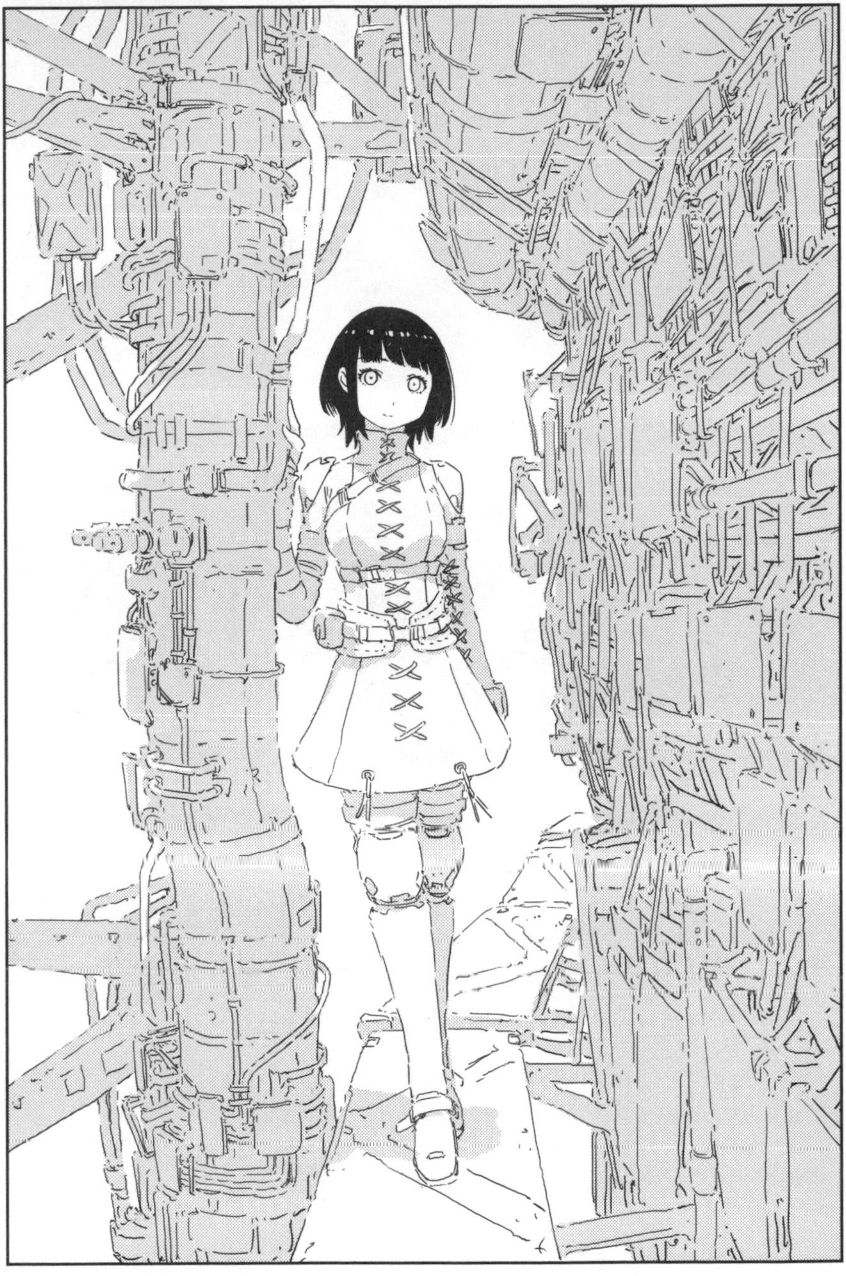

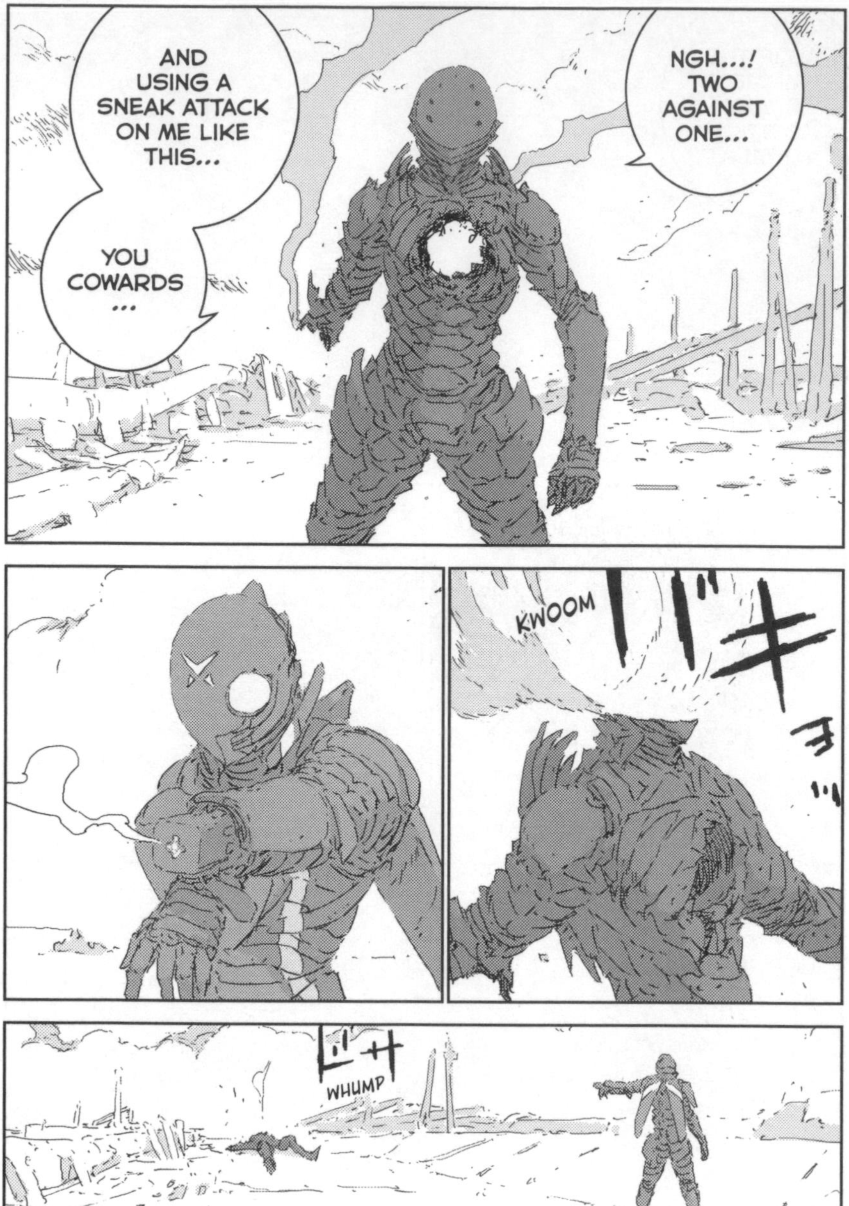
NGH...! TWO AGAINST ONE...
AND USING A SNEAK ATTACK ON ME LIKE THIS...
YOU COWARDS ...
KWOOM
WHUMP

AS IF THE EMPIRE'S IN ANY POSITION TO TALK!
SSSSHHHH

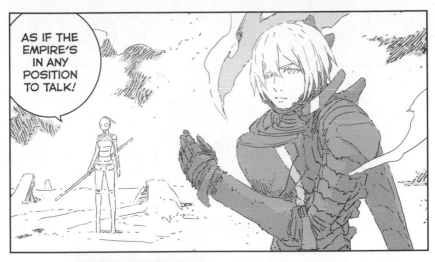

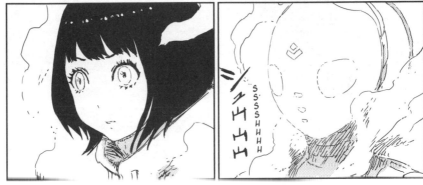

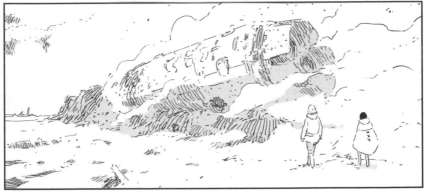

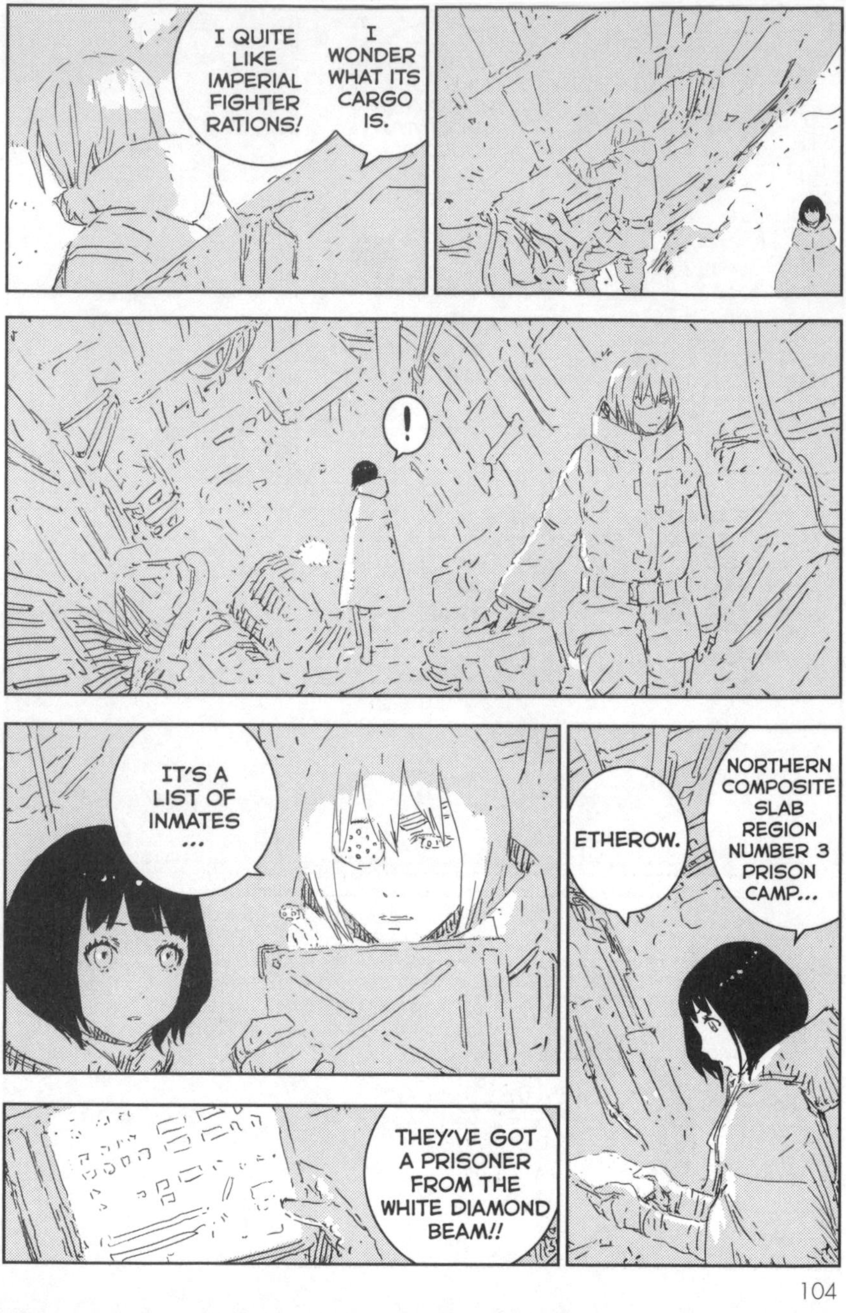
I QUITE LIKE IMPERIAL FIGHTER RATIONS!
I WONDER WHAT ITS CARGO IS.
!
IT'S A LIST OF INMATES ...
NORTHERN COMPOSITE SLAB REGION NUMBER 3 PRISON CAMP...
ETHEROW.
THEY'VE GOT A PRISONER FROM THE WHITE DIAMOND BEAM!!

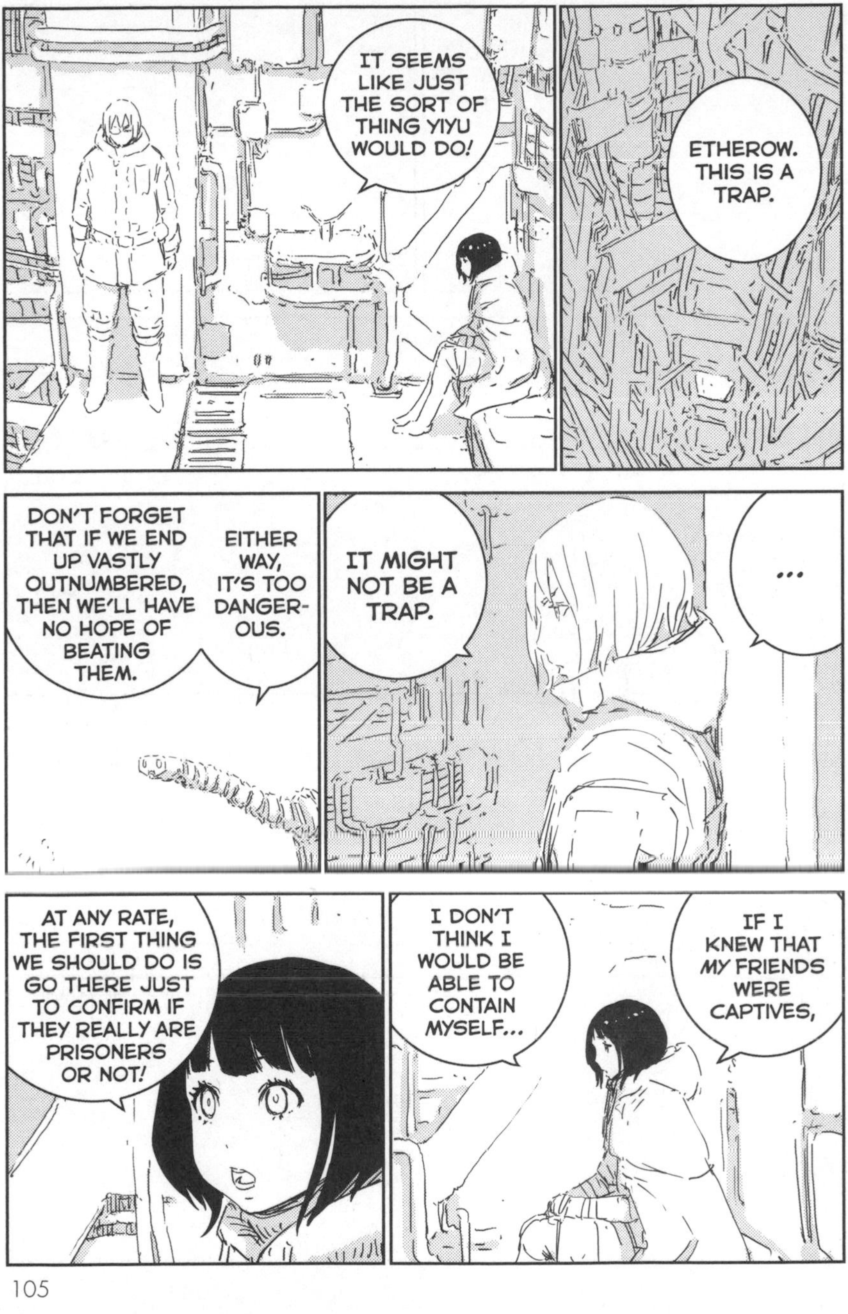
IT SEEMS LIKE JUST THE SORT OF THING YIYU WOULD DO!
ETHEROW. THIS IS A TRAP.
...
IT MIGHT NOT BE A TRAP.
EITHER WAY, IT'S TOO DANGER-OUS.
DON'T FORGET THAT IF WE END UP VASTLY OUTNUMBERED, THEN WE'LL HAVE NO HOPE OF BEATING THEM.
IF I KNEW THAT MY FRIENDS WERE CAPTIVES,
I DON'T THINK I WOULD BE ABLE TO CONTAIN MYSELF...
AT ANY RATE, THE FIRST THING WE SHOULD DO IS GO THERE JUST TO CONFIRM IF THEY REALLY ARE PRISONERS OR NOT!

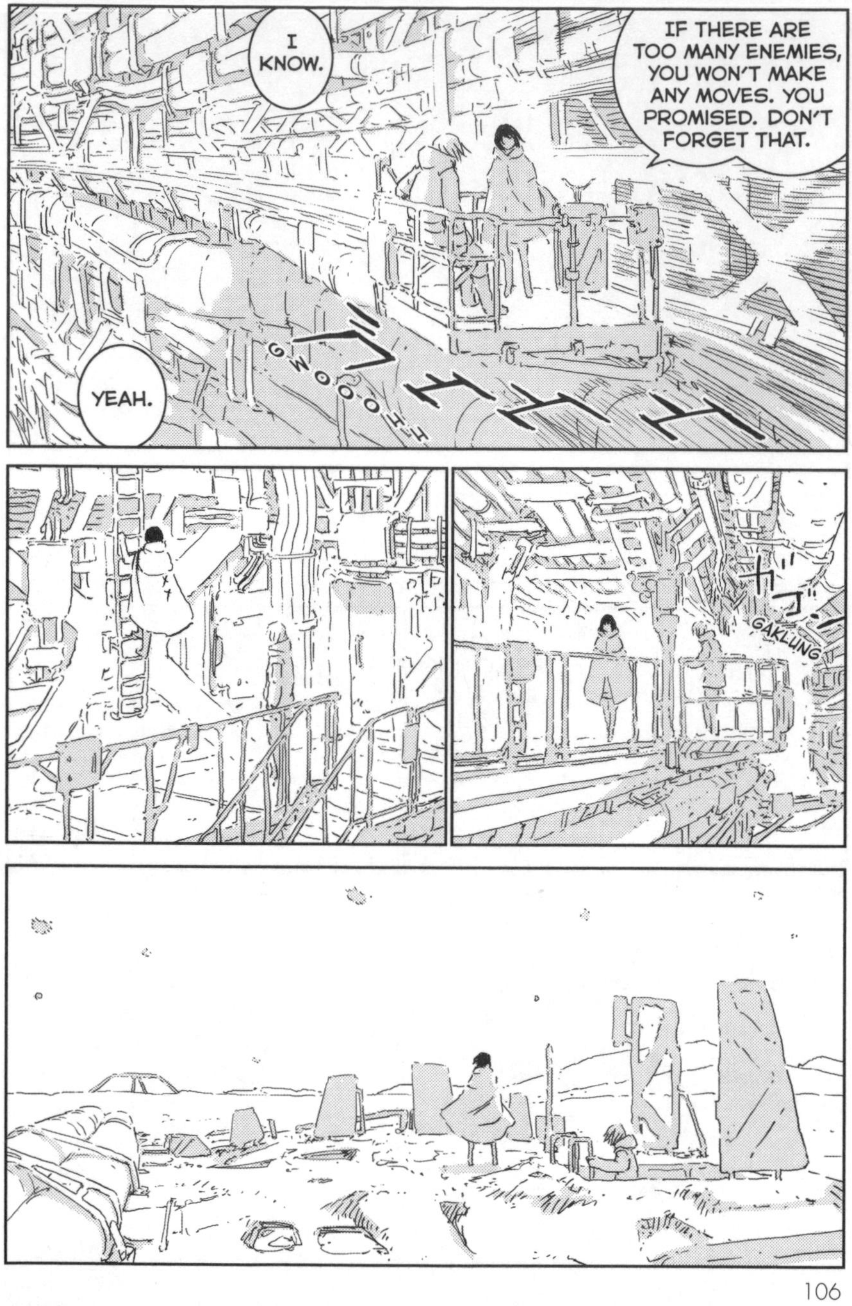
IF THERE ARE TOO MANY ENEMIES, YOU WON'T MAKE ANY MOVES. YOU PROMISED. DON'T FORGET THAT.
I KNOW.
YEAH.
GWOOOOH
GAKLUNG

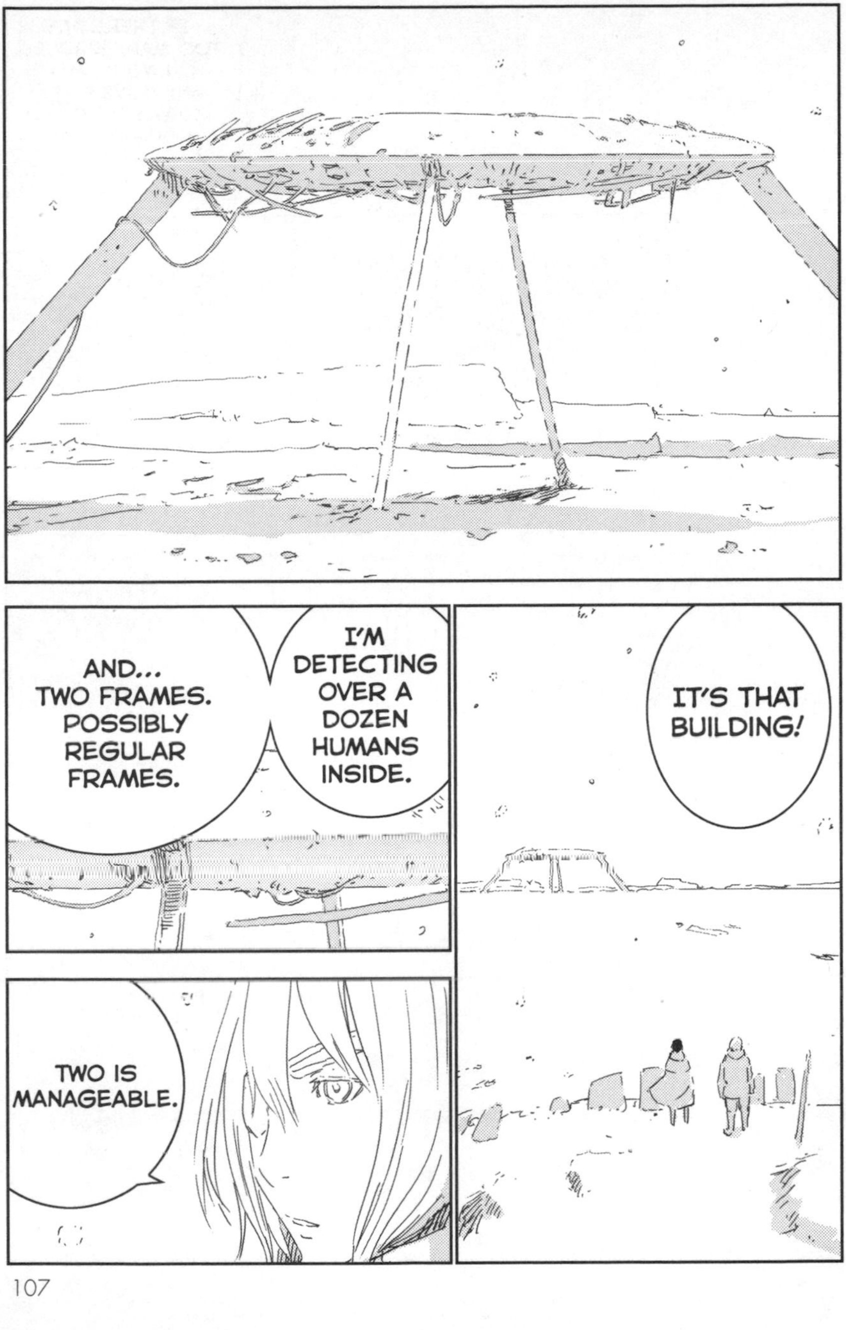
IT'S THAT BUILDING!
I'M DETECTING OVER A DOZEN HUMANS INSIDE.
AND... TWO FRAMES. POSSIBLY REGULAR FRAMES.
TWO IS MANAGEABLE.

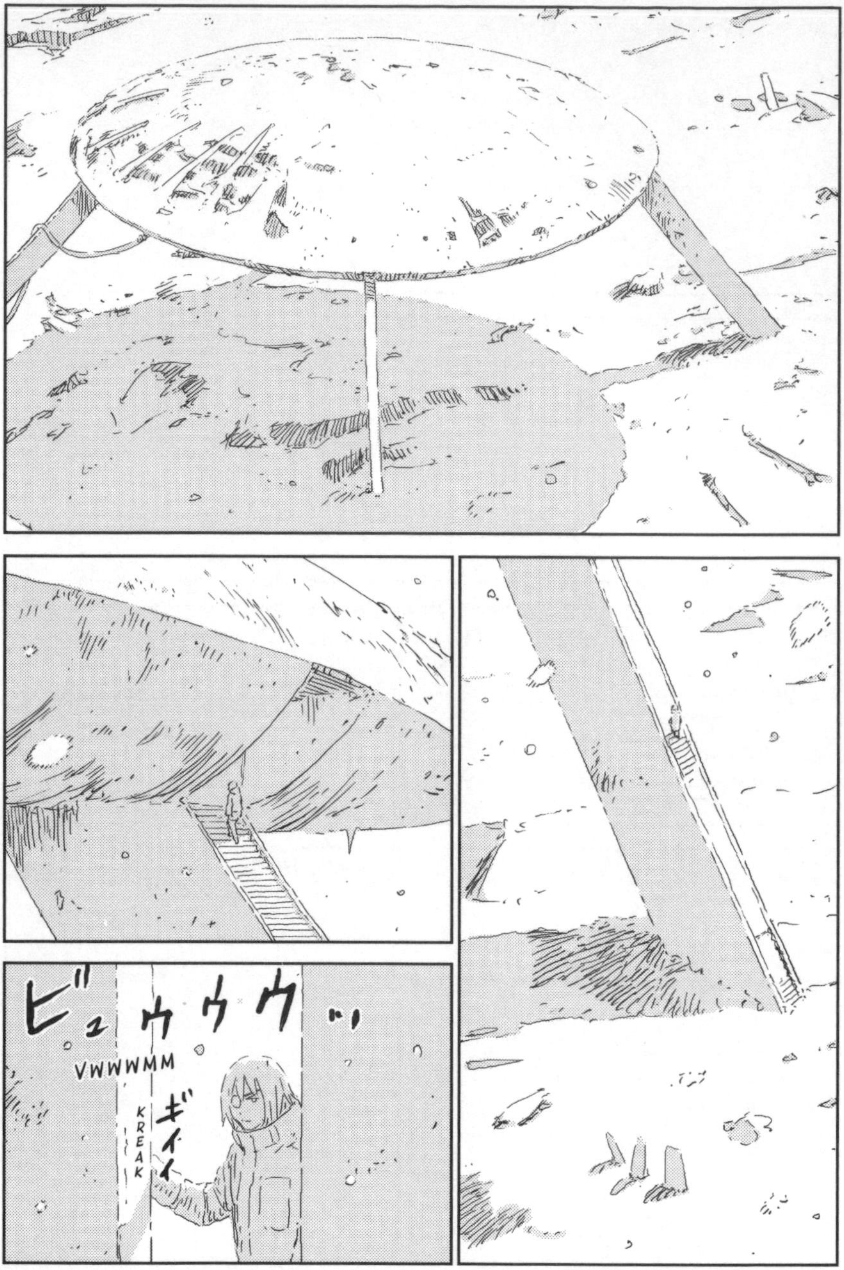
ビュウウウ
VWWWWMM
ギイイ
KREAK

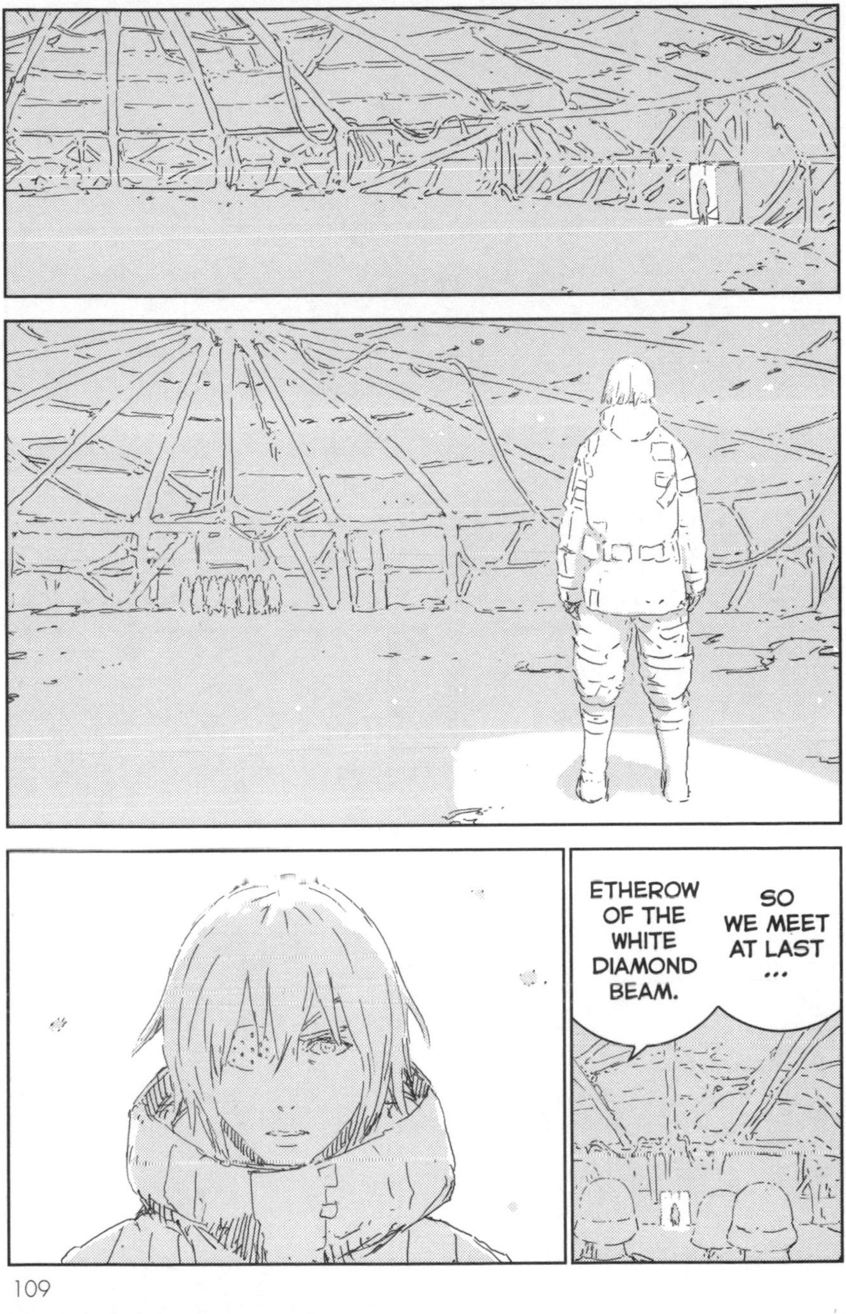
SO WE MEET AT LAST ...
ETHEROW OF THE WHITE DIAMOND BEAM.

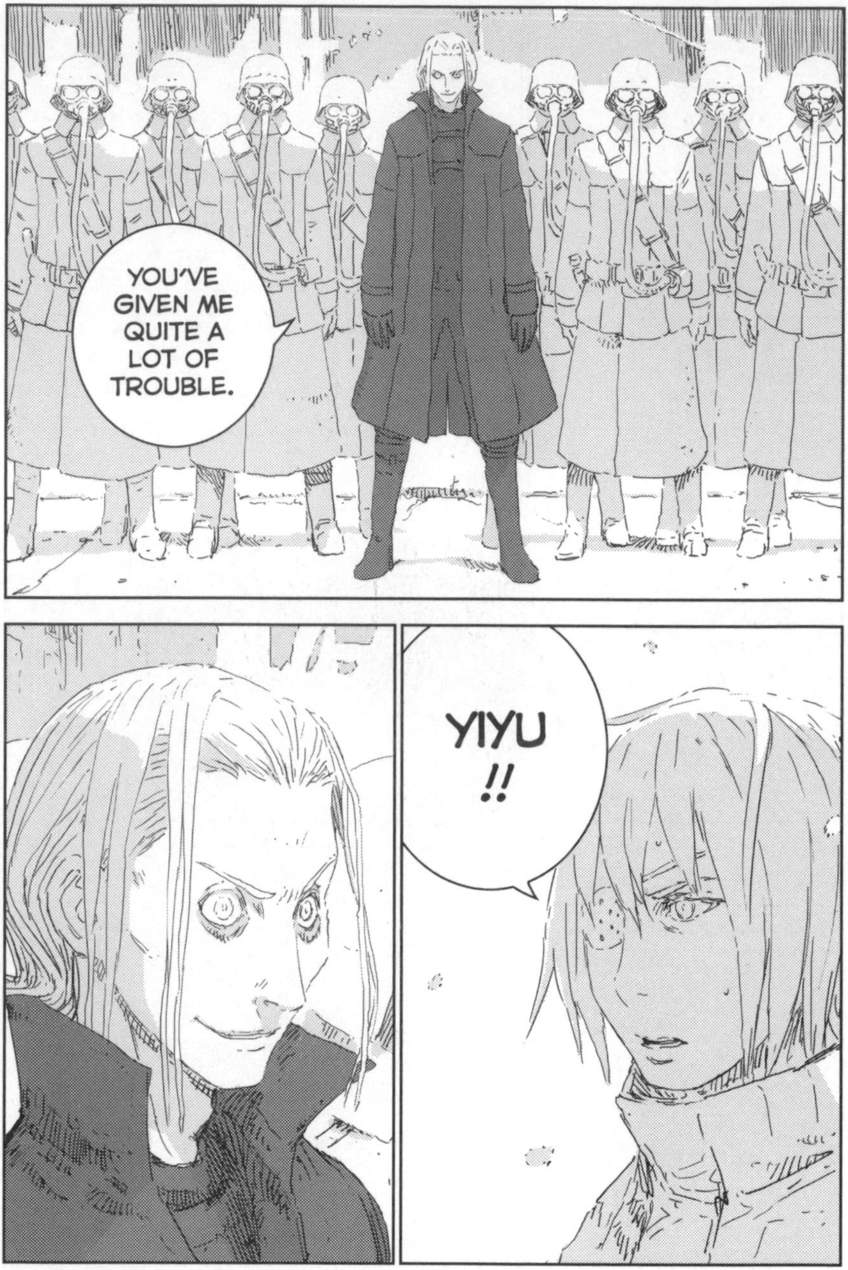
YOU'VE GIVEN ME QUITE A LOT OF TROUBLE.
YIYU !!

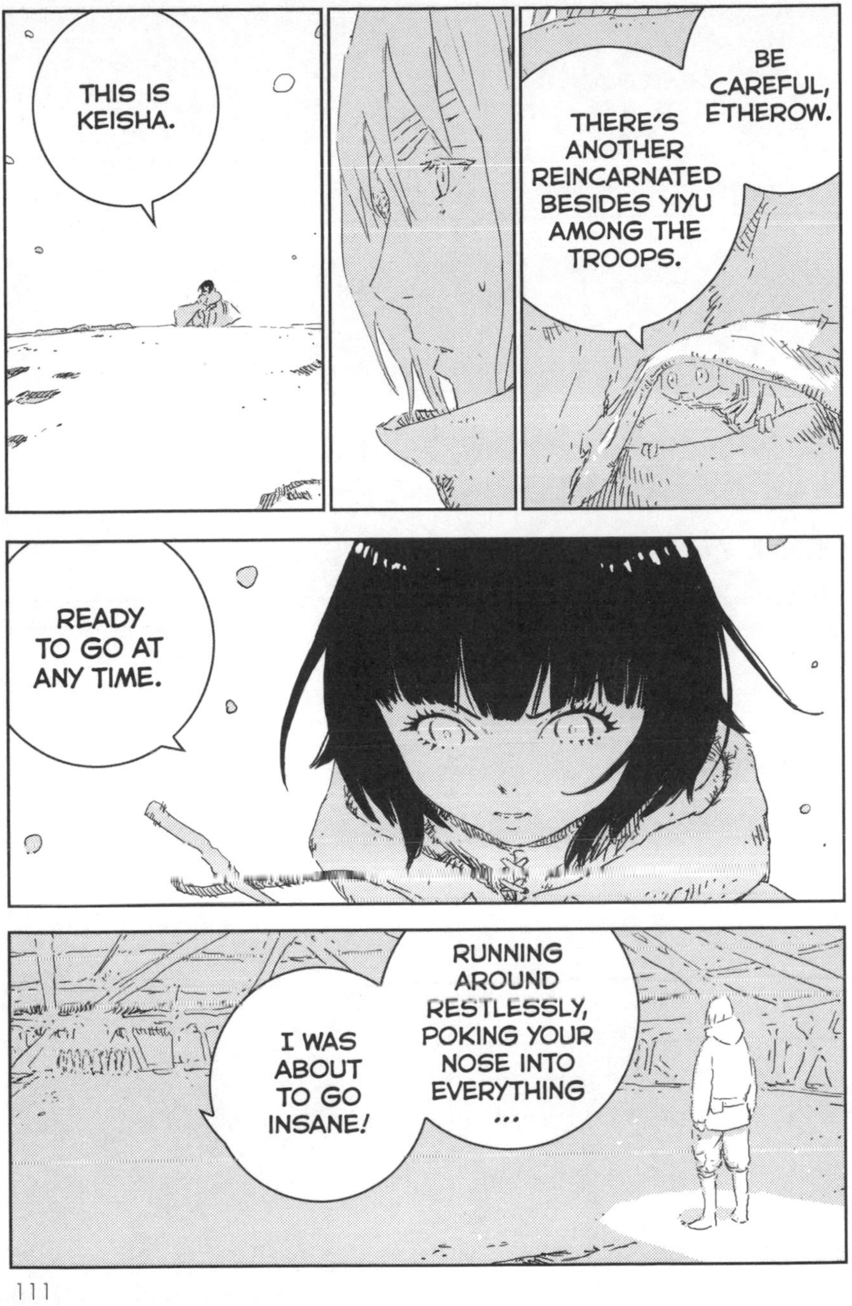
BE CAREFUL, ETHEROW.
THERE'S ANOTHER REINCARNATED BESIDES YIYU AMONG THE TROOPS.
THIS IS KEISHA.
READY TO GO AT ANY TIME.
RUNNING AROUND RESTLESSLY, POKING YOUR NOSE INTO EVERYTHING ...
I WAS ABOUT TO GO INSANE!

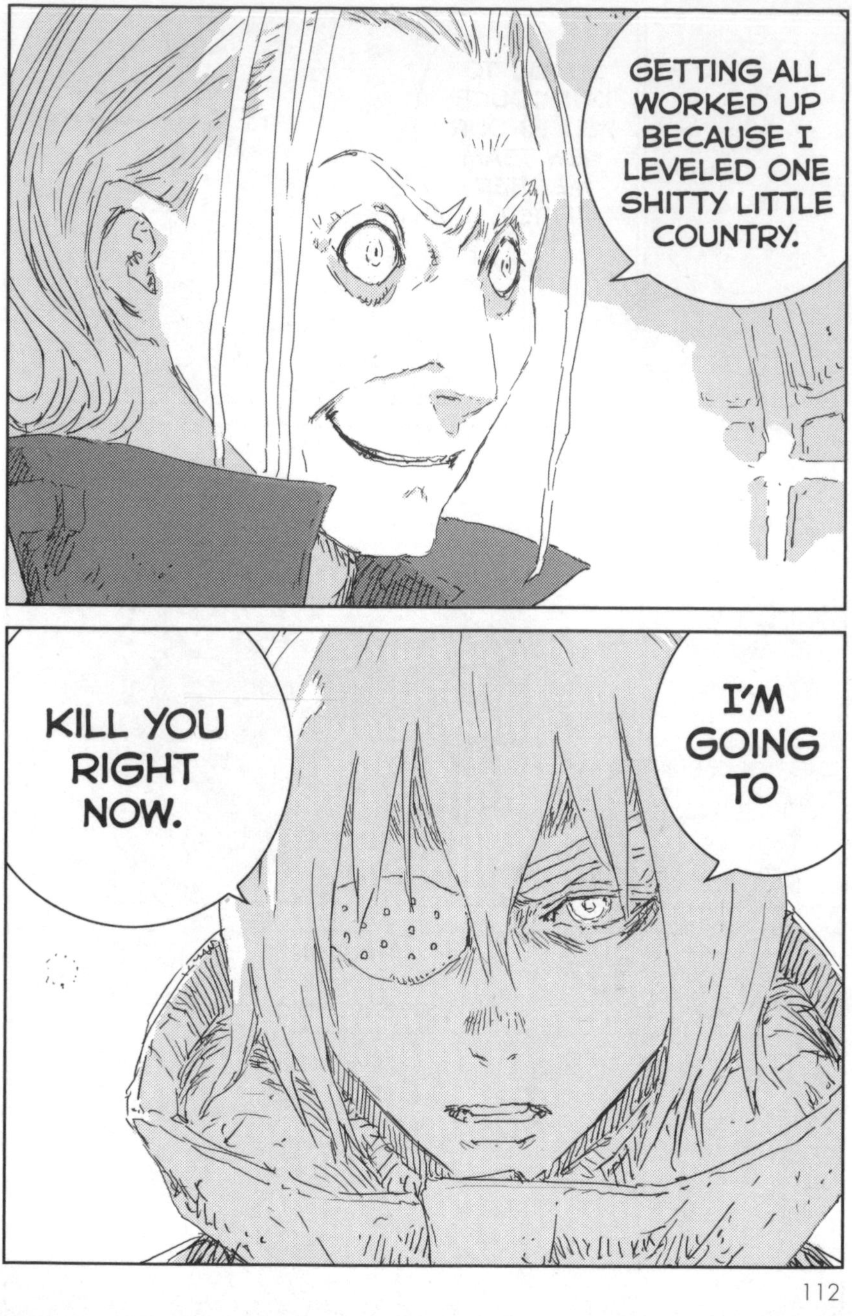
GETTING ALL WORKED UP BECAUSE I LEVELED ONE SHITTY LITTLE COUNTRY.
I'M GOING TO
KILL YOU RIGHT NOW.

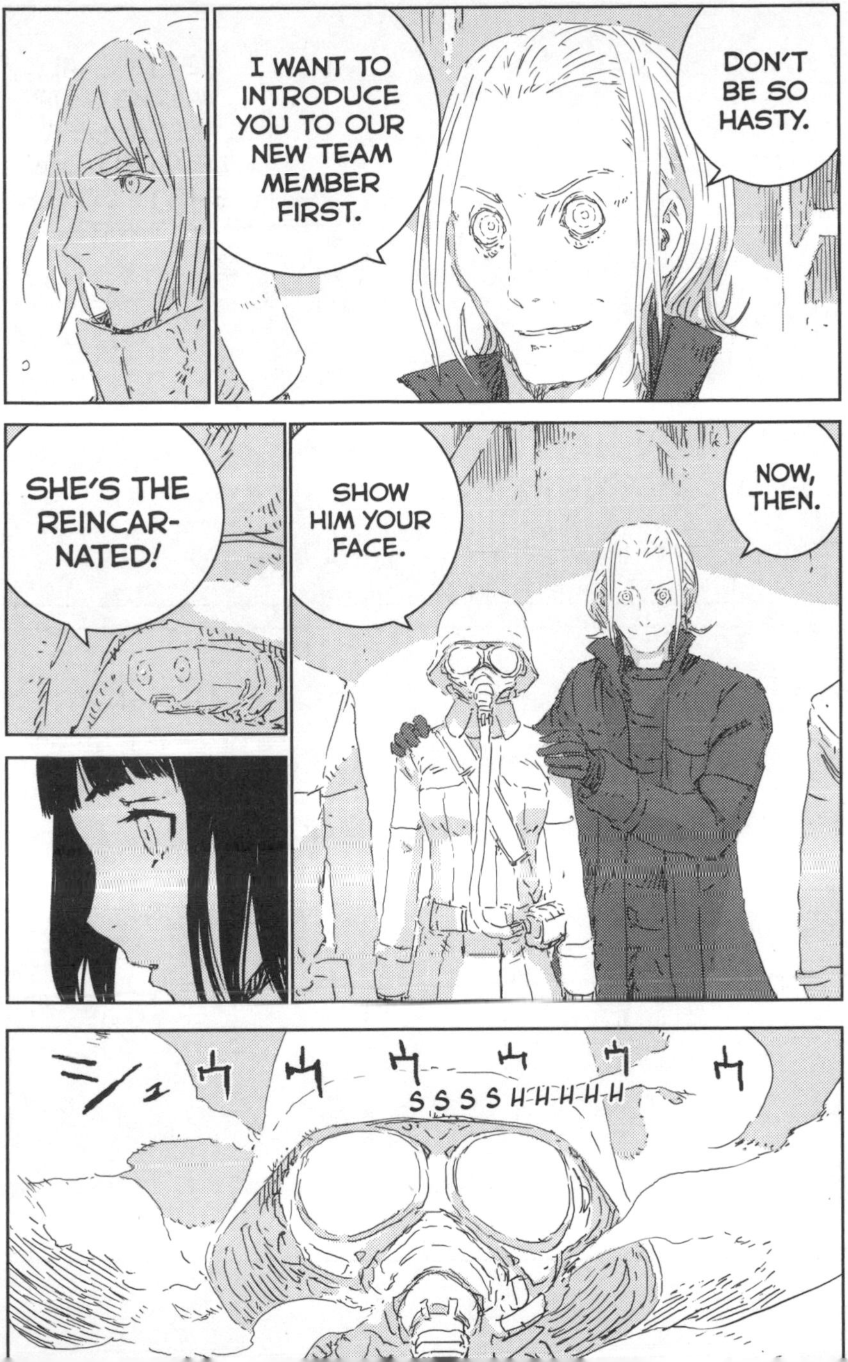
DON'T BE SO HASTY.
I WANT TO INTRODUCE YOU TO OUR NEW TEAM MEMBER FIRST.
NOW, THEN.
SHOW HIM YOUR FACE.
SHE'S THE REINCAR-NATED!
シュウウウウウ
SSSSH-H-H-H-H

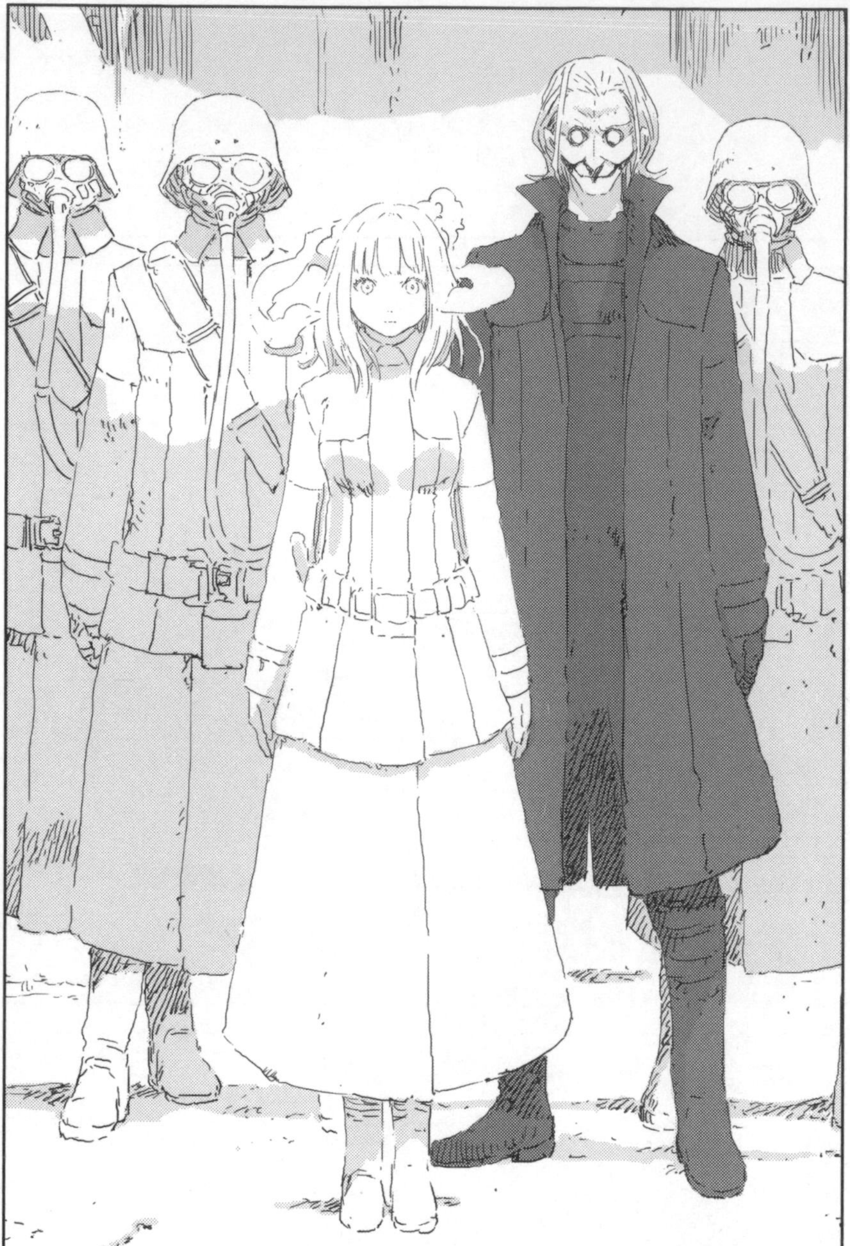

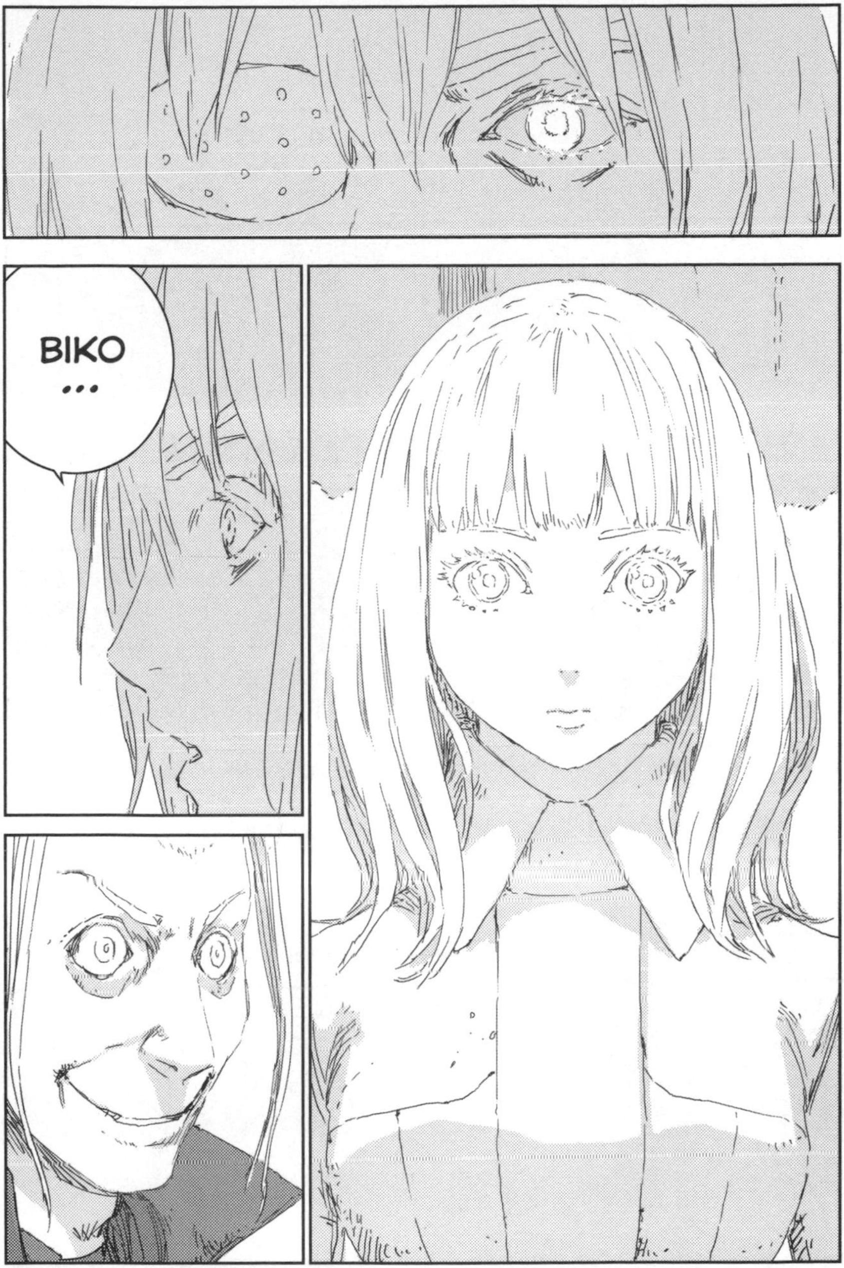
BIKO
...

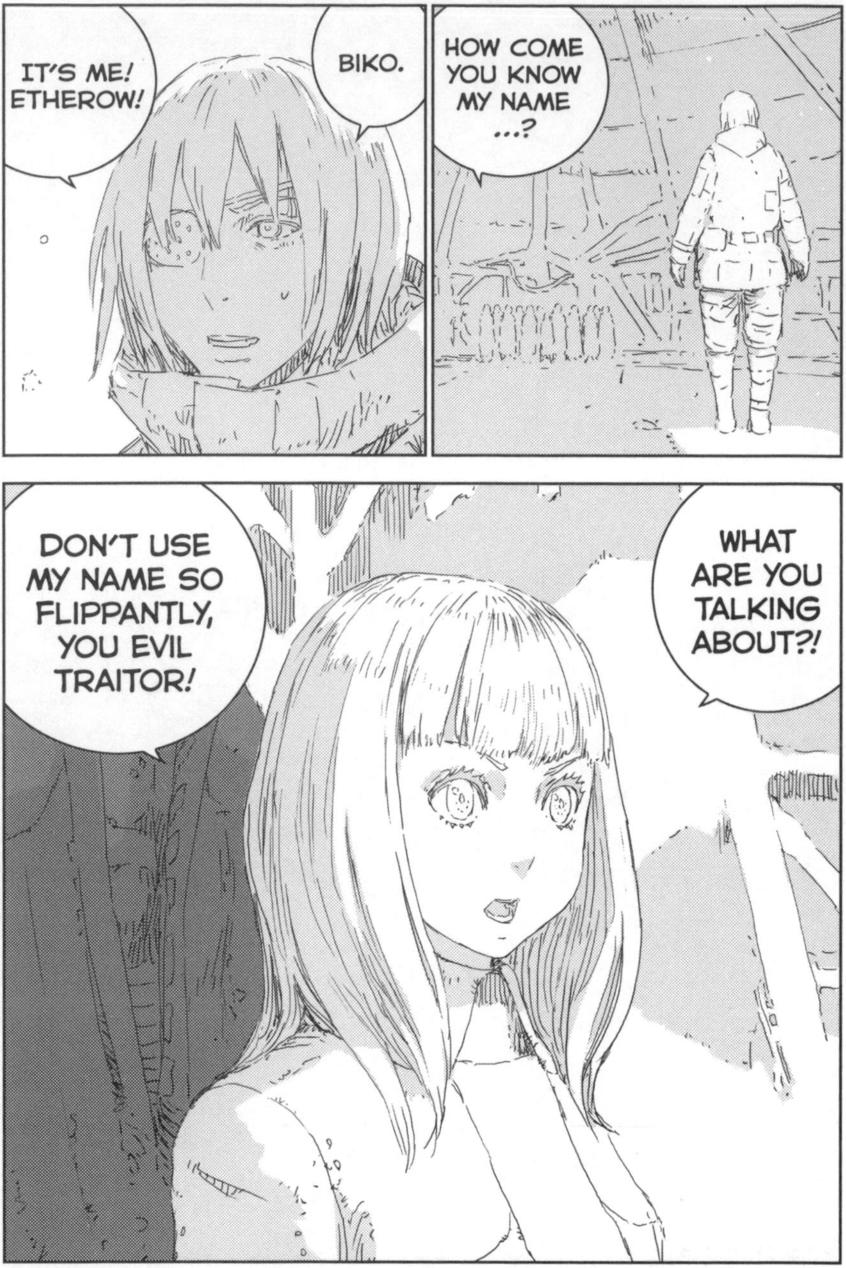
IT'S ME! ETHEROW!
BIKO.
HOW COME YOU KNOW MY NAME ...?
DON'T USE MY NAME SO FLIPPANTLY, YOU EVIL TRAITOR!
WHAT ARE YOU TALKING ABOUT?!

CHAPTER 07 END

APOSIMZ

CHAPTER 08

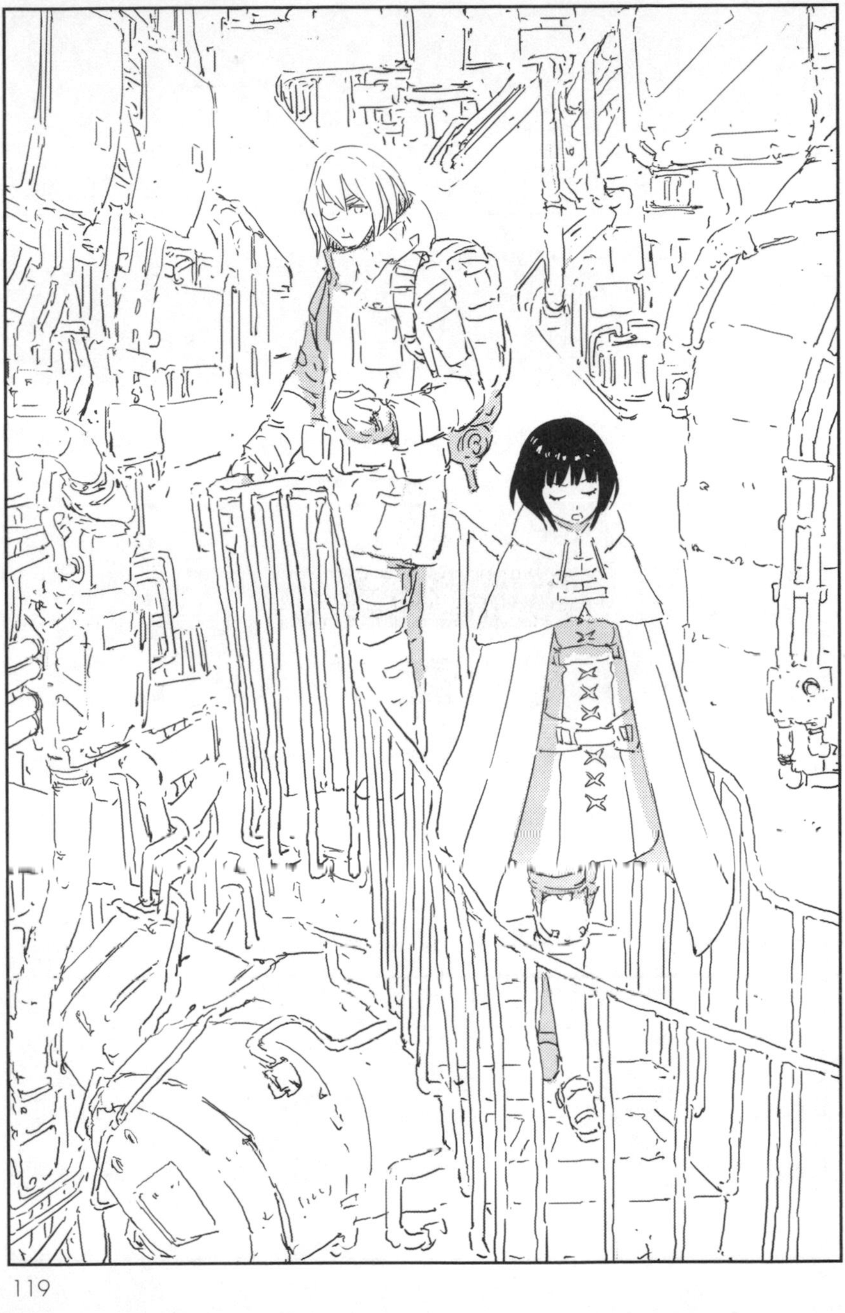

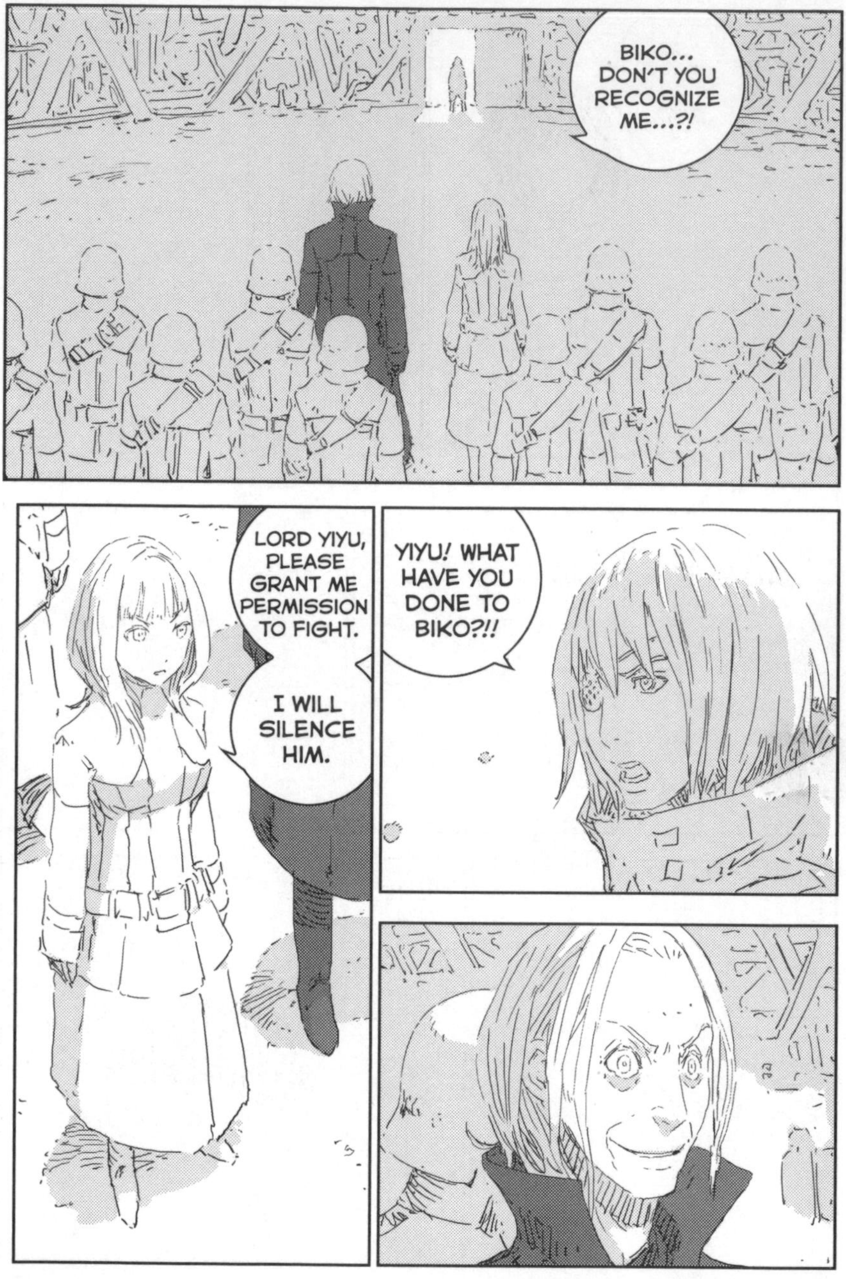
BIKO... DON'T YOU RECOGNIZE ME...?!
LORD YIYU, PLEASE GRANT ME PERMISSION TO FIGHT.
I WILL SILENCE HIM.
YIYU! WHAT HAVE YOU DONE TO BIKO?!!

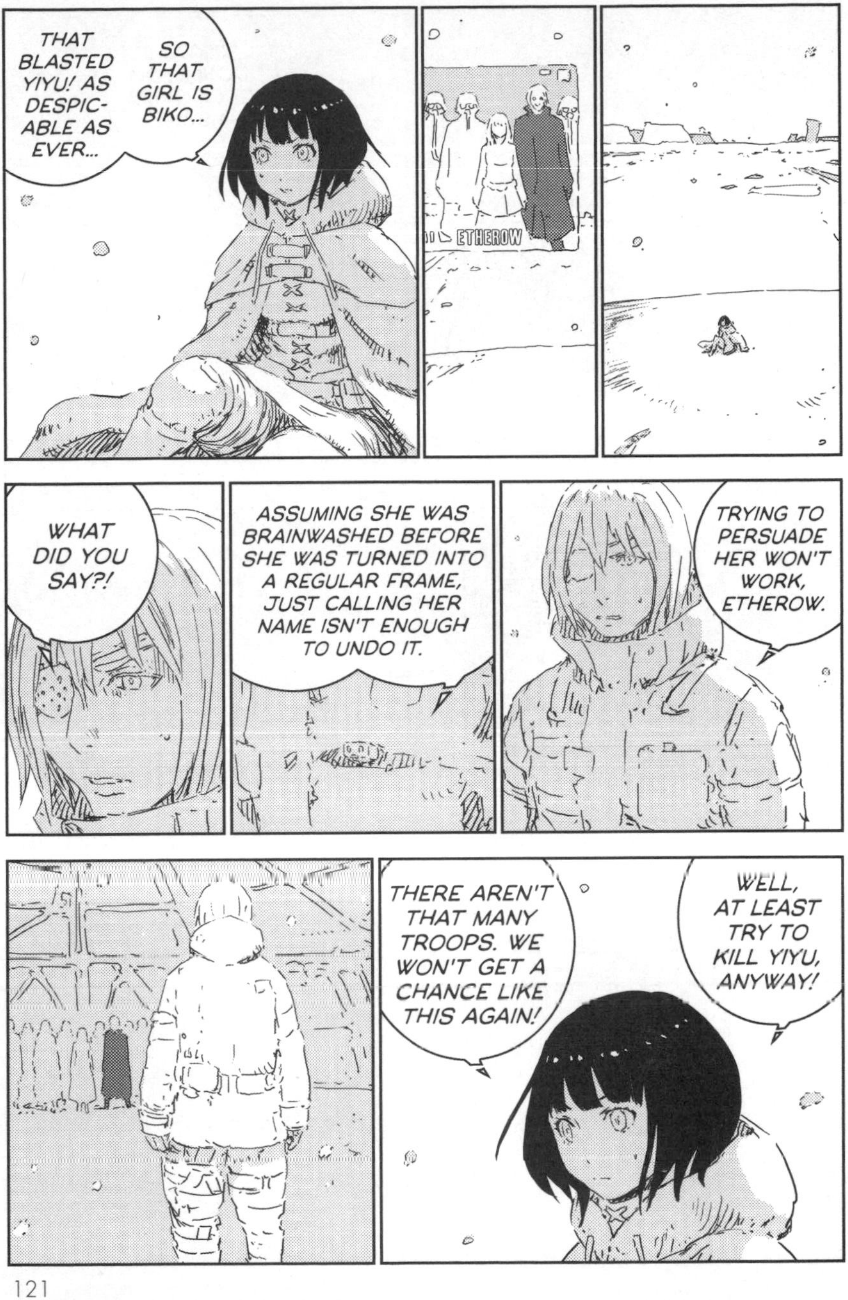
ETHEROW
SO THAT GIRL IS BIKO...
THAT BLASTED YIYU! AS DESPICABLE AS EVER...
TRYING TO PERSUADE HER WON'T WORK, ETHEROW.
ASSUMING SHE WAS BRAINWASHED BEFORE SHE WAS TURNED INTO A REGULAR FRAME, JUST CALLING HER NAME ISN'T ENOUGH TO UNDO IT.
WHAT DID YOU SAY?!
WELL, AT LEAST TRY TO KILL YIYU, ANYWAY!
THERE AREN'T THAT MANY TROOPS. WE WON'T GET A CHANCE LIKE THIS AGAIN!

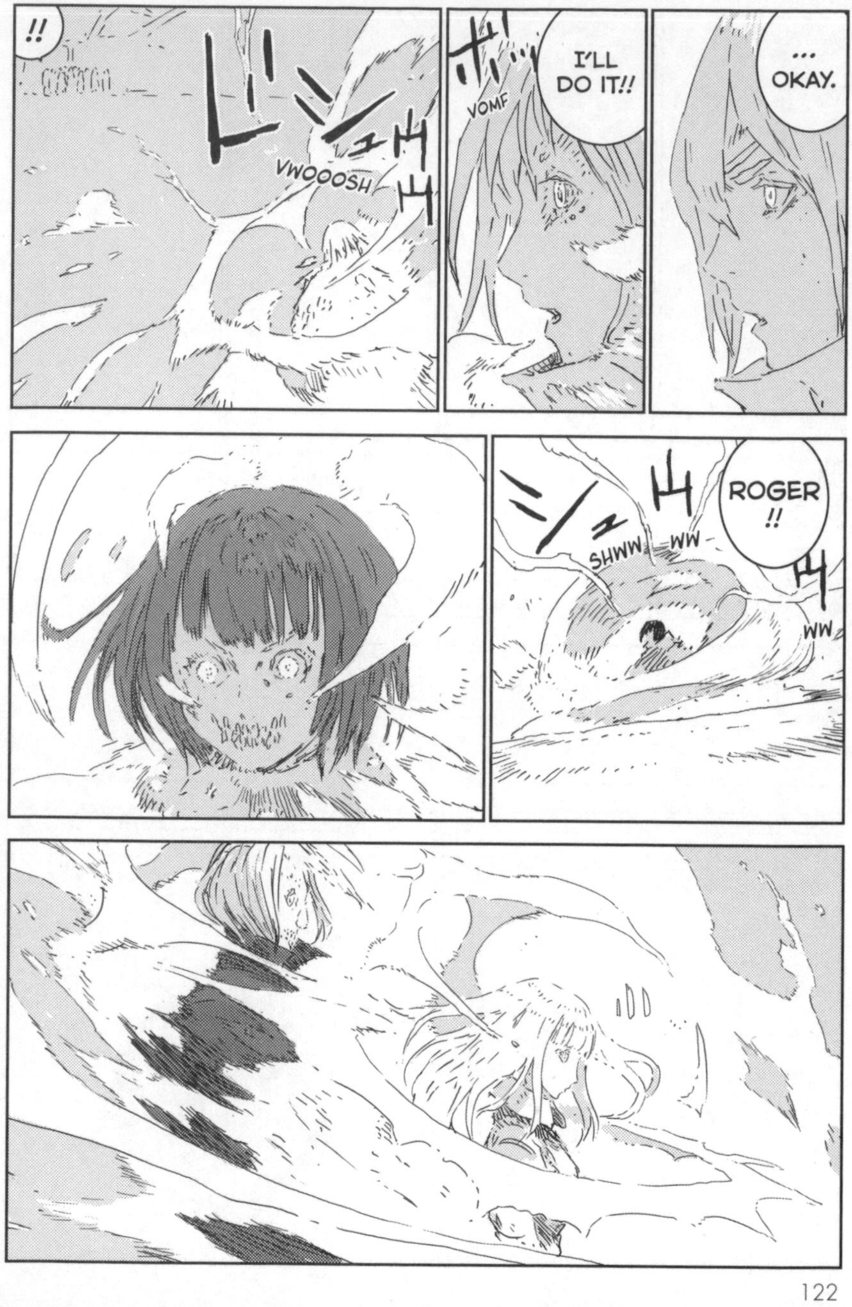
!!
VWOOOSH
VOMF
I'LL DO IT!!
... OKAY.
SHWWWWW
ROGER !!
WW

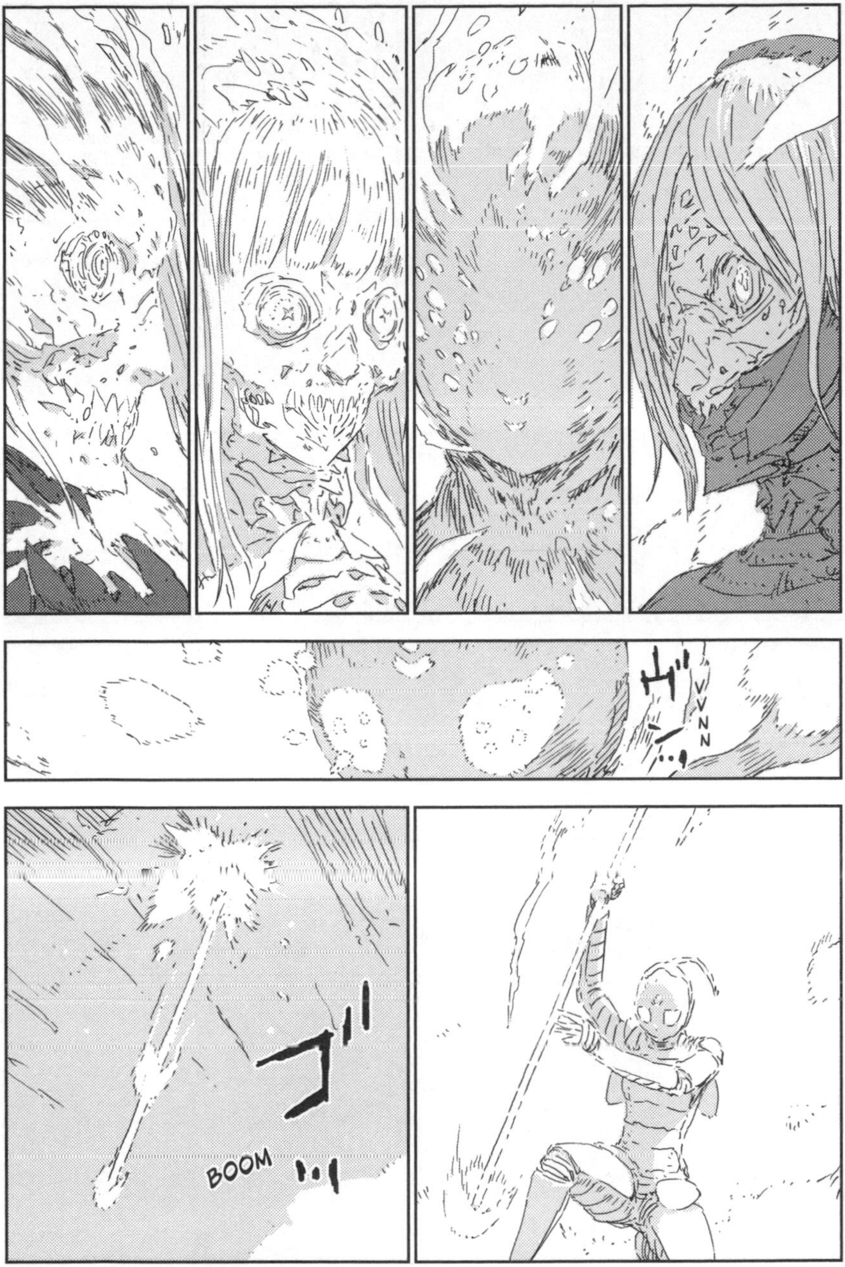
VVVNN
BOOM

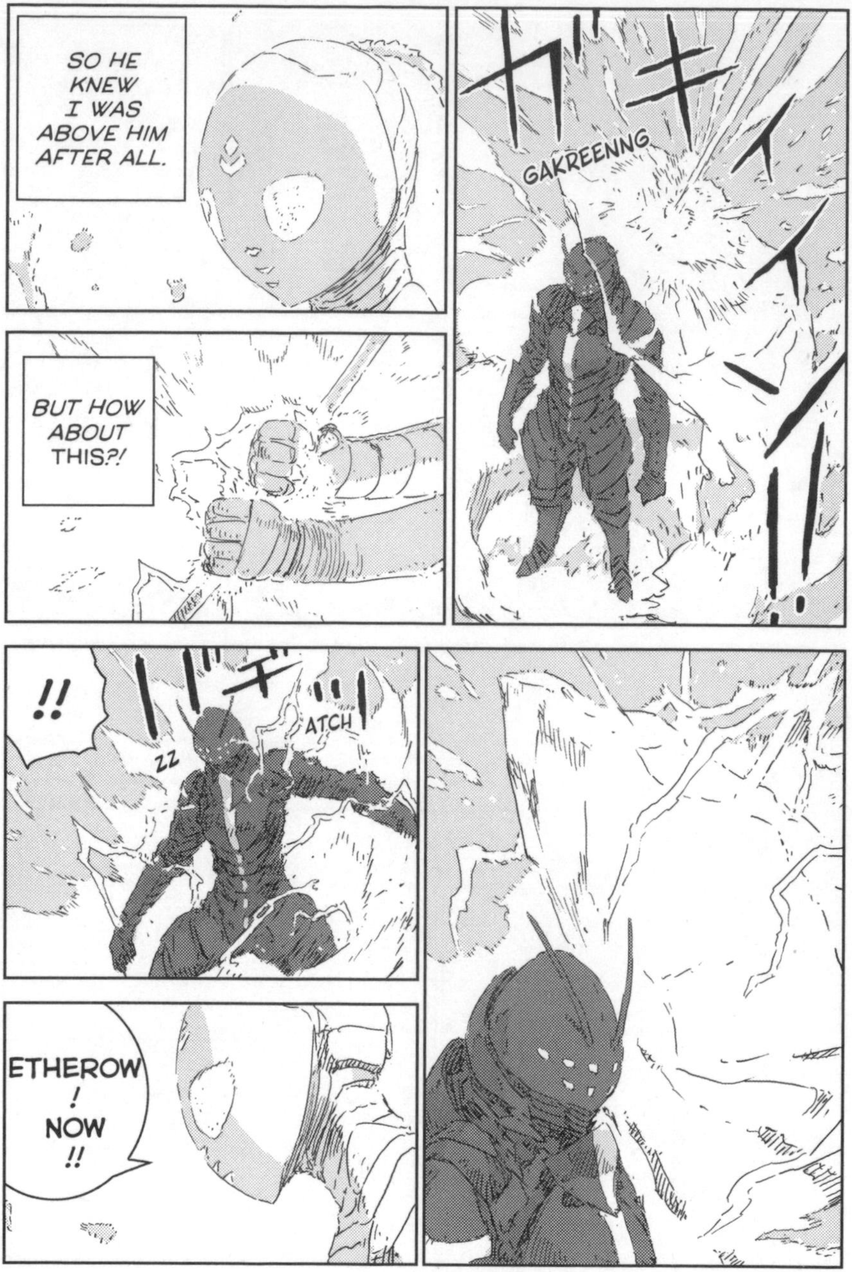
SO HE KNEW I WAS ABOVE HIM AFTER ALL.
BUT HOW ABOUT THIS?!
GAKREENNG
!!
ZZ
ATCH
ETHEROW! NOW!!

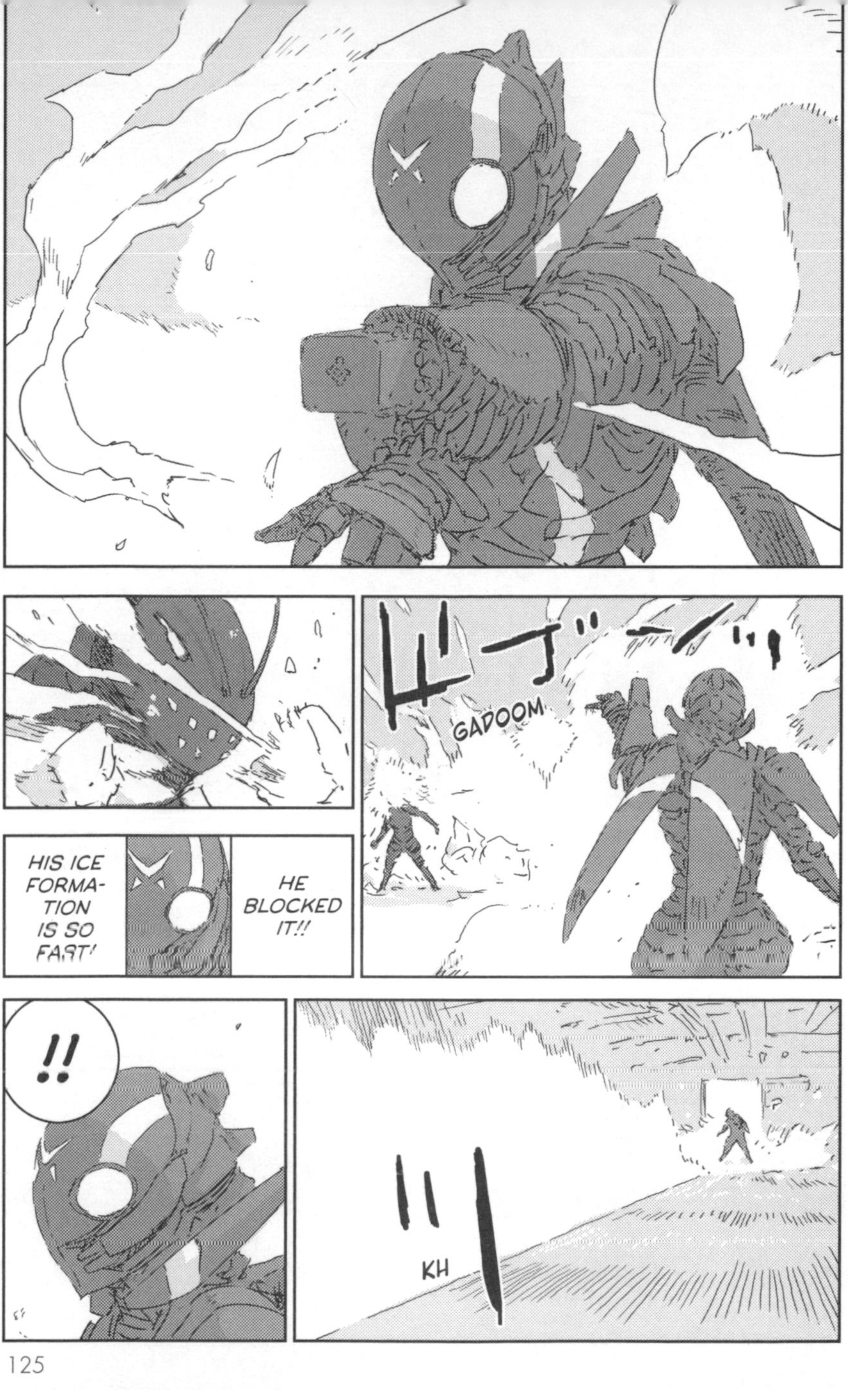

GADOOM
HE BLOCKED IT!!
HIS ICE FORMATION IS SO FAST!
KH
!!

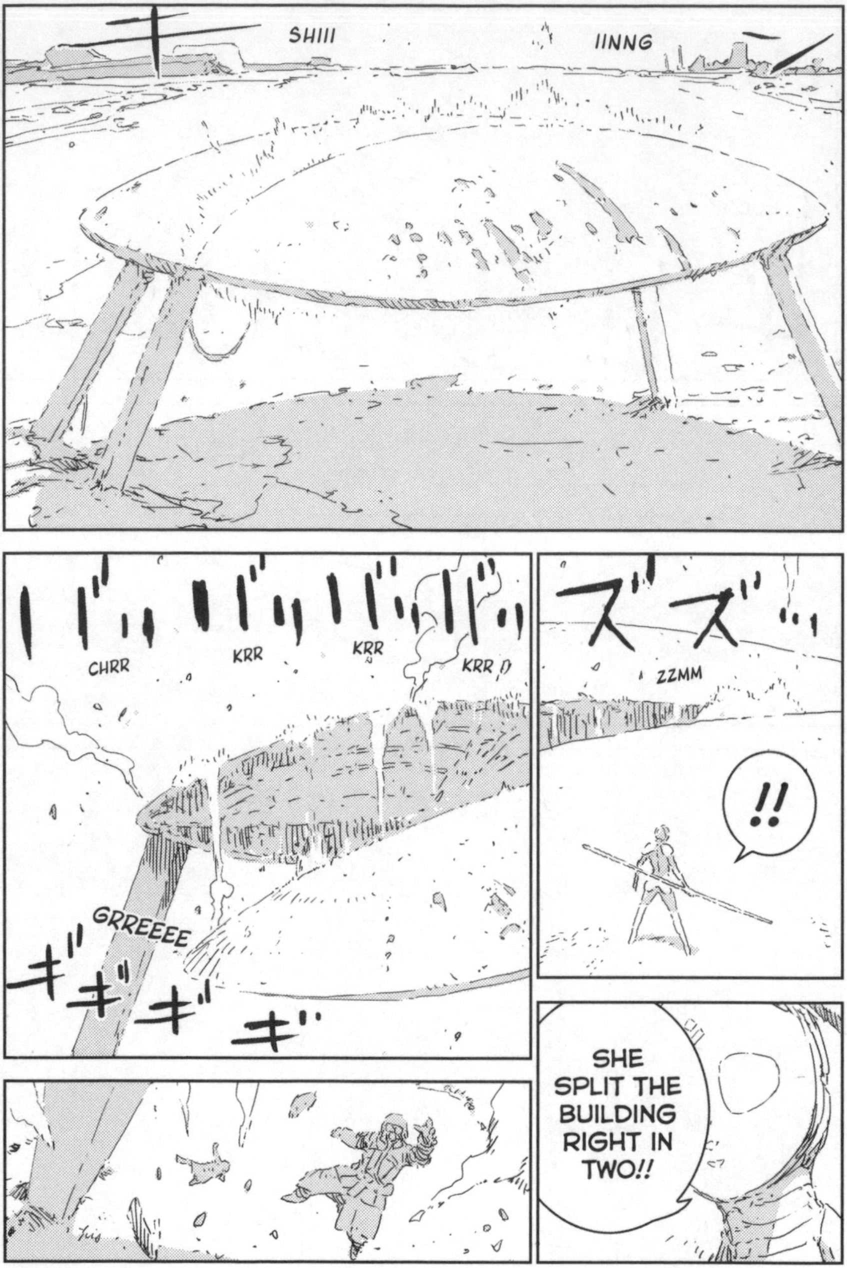
SHIII
IINNG
CHRR
KRR
KRR
KRR
GRREEEE
ギギギギ
ズズッ
ZZMM
!!
SHE SPLIT THE BUILDING RIGHT IN TWO!!

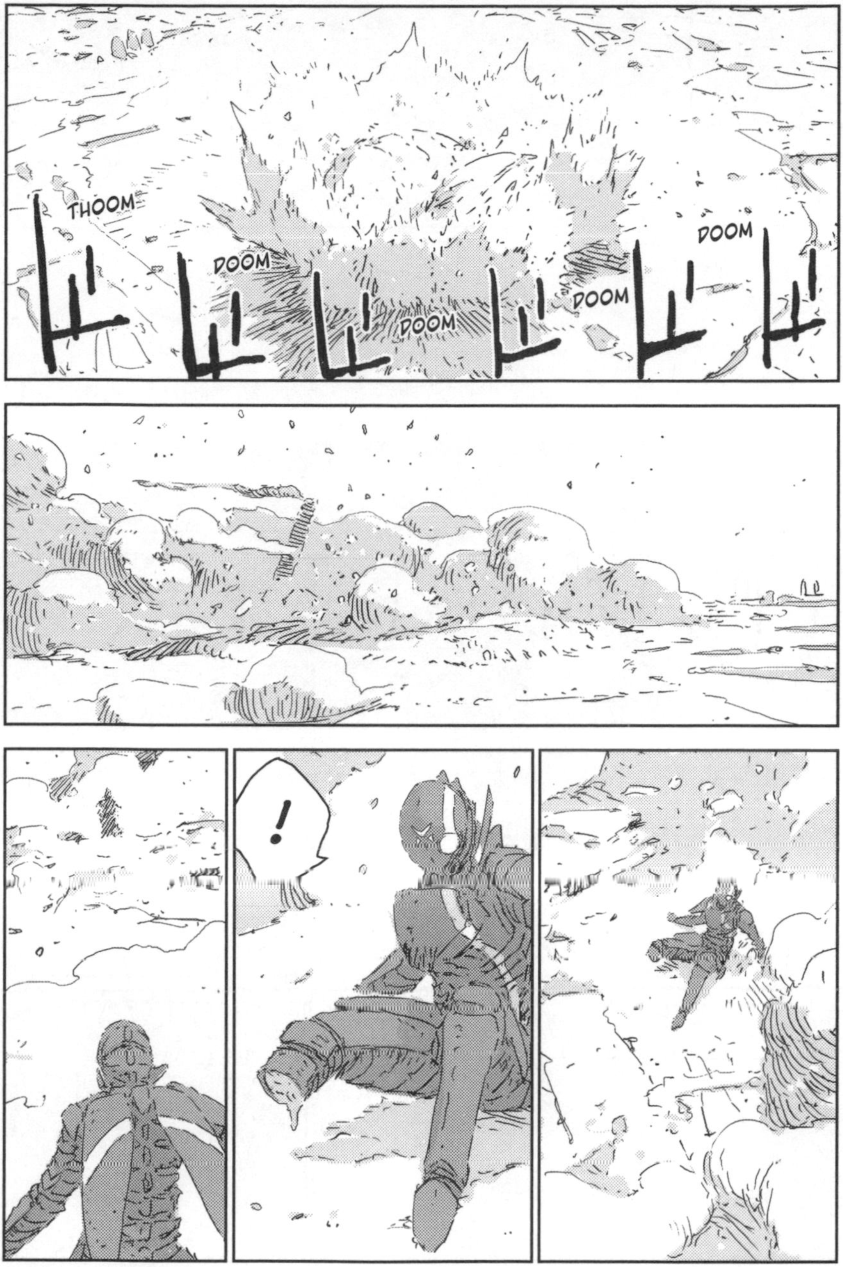
THOOM
DOOM
DOOM
DOOM
DOOM
DOOM
!

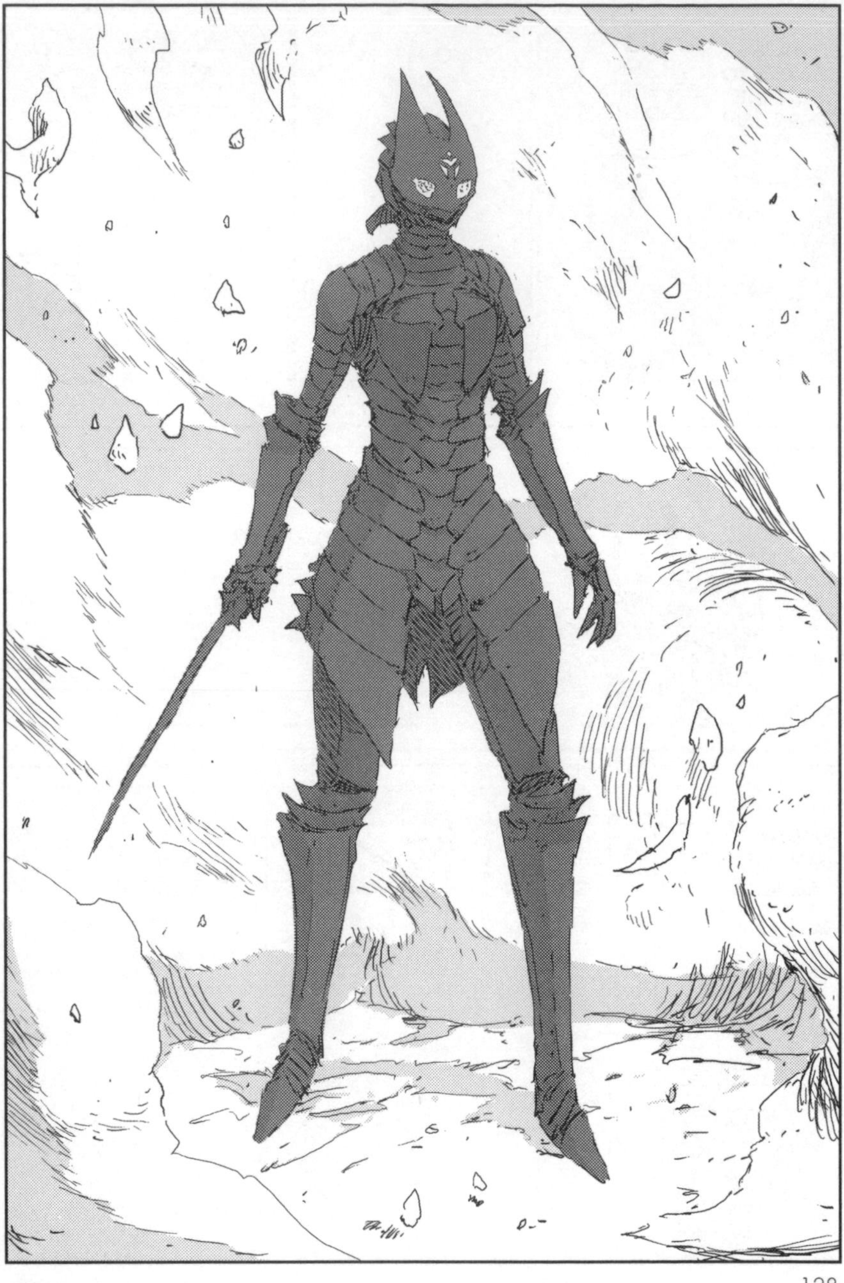

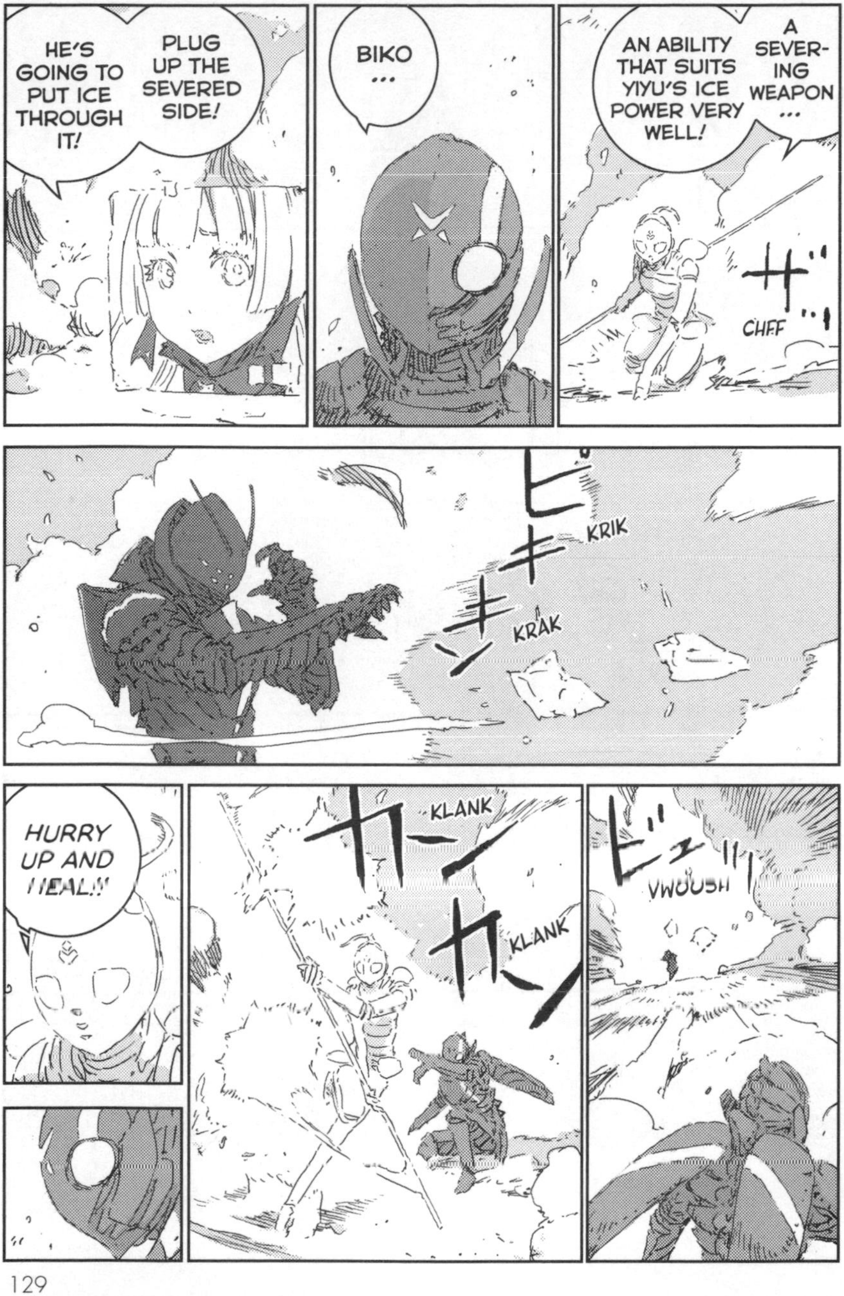
A SEVERING WEAPON...
AN ABILITY THAT SUITS YIYU'S ICE POWER VERY WELL!
CHFF
BIKO...
PLUG UP THE SEVERED SIDE!
HE'S GOING TO PUT ICE THROUGH IT!
KRIK
KRAK
VWOUSH
KLANK
KLANK
HURRY UP AND HEAL!!

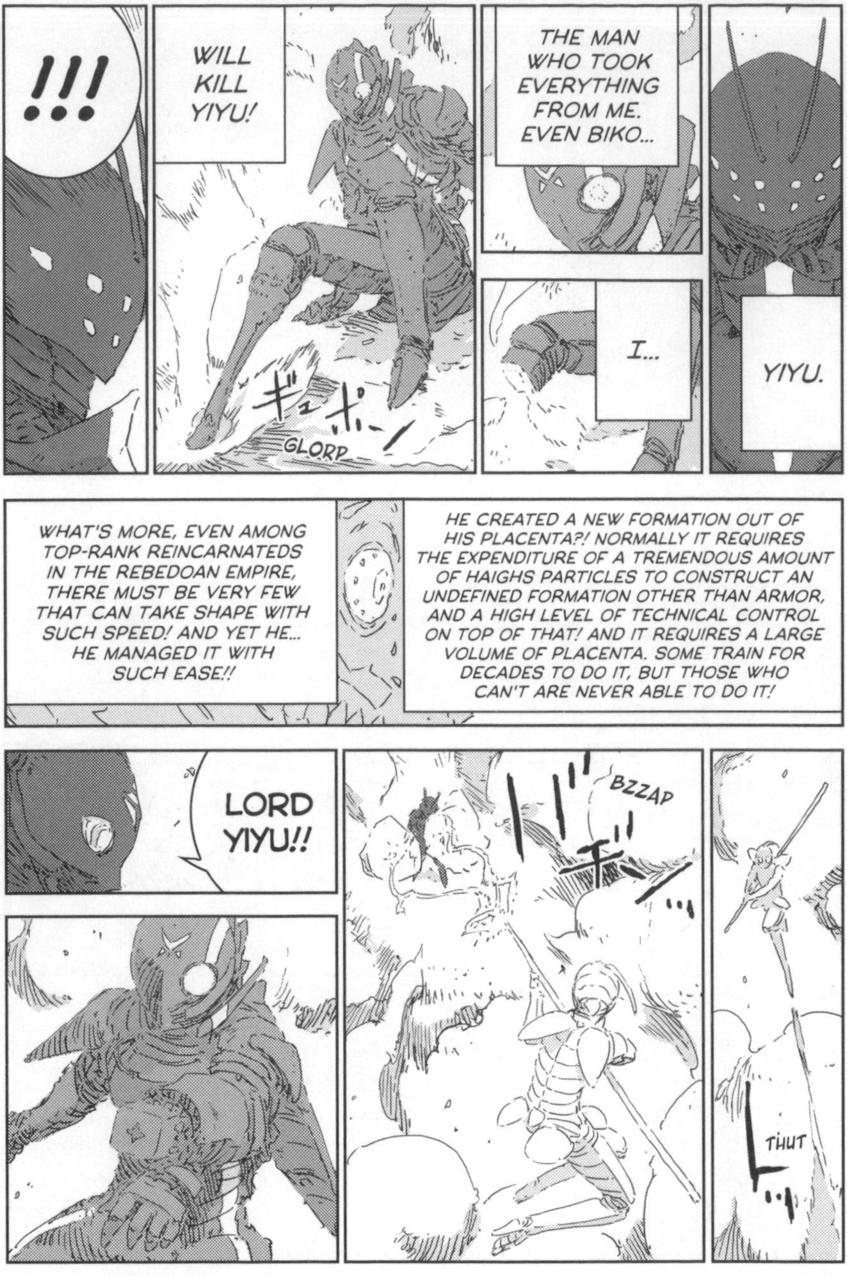
!!!
WILL KILL YIYU!
GLORP
THE MAN WHO TOOK EVERYTHING FROM ME. EVEN BIKO...
I...
YIYU.
WHAT'S MORE, EVEN AMONG TOP-RANK REINCARNATEDS IN THE REBEDOAN EMPIRE, THERE MUST BE VERY FEW THAT CAN TAKE SHAPE WITH SUCH SPEED! AND YET HE... HE MANAGED IT WITH SUCH EASE!!
HE CREATED A NEW FORMATION OUT OF HIS PLACENTA?! NORMALLY IT REQUIRES THE EXPENDITURE OF A TREMENDOUS AMOUNT OF HAIGHS PARTICLES TO CONSTRUCT AN UNDEFINED FORMATION OTHER THAN ARMOR, AND A HIGH LEVEL OF TECHNICAL CONTROL ON TOP OF THAT! AND IT REQUIRES A LARGE VOLUME OF PLACENTA. SOME TRAIN FOR DECADES TO DO IT, BUT THOSE WHO CAN'T ARE NEVER ABLE TO DO IT!
LORD YIYU!!
BZZAP
THUT

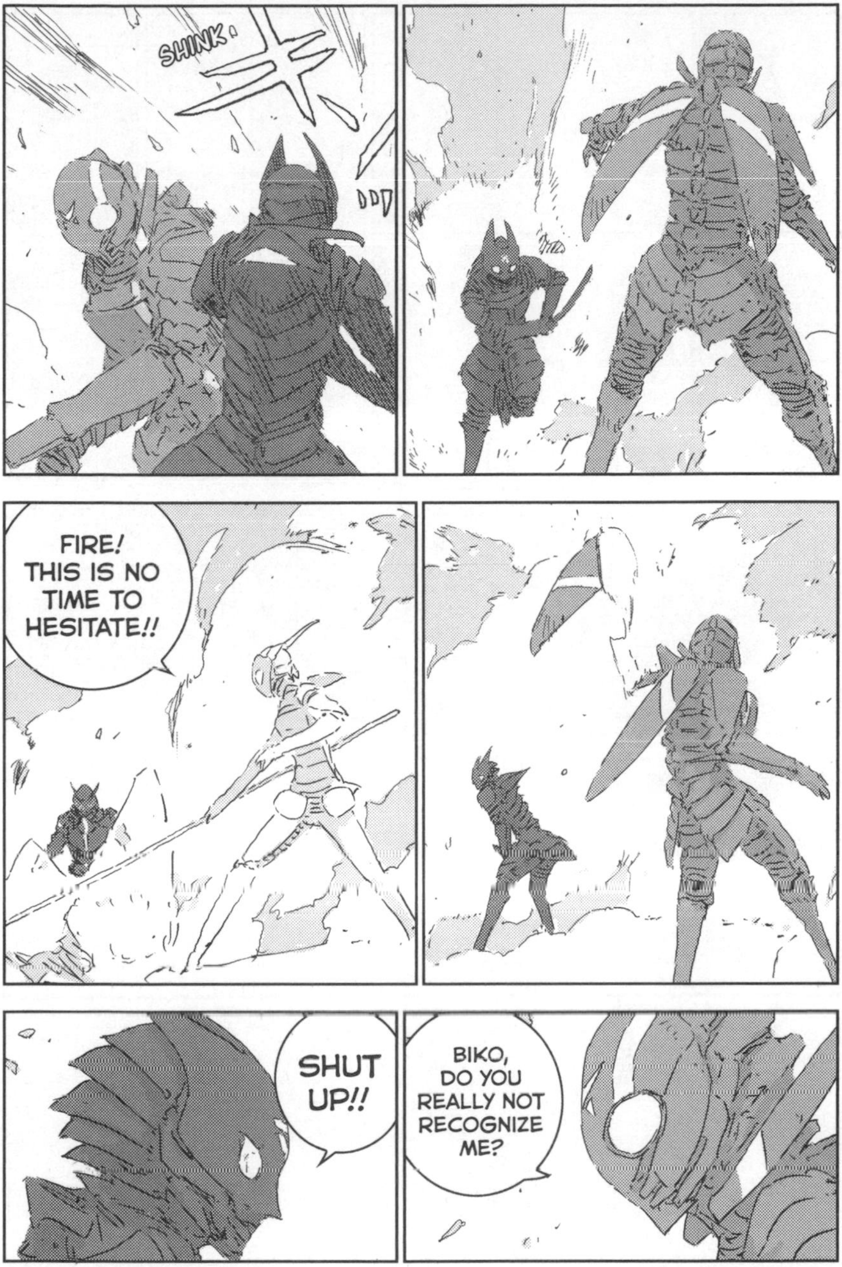
SHINK
FIRE! THIS IS NO TIME TO HESITATE!!
SHUT UP!!
BIKO, DO YOU REALLY NOT RECOGNIZE ME?

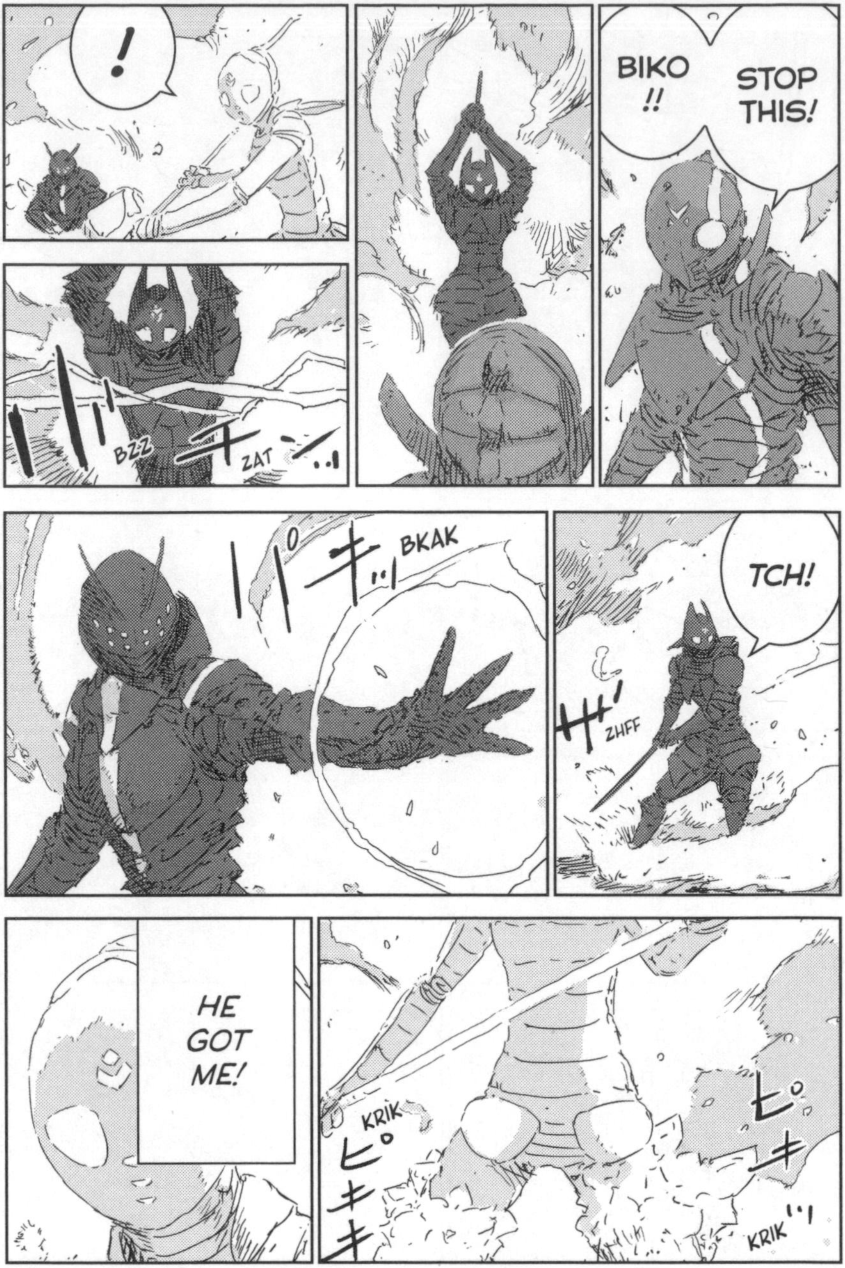
!
BIKO !!
STOP THIS!
BZZ
ZAT
BKAK
TCH!
ZHFF
HE GOT ME!
KRIK
KRIK

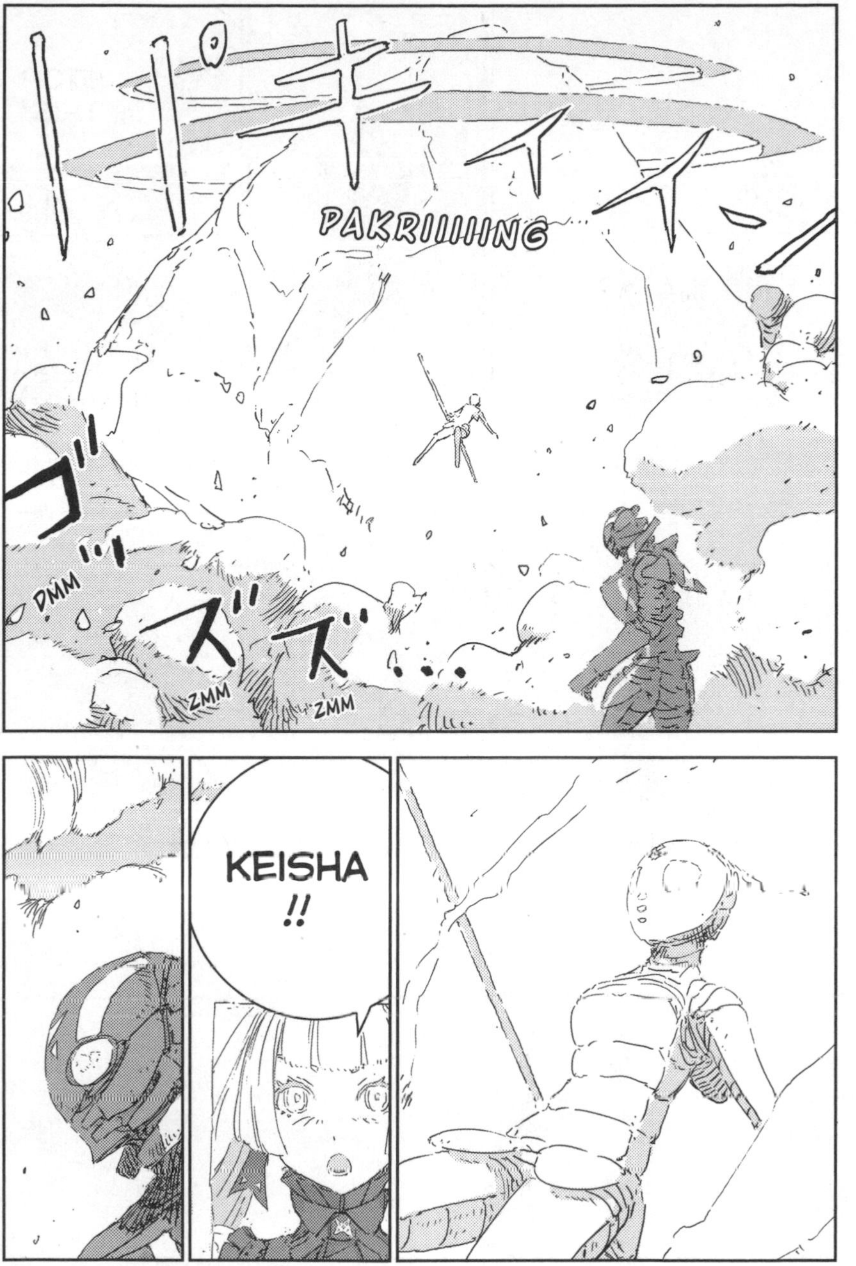
パキィィ
PAKRIIIIIING
ゴゴ
DMM
ズズ…
ZMM
ZMM
KEISHA
!!

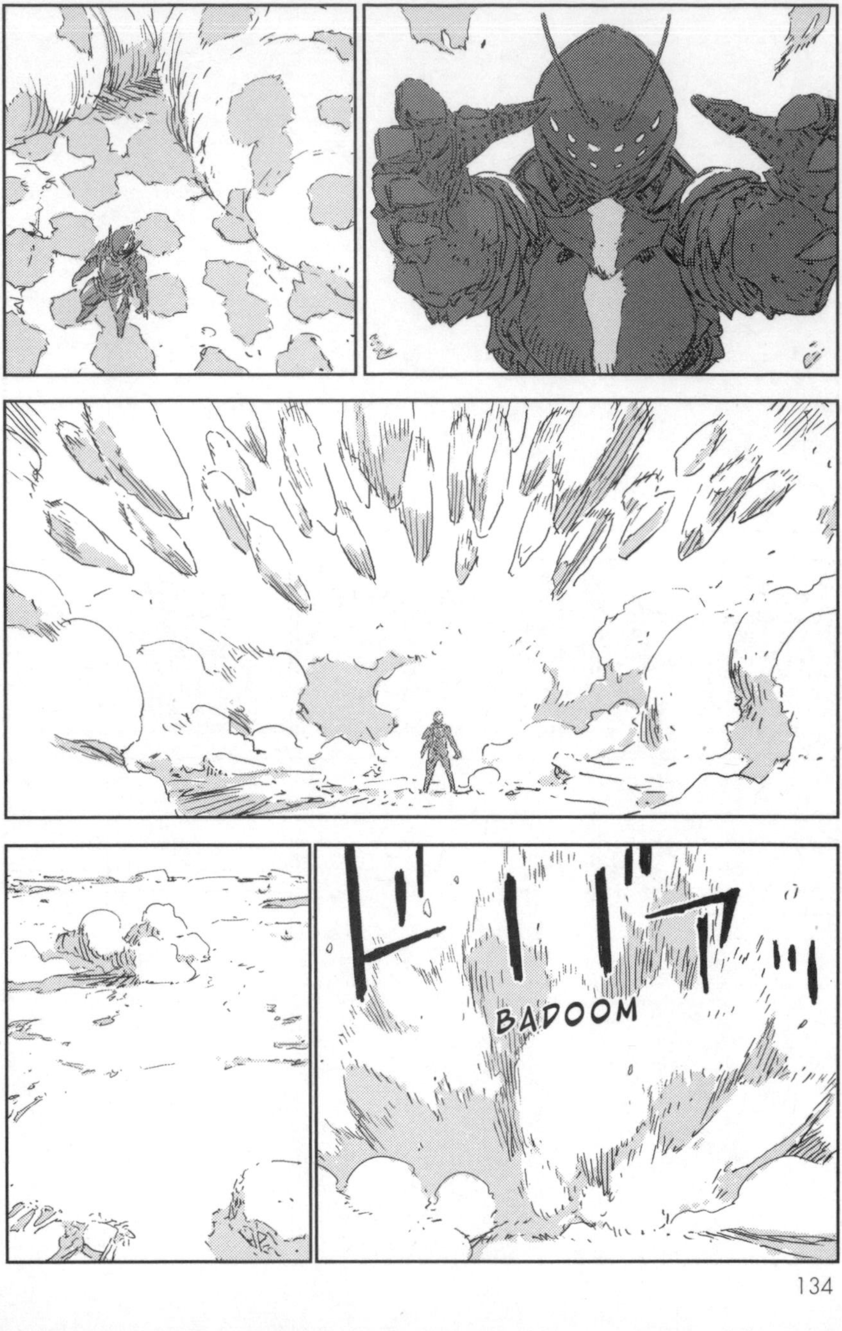
BADOOM

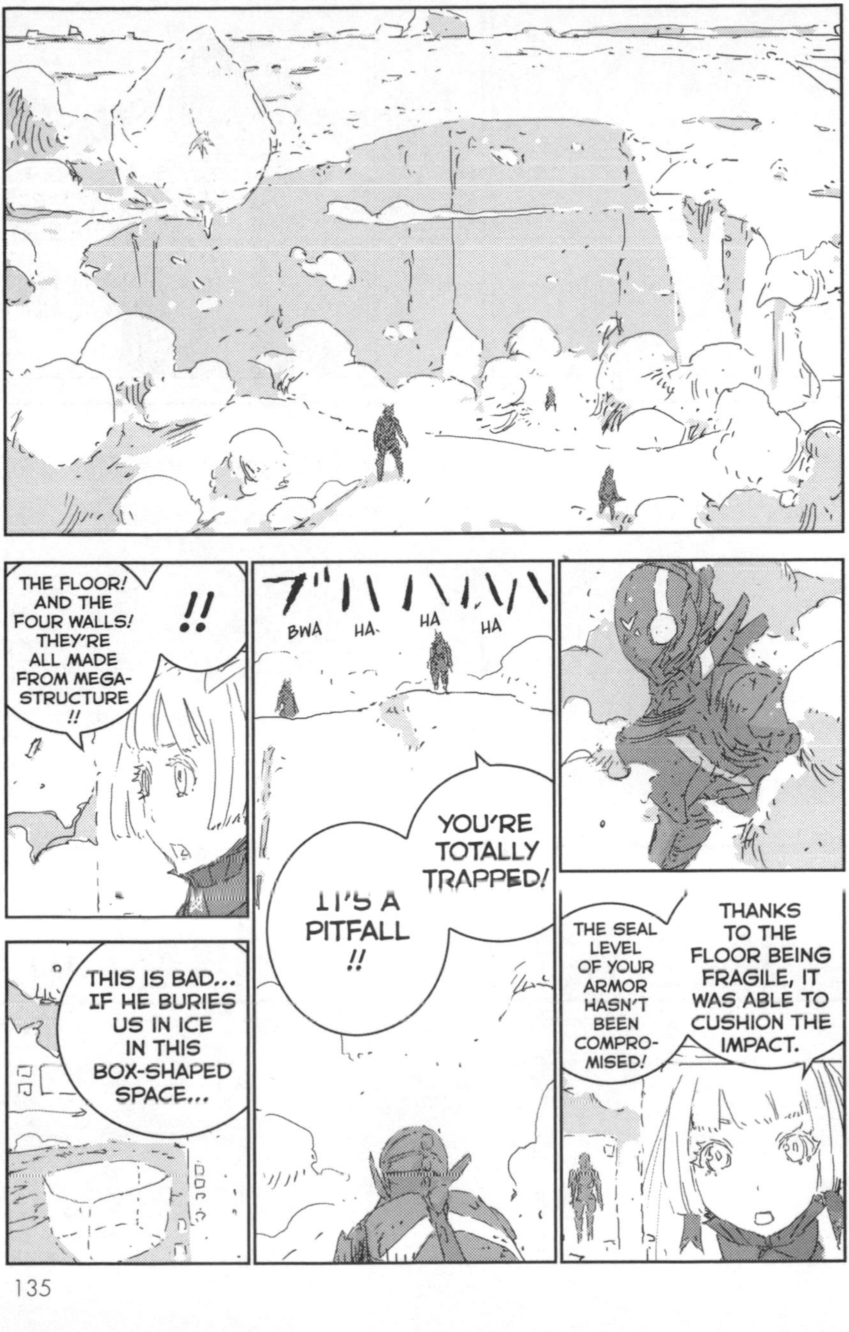
ブハハハハ
BWA HA HA HA
YOU'RE TOTALLY TRAPPED!
IT'S A PITFALL !!
THE FLOOR! AND THE FOUR WALLS! THEY'RE ALL MADE FROM MEGA-STRUCTURE !!
!!
THANKS TO THE FLOOR BEING FRAGILE, IT WAS ABLE TO CUSHION THE IMPACT.
THE SEAL LEVEL OF YOUR ARMOR HASN'T BEEN COMPROMISED!
THIS IS BAD... IF HE BURIES US IN ICE IN THIS BOX-SHAPED SPACE...

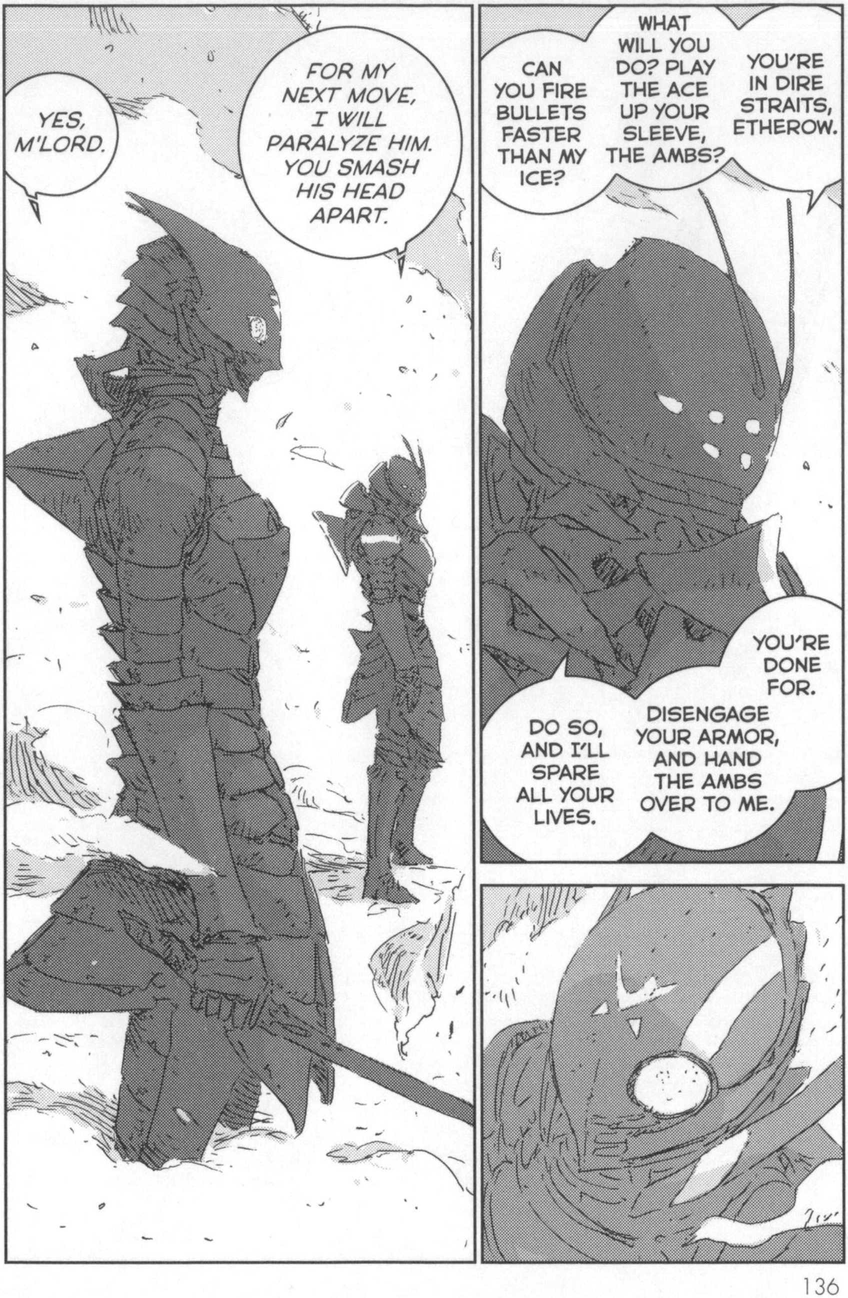
FOR MY NEXT MOVE, I WILL PARALYZE HIM. YOU SMASH HIS HEAD APART.
YES, M'LORD.
YOU'RE IN DIRE STRAITS, ETHEROW.
WHAT WILL YOU DO? PLAY THE ACE UP YOUR SLEEVE, THE AMBS?
CAN YOU FIRE BULLETS FASTER THAN MY ICE?
YOU'RE DONE FOR.
DISENGAGE YOUR ARMOR, AND HAND THE AMBS OVER TO ME.
DO SO, AND I'LL SPARE ALL YOUR LIVES.

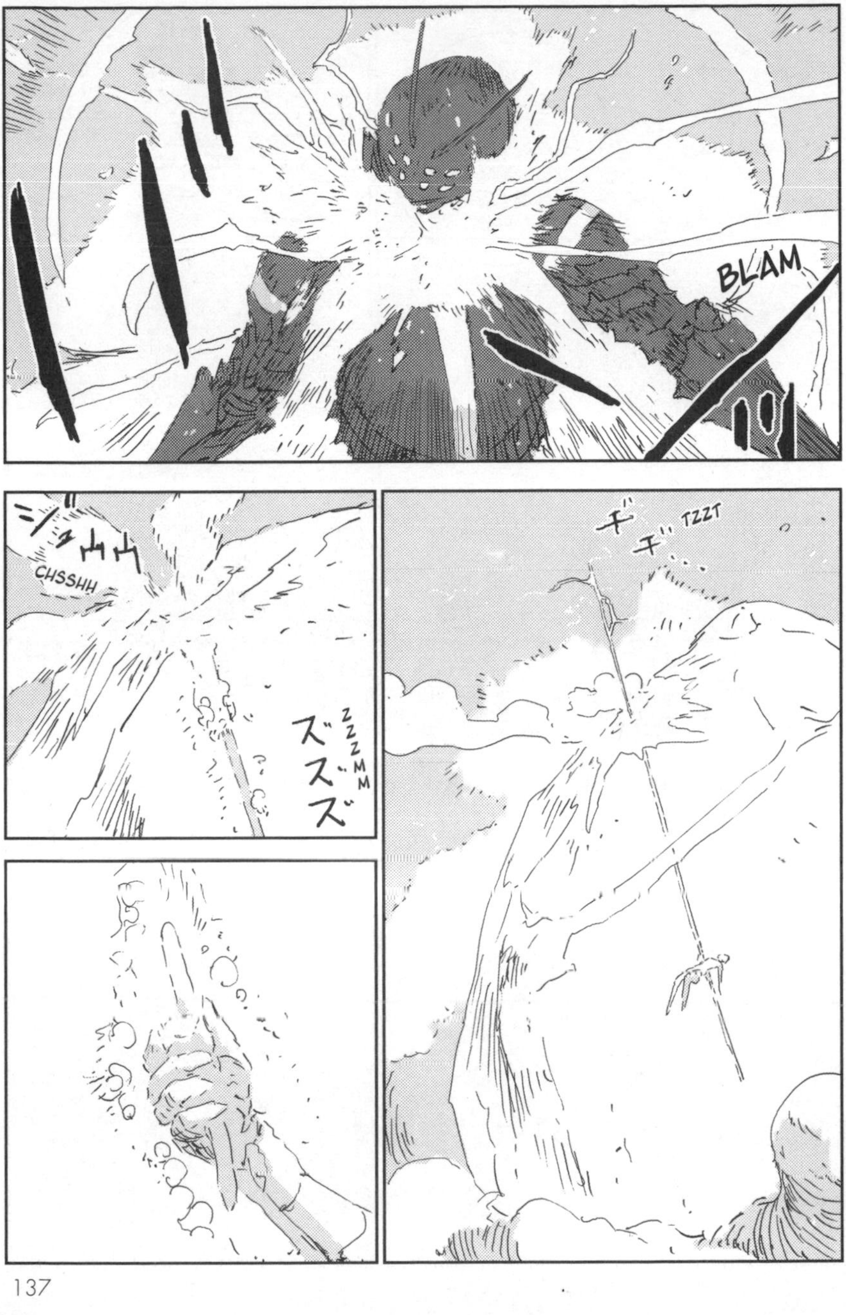
BLAM
シュゥゥ
CHSSHH
ズズズ
ZZZMM
ヂヂ…
TZZT

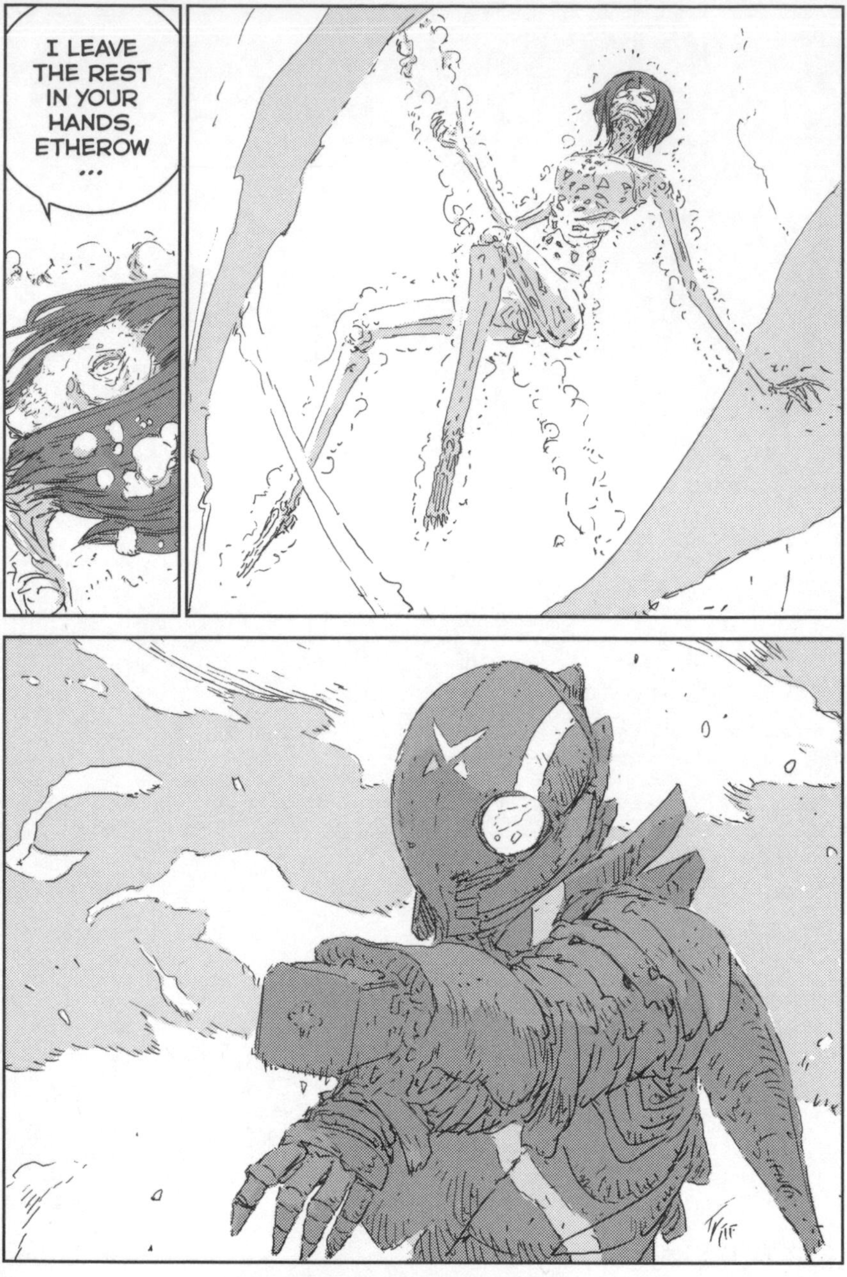
I LEAVE THE REST IN YOUR HANDS, ETHEROW ...

CHAPTER 08 END

APOSIMZ

CHAPTER 09

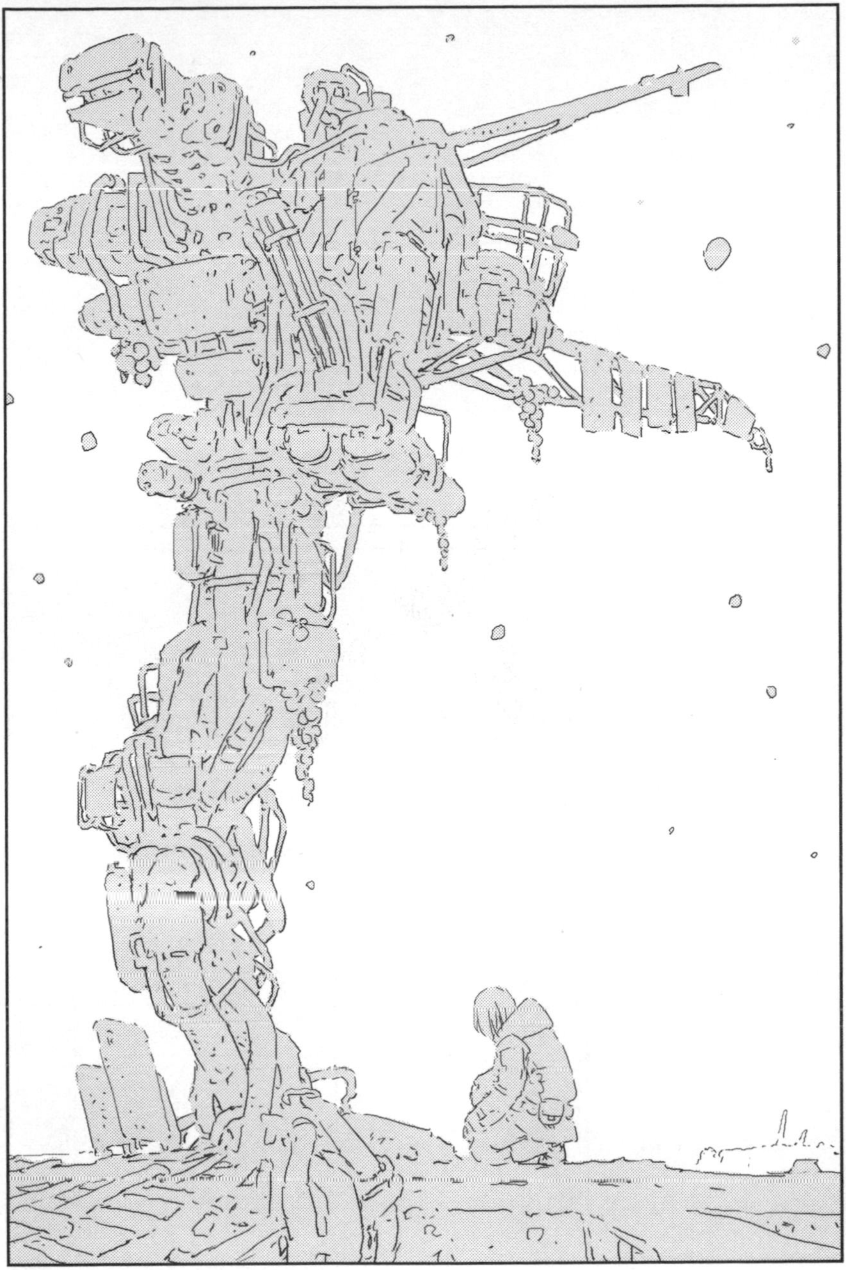

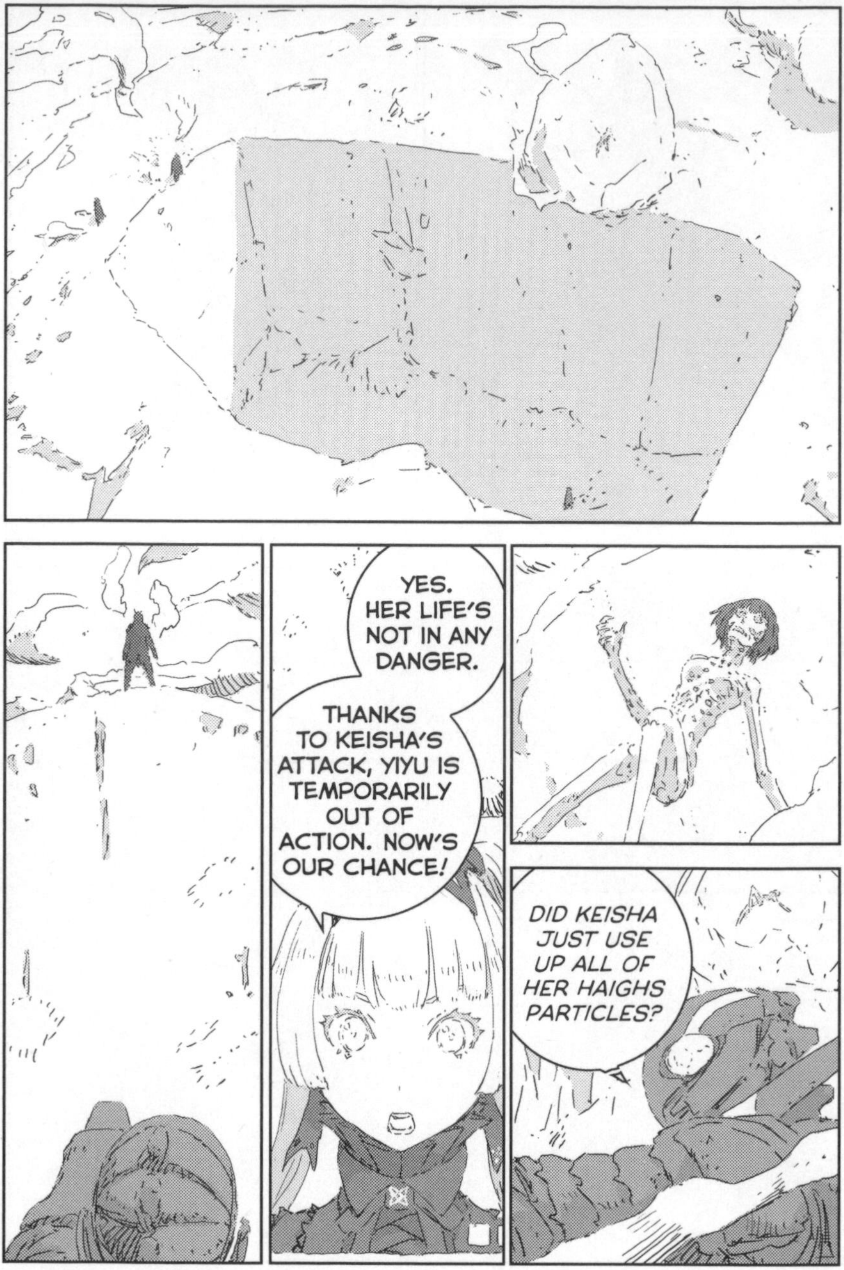
YES. HER LIFE'S NOT IN ANY DANGER.
THANKS TO KEISHA'S ATTACK, YIYU IS TEMPORARILY OUT OF ACTION. NOW'S OUR CHANCE!
DID KEISHA JUST USE UP ALL OF HER HAIGHS PARTICLES?

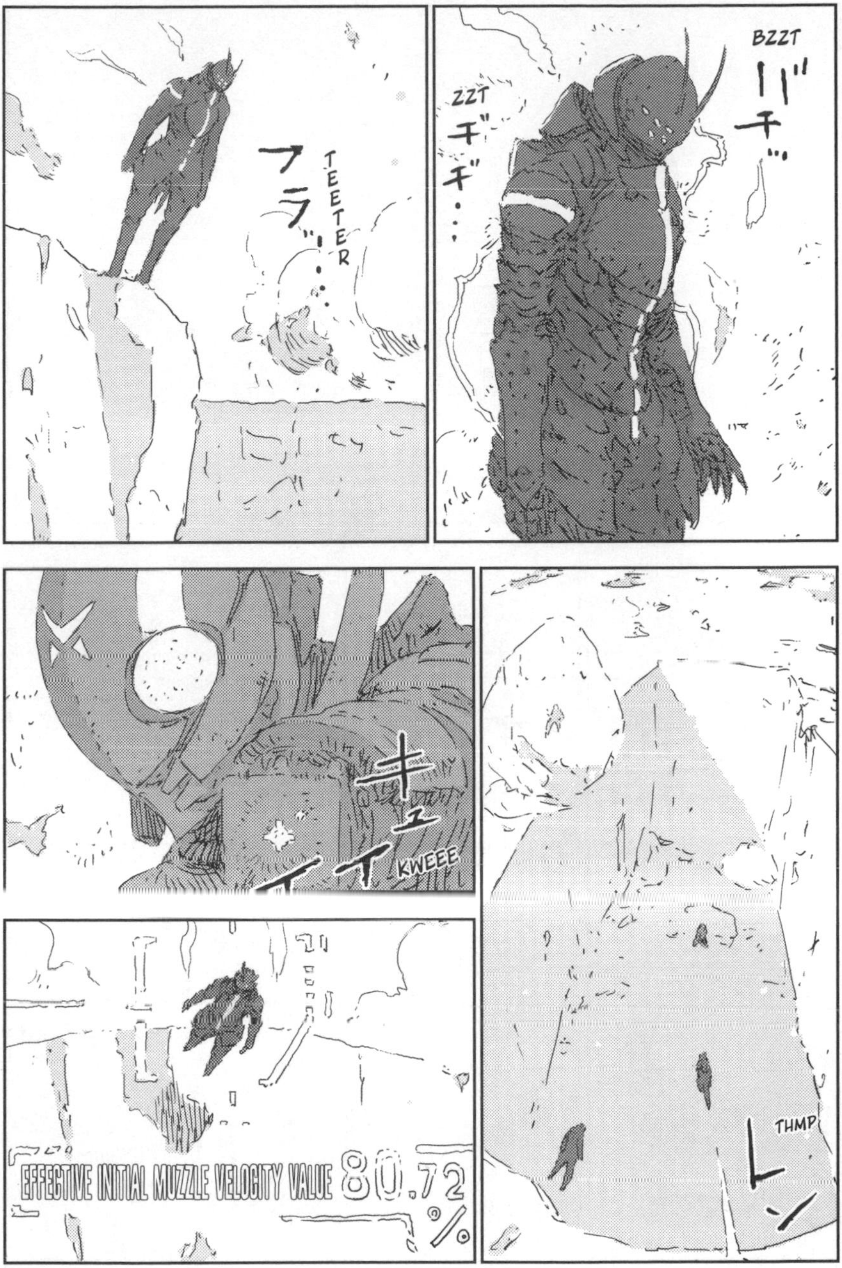
BZZT
ZZT
フラ…
TEETER
THMP
ドン
キュイイ
KWEEE
EFFECTIVE INITIAL MUZZLE VELOCITY VALUE 80.72 %

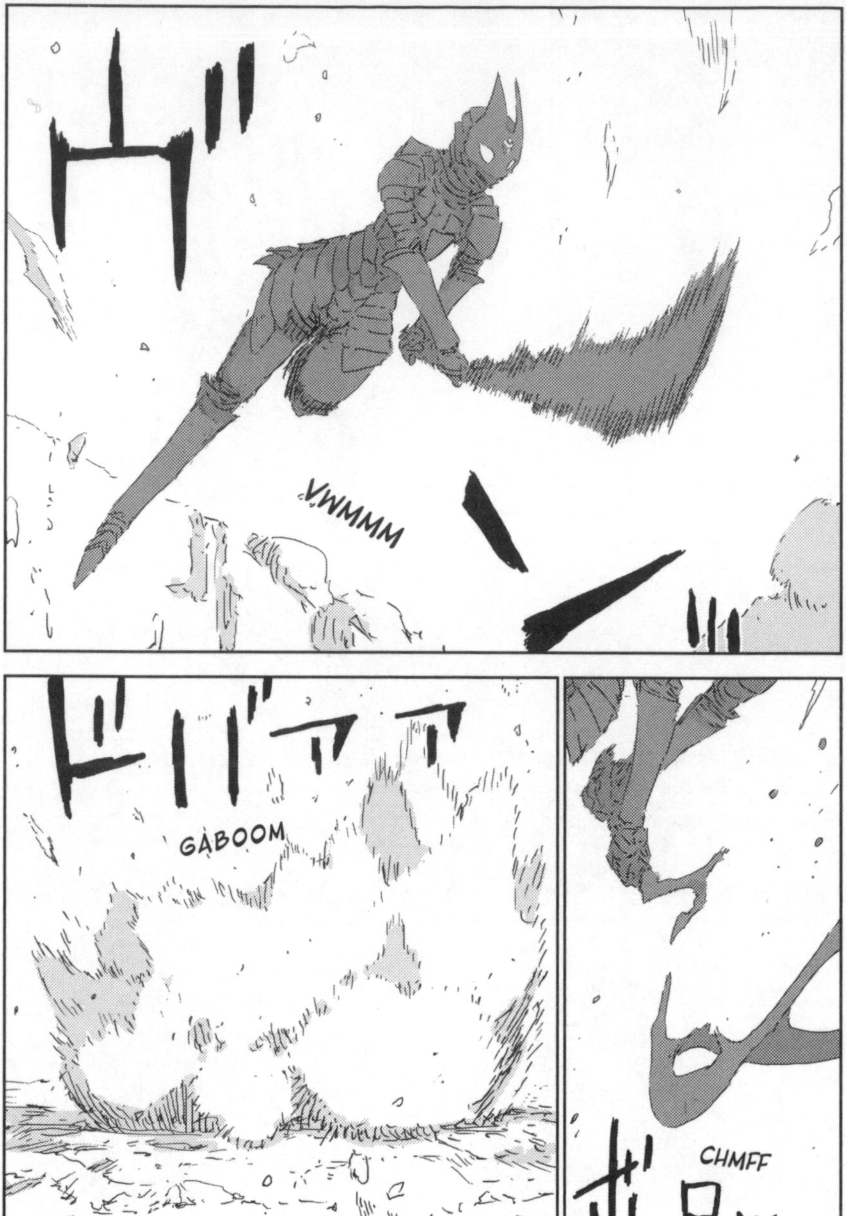
VWMMM
CHMFF
GABOOM

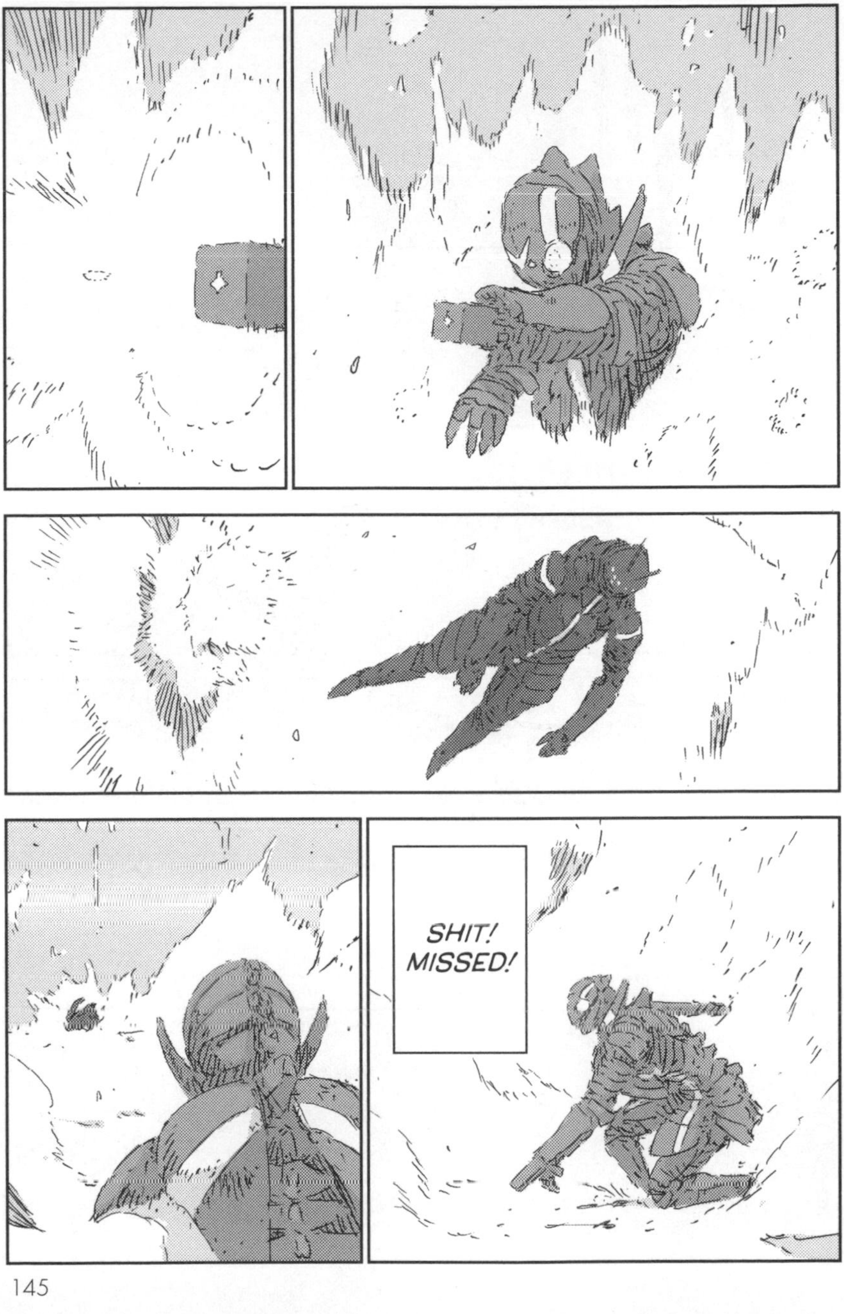
SHIT!
MISSED!

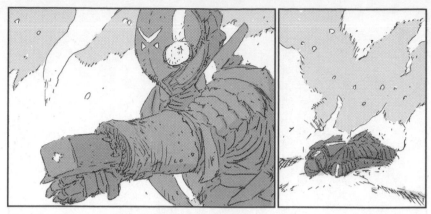

GABAM

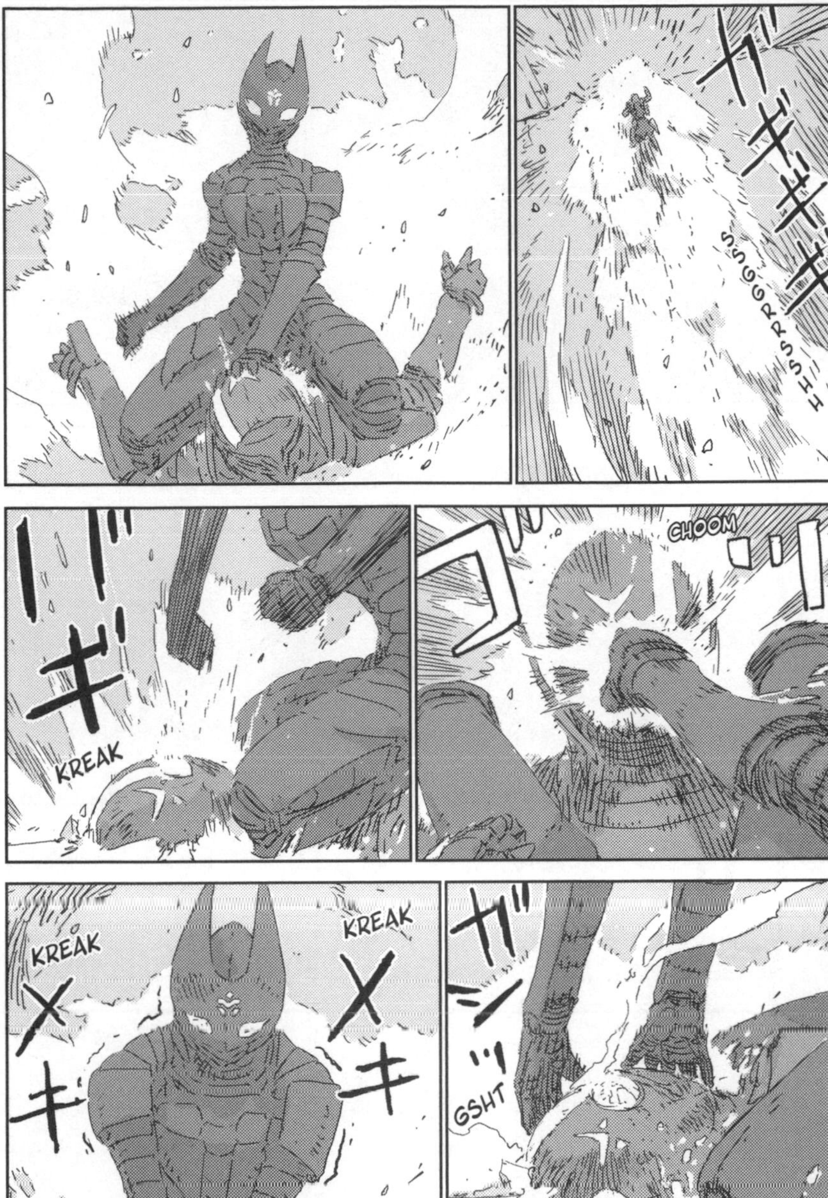
SSGGRRSSHH
CHOOM
KREAK
GSHT
KREAK
KREAK

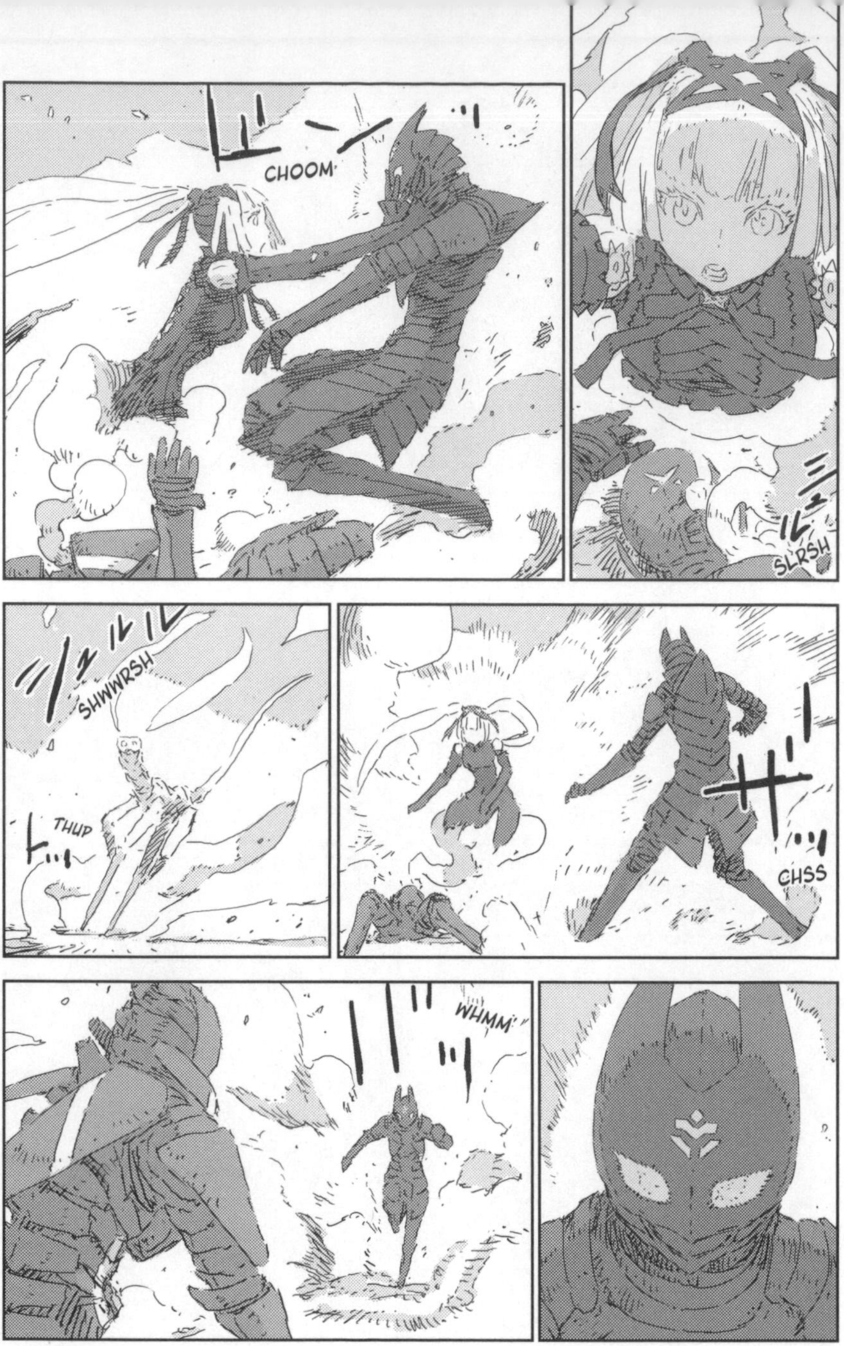
SLRSH
CHOOM
CHSS
SHWWRSH
THUP
WHMM

SHIT ...!
YIYU'S ON THE MOVE AGAIN!

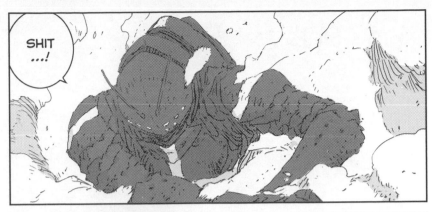

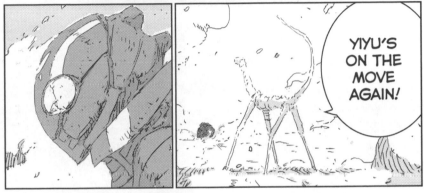

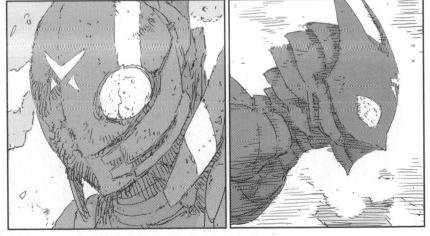

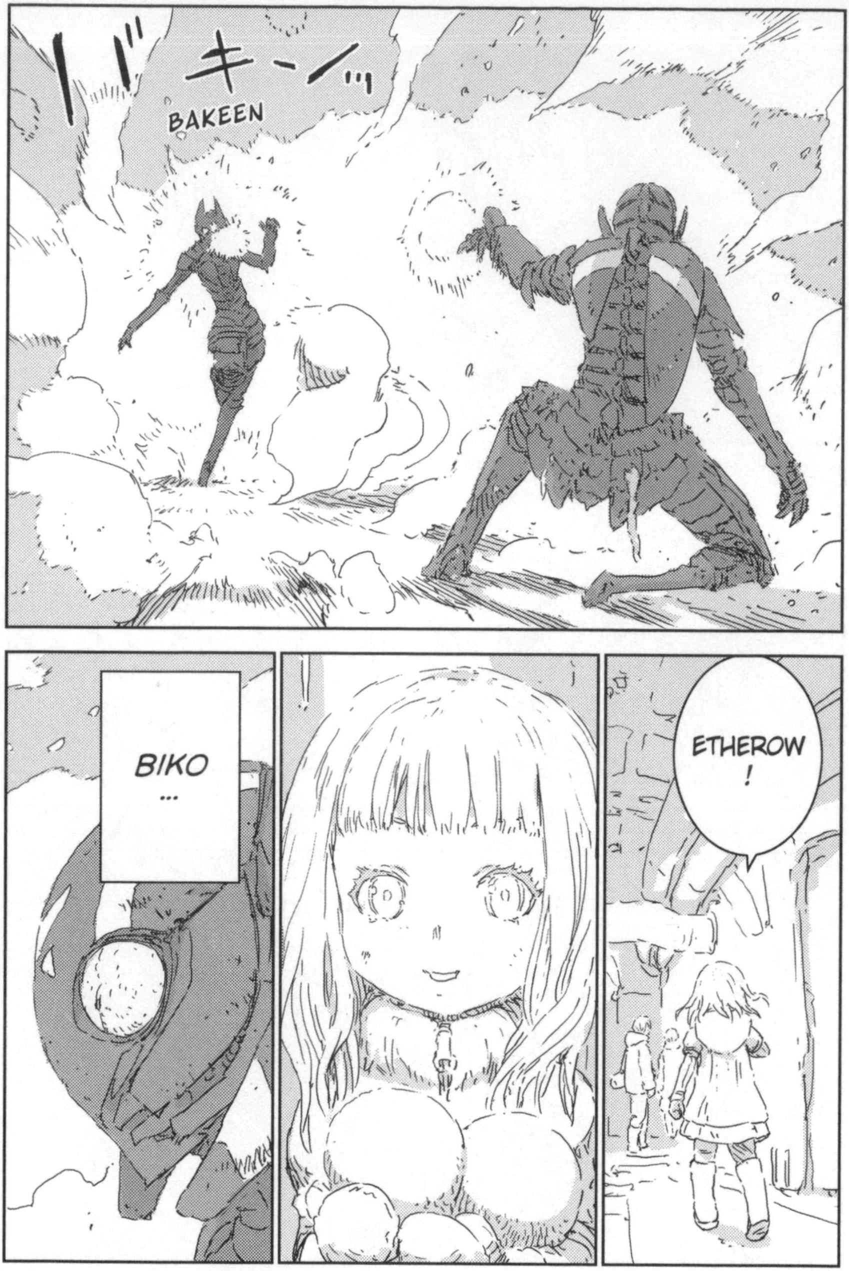
バキーンッ
BAKEEN
ETHEROW !
BIKO ...

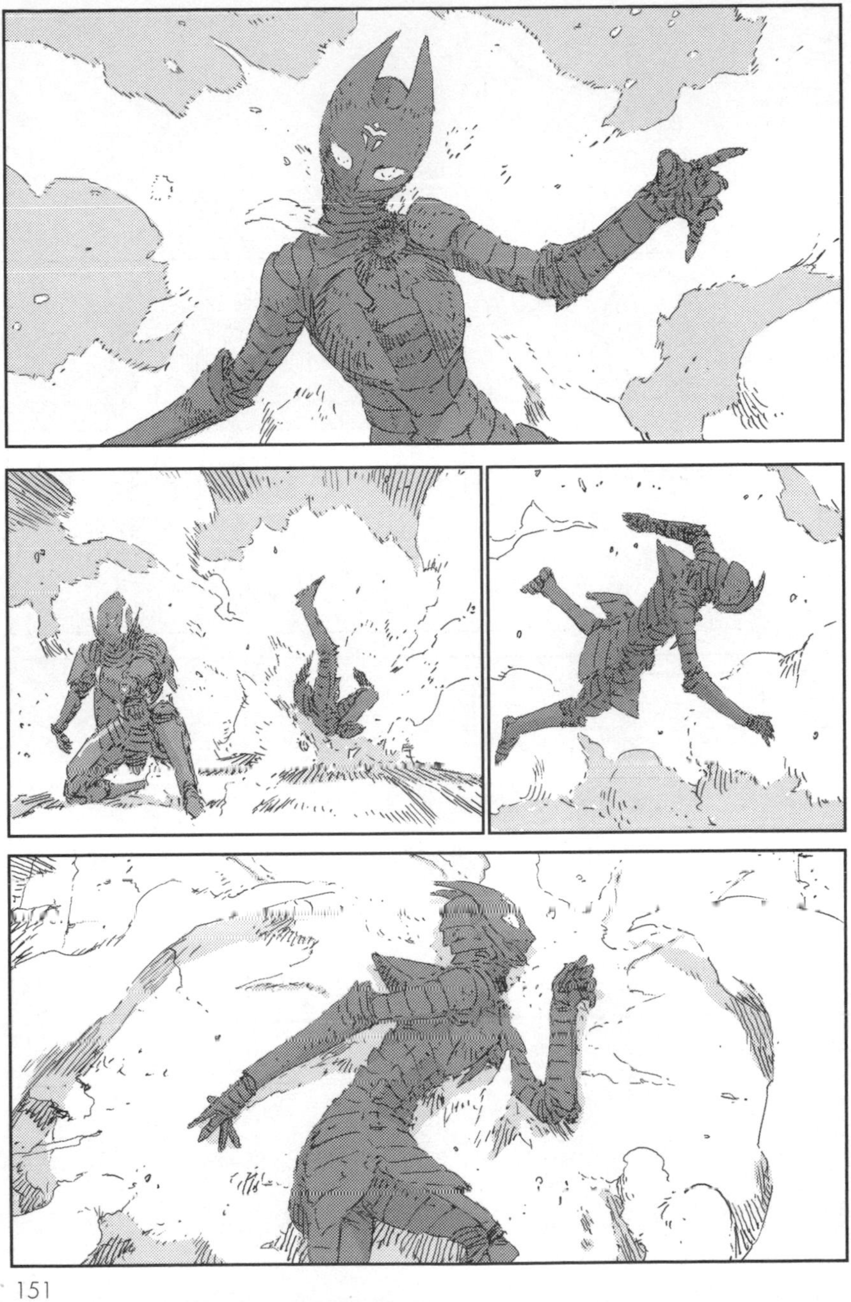

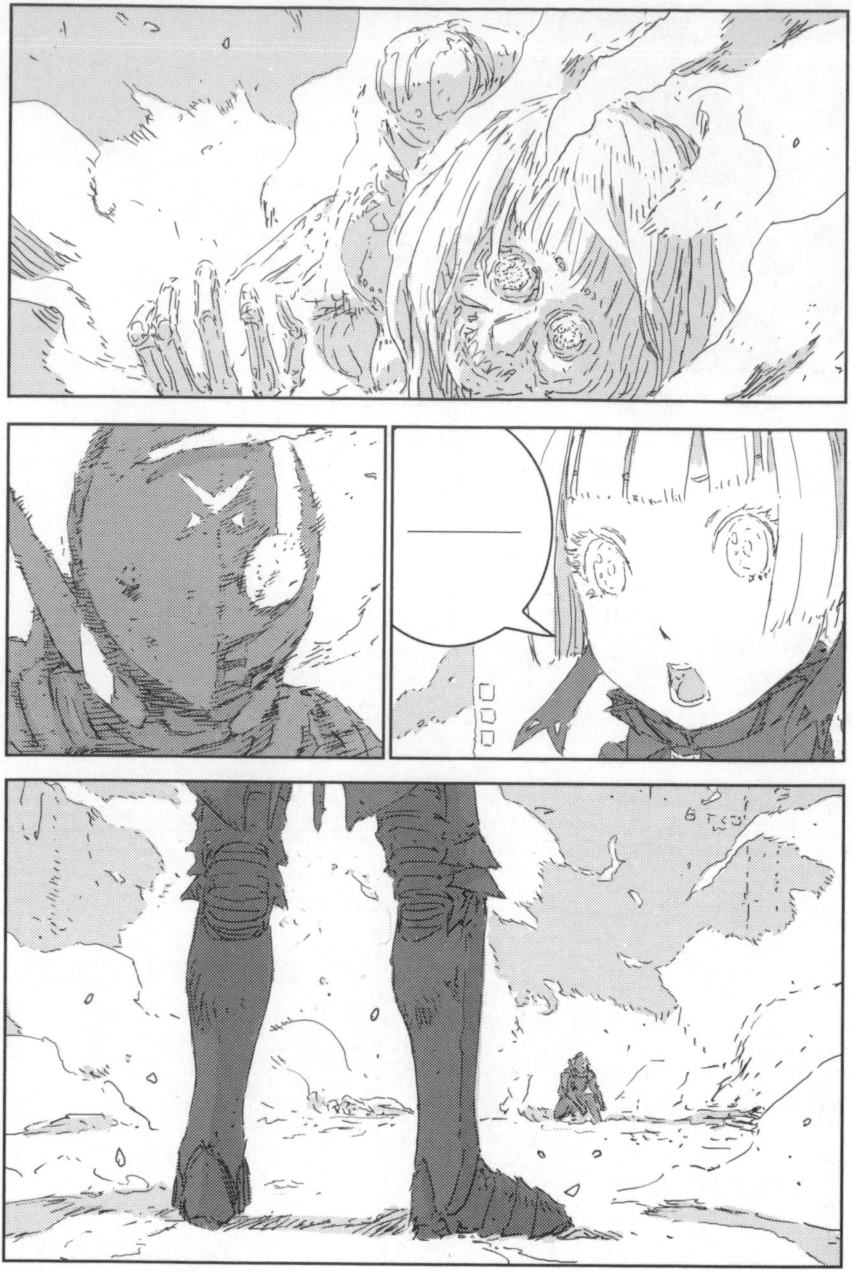

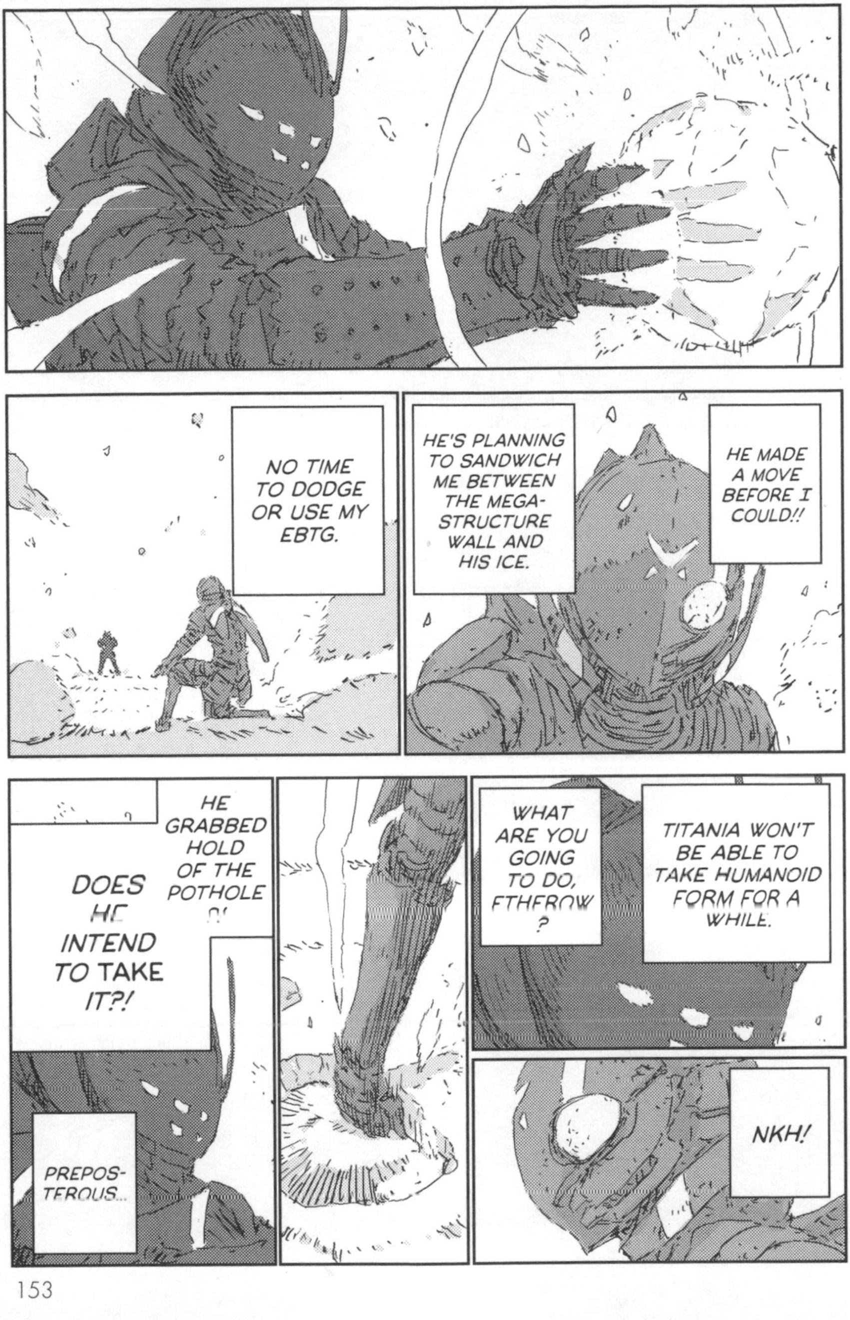
NO TIME TO DODGE OR USE MY EBTG.
HE'S PLANNING TO SANDWICH ME BETWEEN THE MEGA-STRUCTURE WALL AND HIS ICE.
HE MADE A MOVE BEFORE I COULD!!
HE GRABBED HOLD OF THE POTHOLE ?!
DOES HE INTEND TO TAKE IT?!
PREPOS-TEROUS...
WHAT ARE YOU GOING TO DO, ETHEROW ?
TITANIA WON'T BE ABLE TO TAKE HUMANOID FORM FOR A WHILE.
NKH!

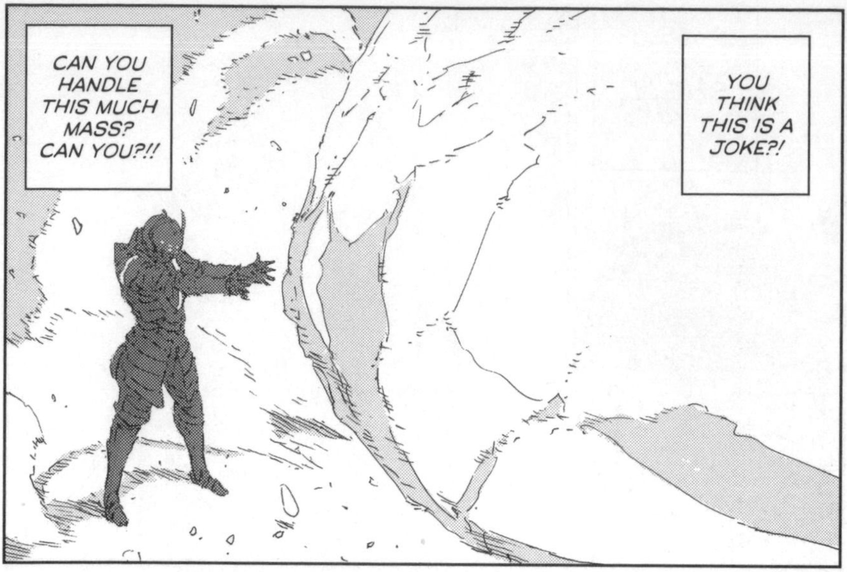
YOU THINK THIS IS A JOKE?!
CAN YOU HANDLE THIS MUCH MASS? CAN YOU?!!
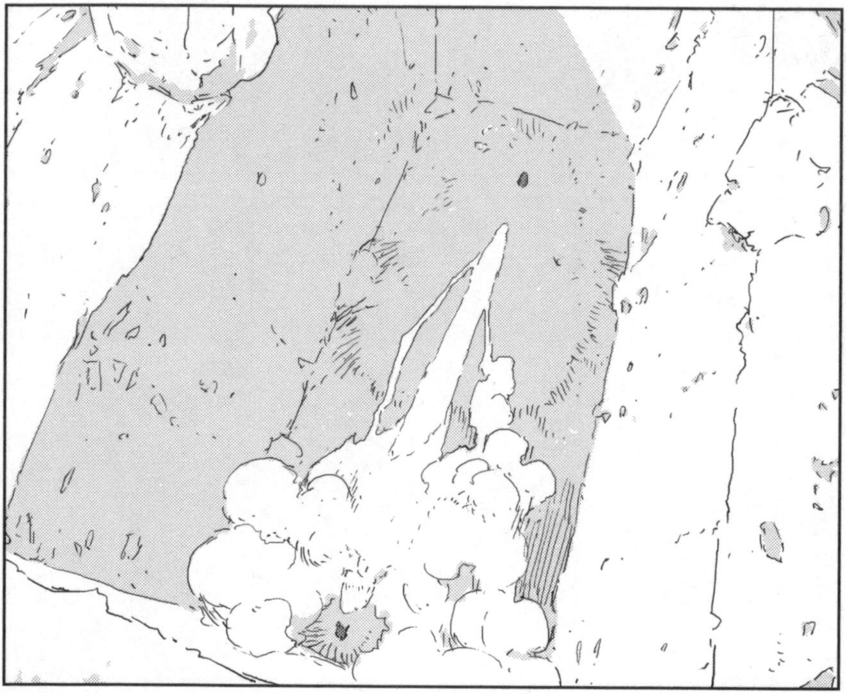

A
SHIELD
!!!

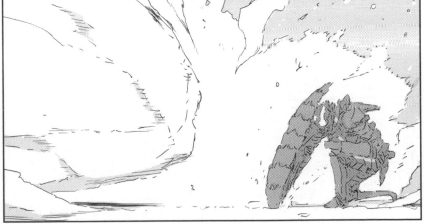

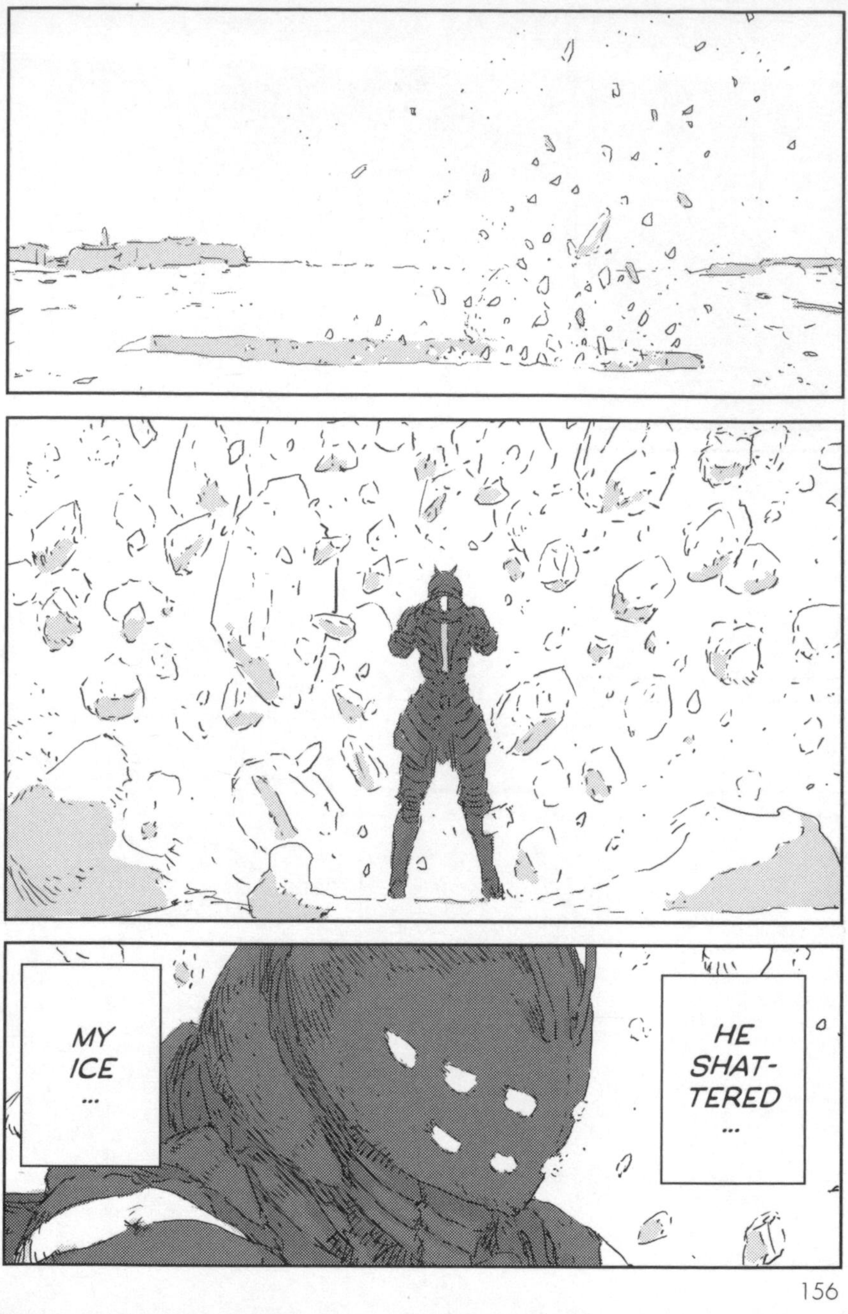
MY ICE ...
HE SHATTERED ...

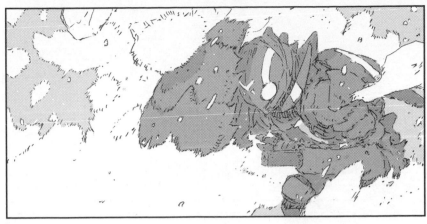

HAVING THE ACCELERATED PERCEPTION AND THOUGHT PROCESS OF A REGULAR FRAME, YIYU FORESAW THAT THE BULLET FIRED AT HIM WOULD STRIKE HIM PRECISELY IN THE MIDDLE OF HIS FOREHEAD

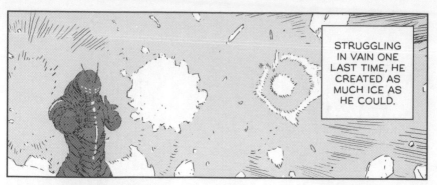

STRUGGLING IN VAIN ONE LAST TIME, HE CREATED AS MUCH ICE AS HE COULD.

BUT NOW THE BULLET'S TRAJECTORY HAD VEERED EVER SO SLIGHTLY...

AND THE PLACENTA BULLET HIT HIS RIGHT EYE AND DISPERSED INSIDE HIS HEAD, A VITAL PART FOR FRAMES.

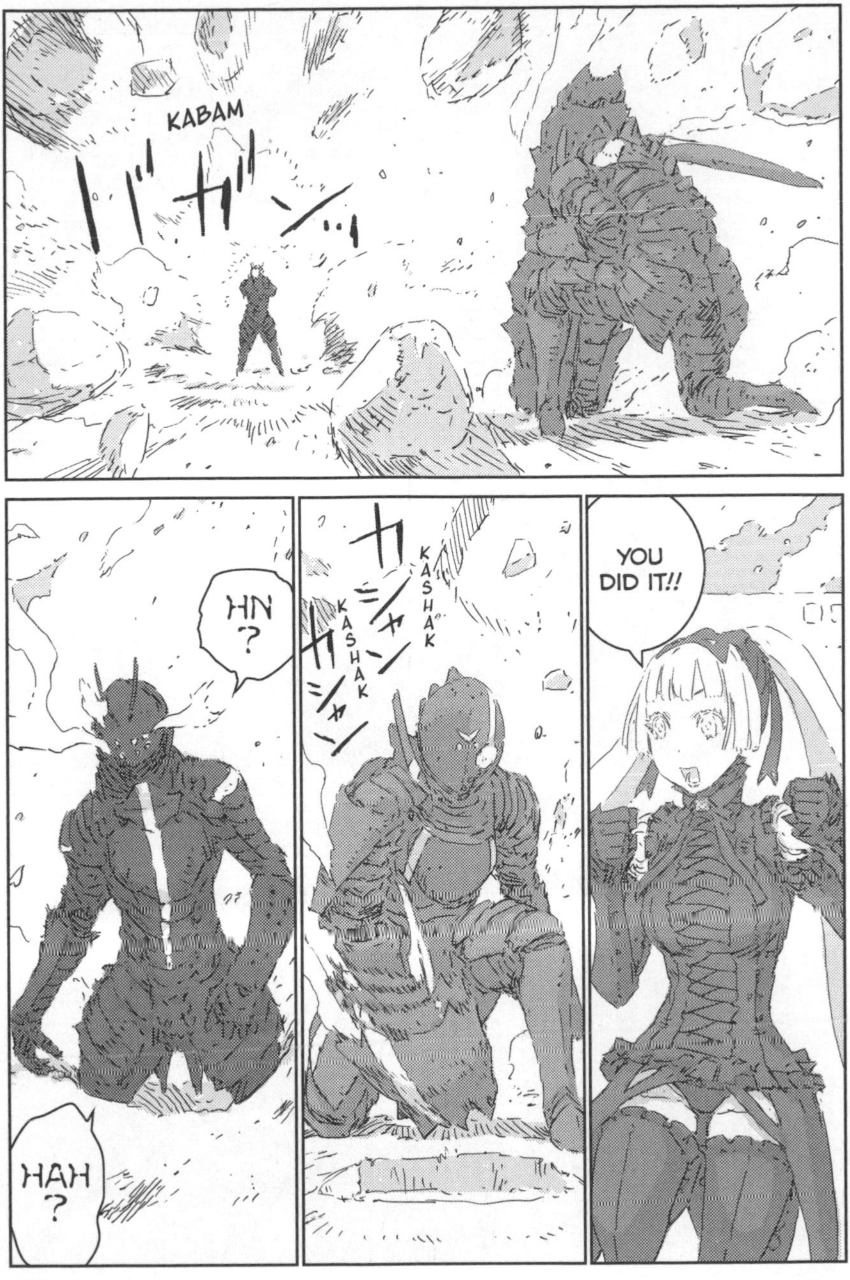
KABAM
YOU DID IT!!
KASHAK
KASHAK
HN?
HAH?

GLURGLRGL
BAKAM
BAGAK
BLAM
BLAM
BKOOM
BAGAK
BLAM

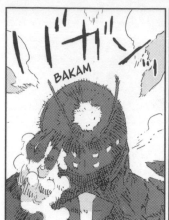

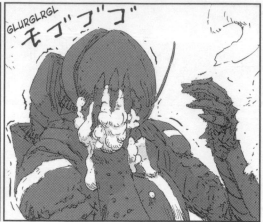

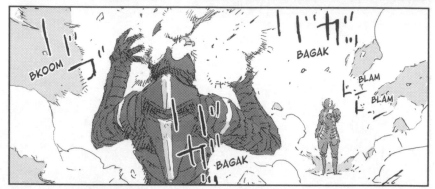

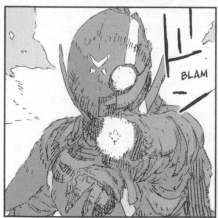

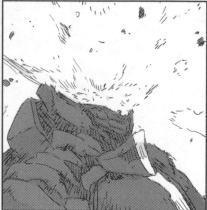

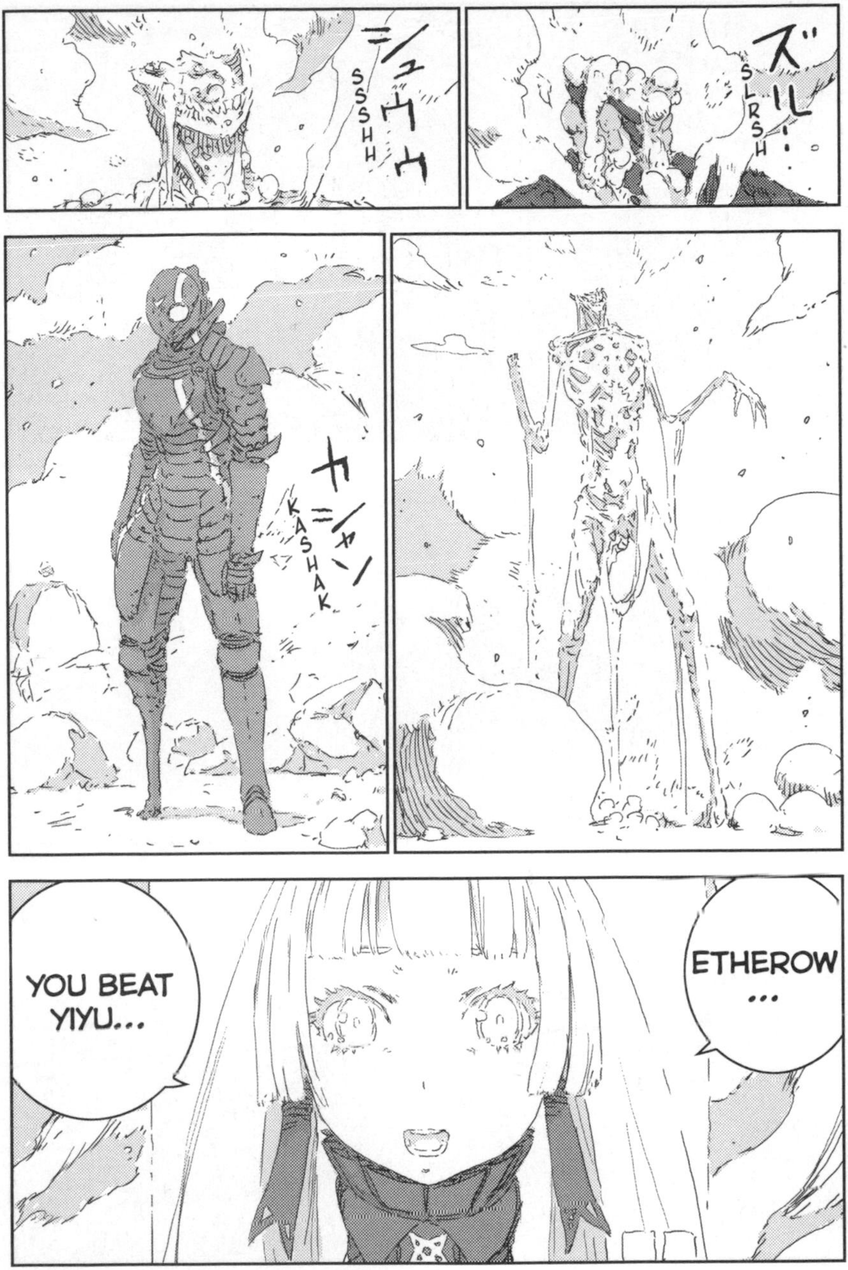
ズル…
SLRSH
シュウウ
SSSHH
ガシャン
KASHAK
ETHEROW...
YOU BEAT YIYU...

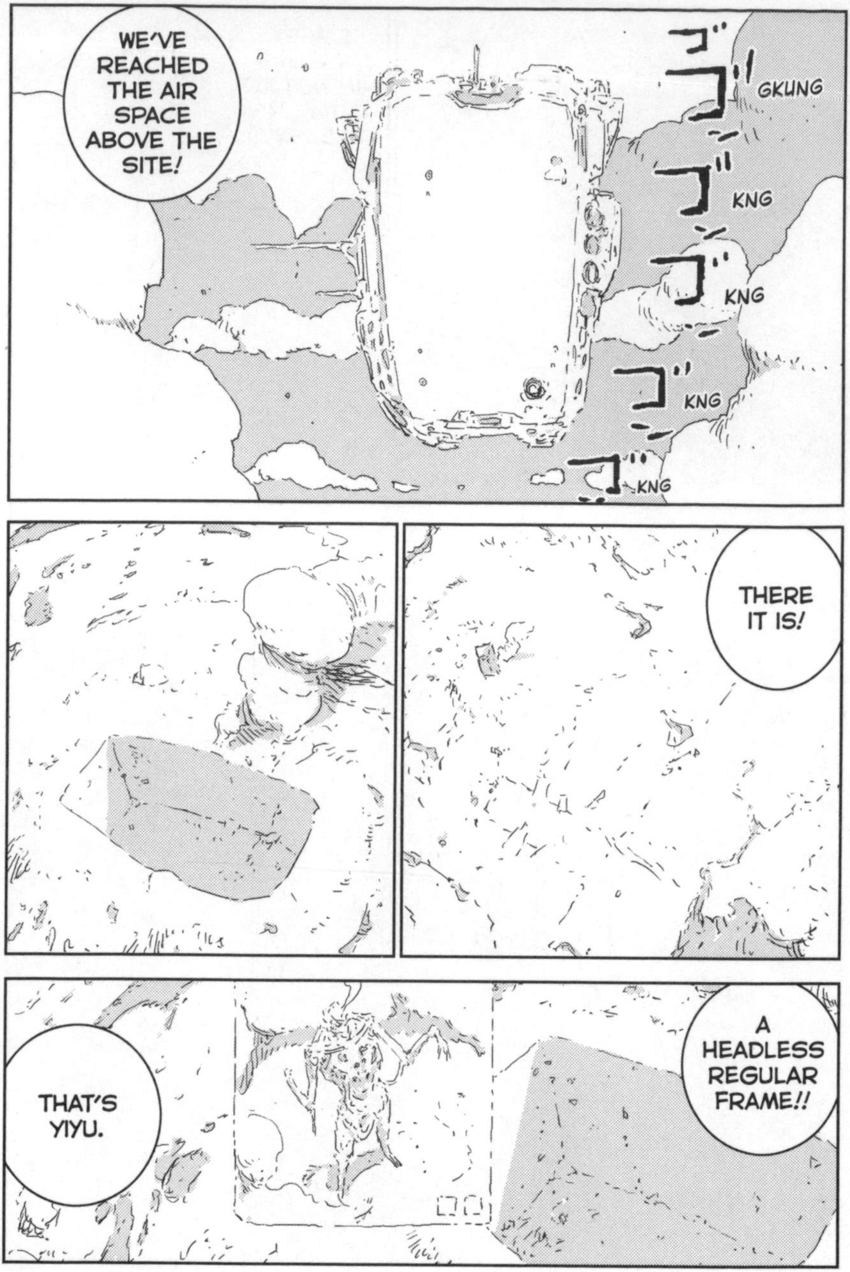
WE'VE REACHED THE AIR SPACE ABOVE THE SITE!
GKUNG
KNG
KNG
KNG
KNG
THERE IT IS!
A HEADLESS REGULAR FRAME!!
THAT'S YIYU.

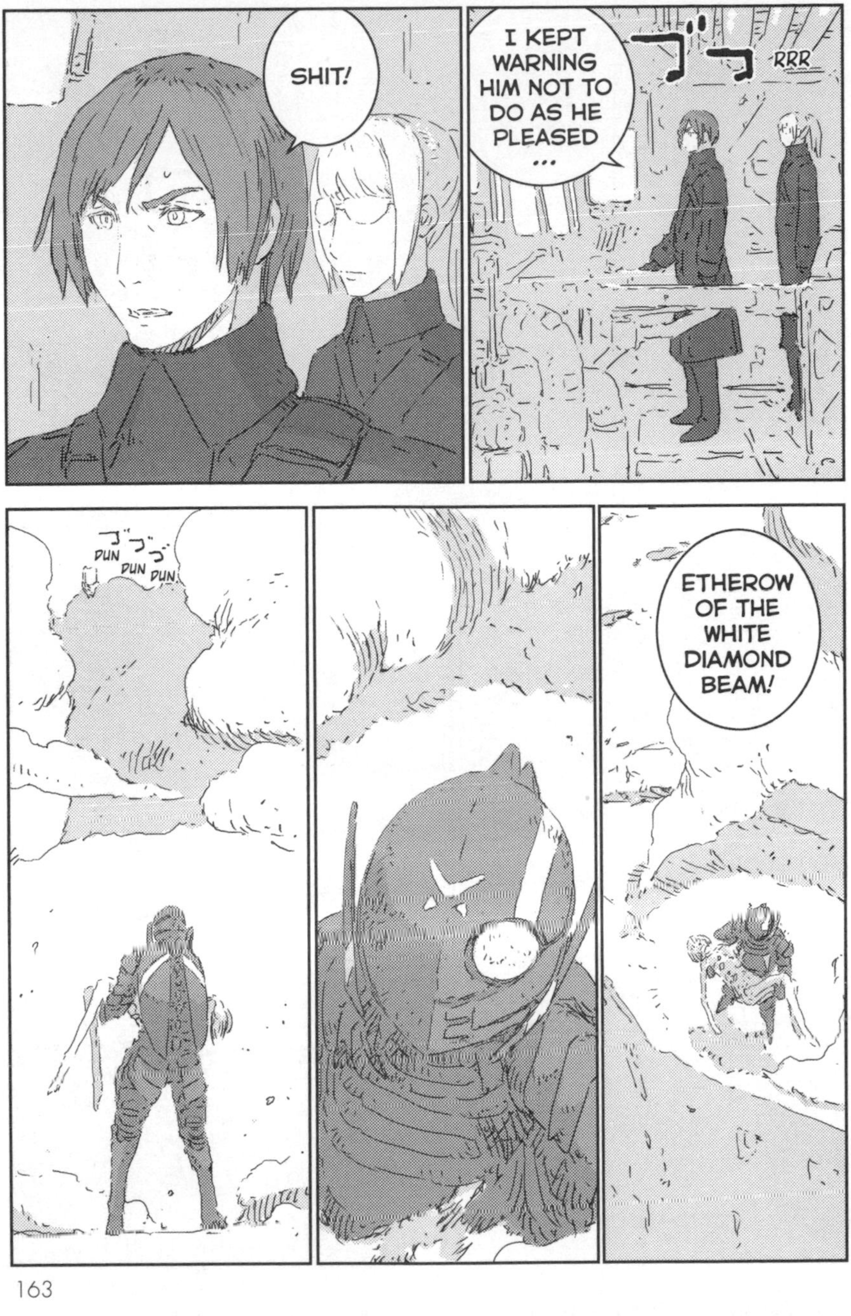

SHIT!
I KEPT WARNING HIM NOT TO DO AS HE PLEASED ...
ゴゴ
RRR
ゴゴゴ
DUN DUN DUN
ETHEROW OF THE WHITE DIAMOND BEAM!

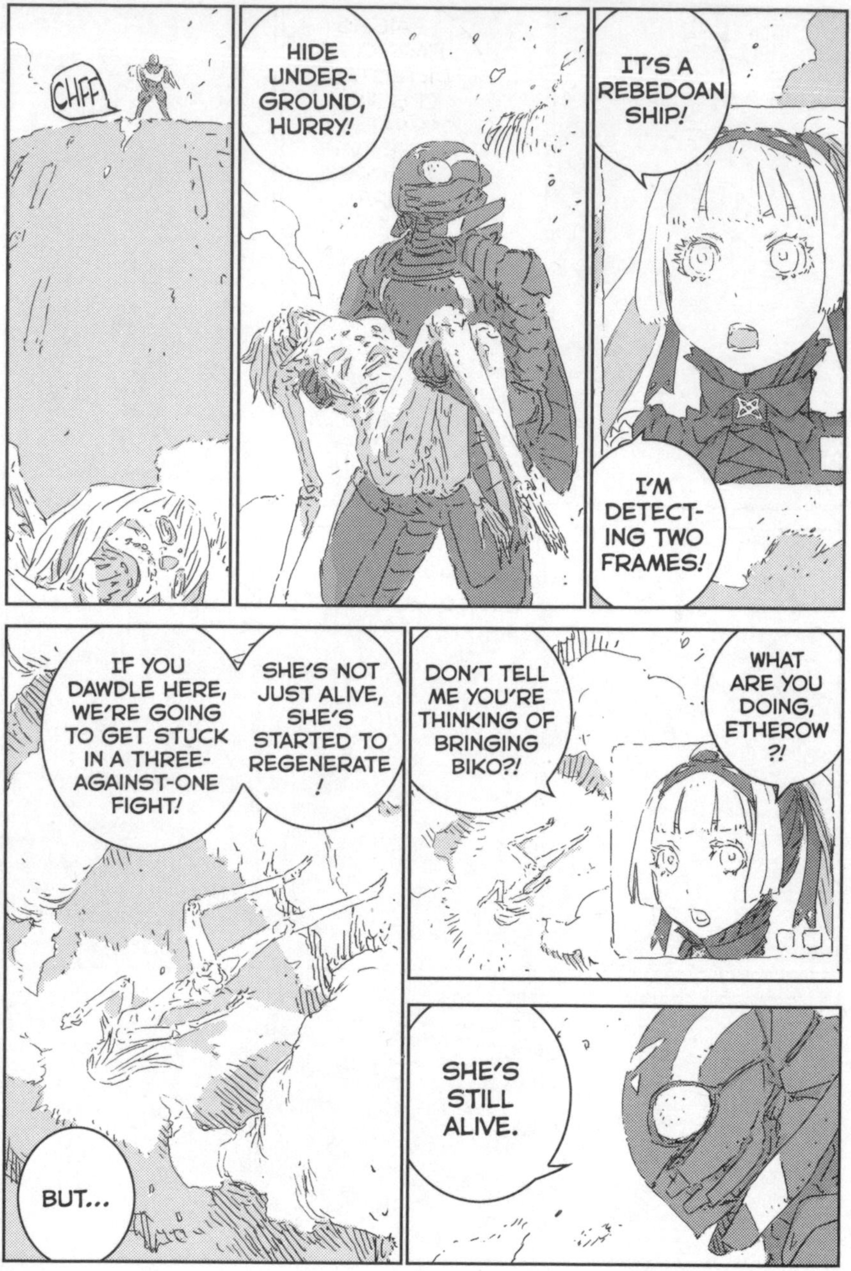
IT'S A REBEDOAN SHIP!
I'M DETECTING TWO FRAMES!
HIDE UNDERGROUND, HURRY!
CHFF
WHAT ARE YOU DOING, ETHEROW?!
DON'T TELL ME YOU'RE THINKING OF BRINGING BIKO?!
SHE'S STILL ALIVE.
SHE'S NOT JUST ALIVE, SHE'S STARTED TO REGENERATE!
IF YOU DAWDLE HERE, WE'RE GOING TO GET STUCK IN A THREE-AGAINST-ONE FIGHT!
BUT...

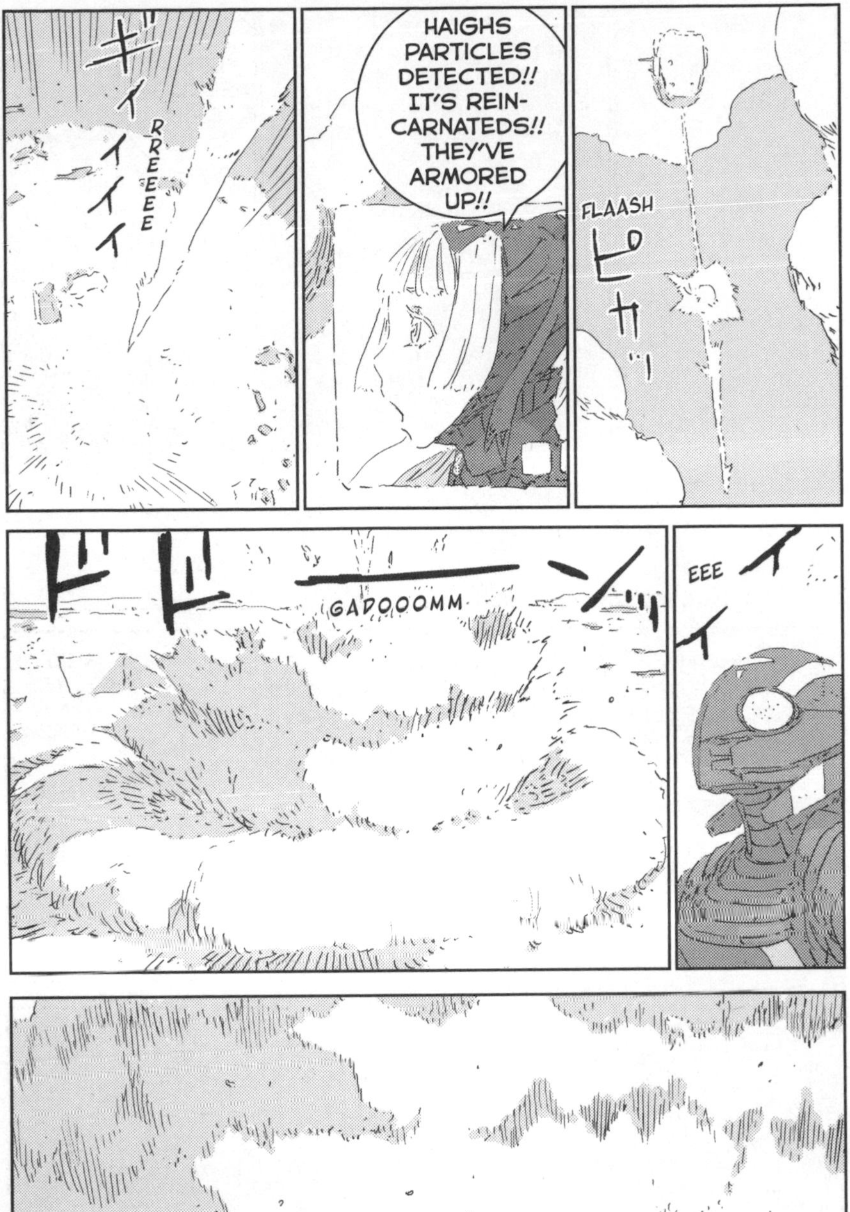
FLAASH
ピカッ
HAIGHS PARTICLES DETECTED!! IT'S REIN-CARNATEDS!! THEY'VE ARMORED UP!!
ギィイイイ
RREEEE
EEE
イイ
ドドーンッ
GADOOOMM

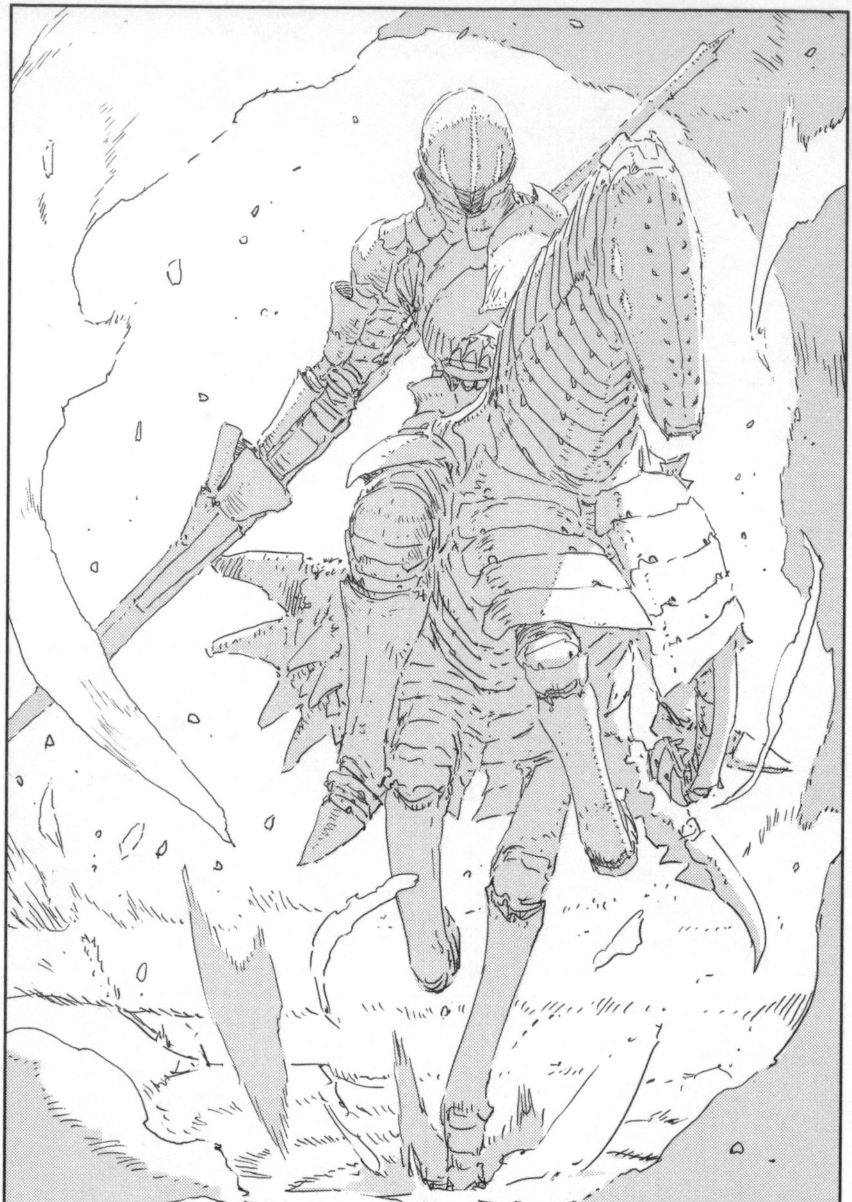

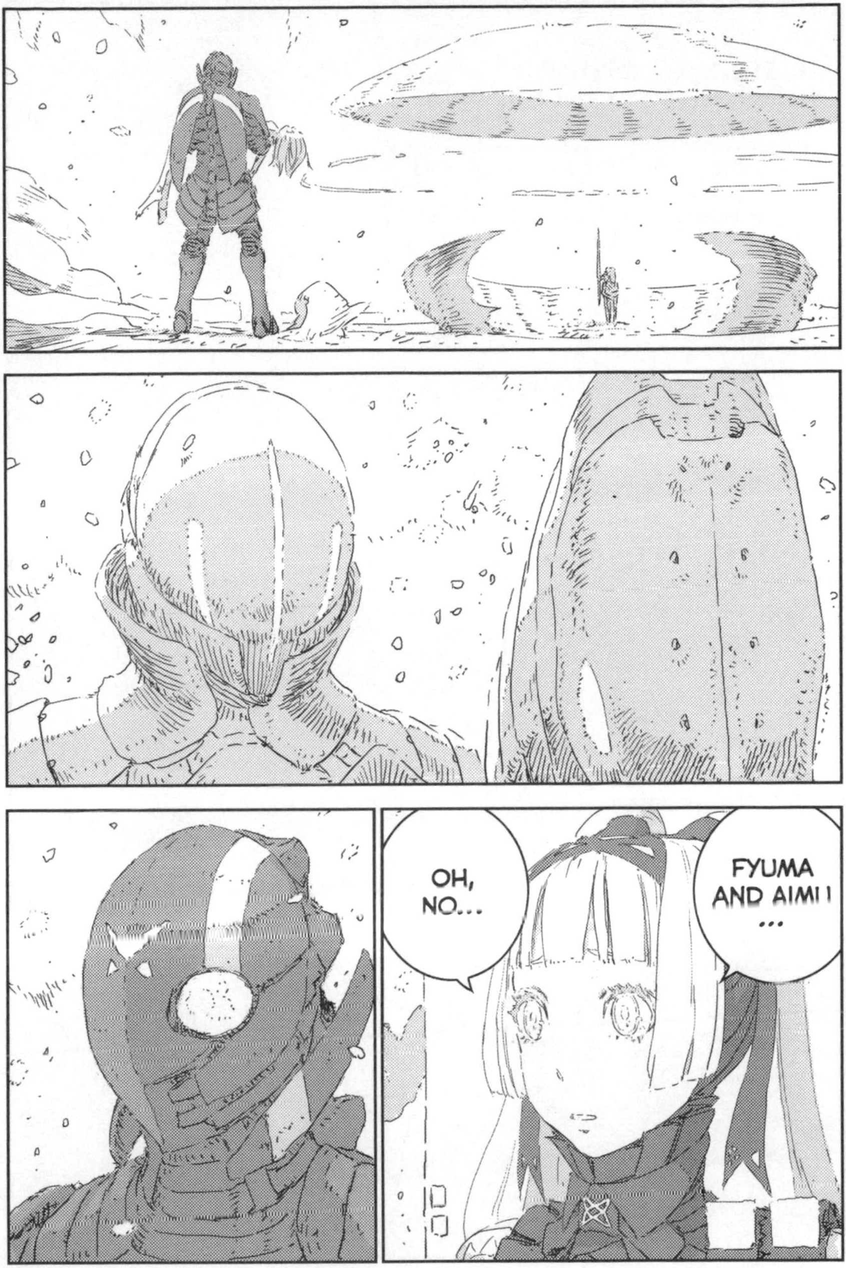
FYUMA AND AIMU ...
OH, NO...

CHAPTER 09 END

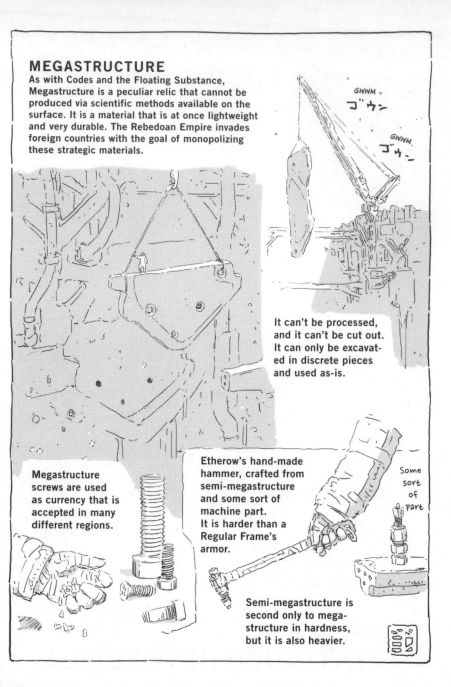

MEGASTRUCTURE

As with Codes and the Floating Substance, Megastructure is a peculiar relic that cannot be produced via scientific methods available on the surface. It is a material that is at once lightweight and very durable. The Rebedoan Empire invades foreign countries with the goal of monopolizing these strategic materials.

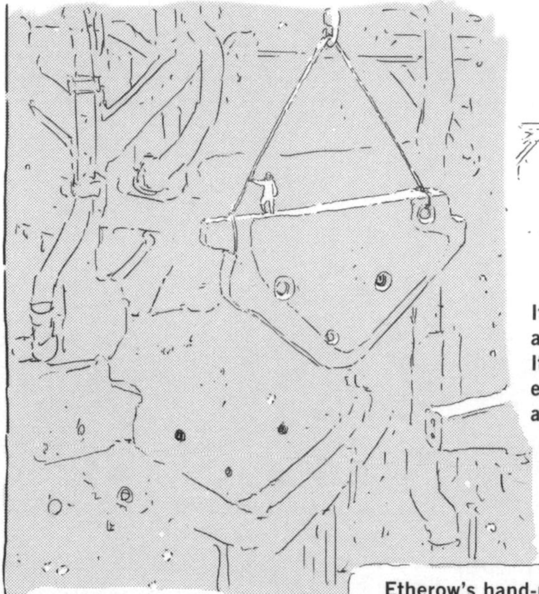

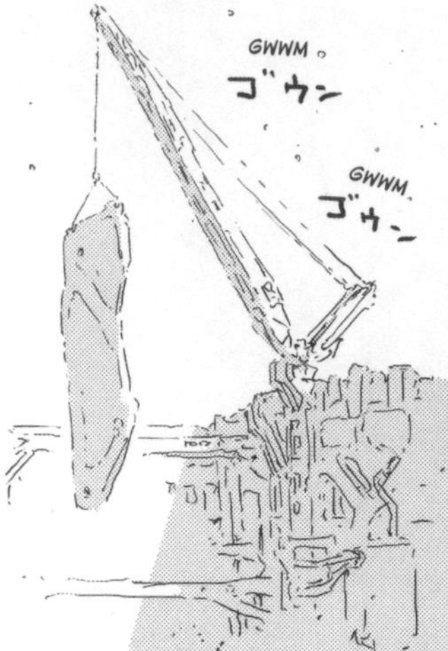
GWWM
ゴウン
GWWM
ゴウン

It can't be processed, and it can't be cut out. It can only be excavated in discrete pieces and used as-is.

Megastructure screws are used as currency that is accepted in many different regions.

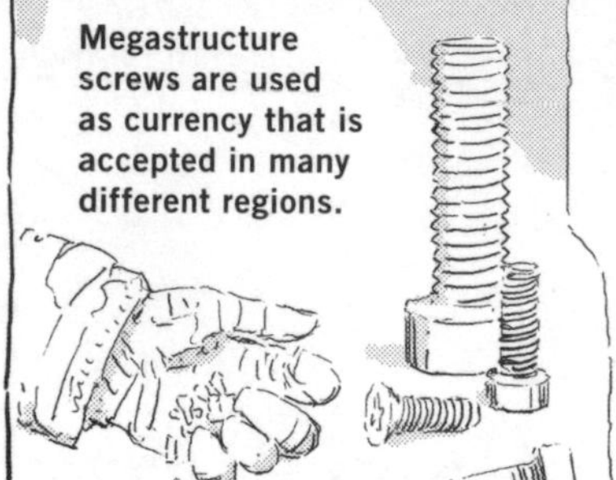

Etherow's hand-made hammer, crafted from semi-megastructure and some sort of machine part. It is harder than a Regular Frame's armor.

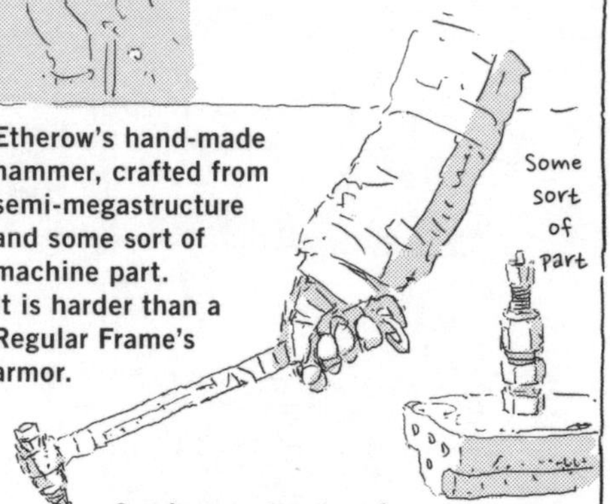
Some sort of part

Semi-megastructure is second only to megastructure in hardness, but it is also heavier.

CONTINUED IN VOLUME 3

NEXT VOLUME

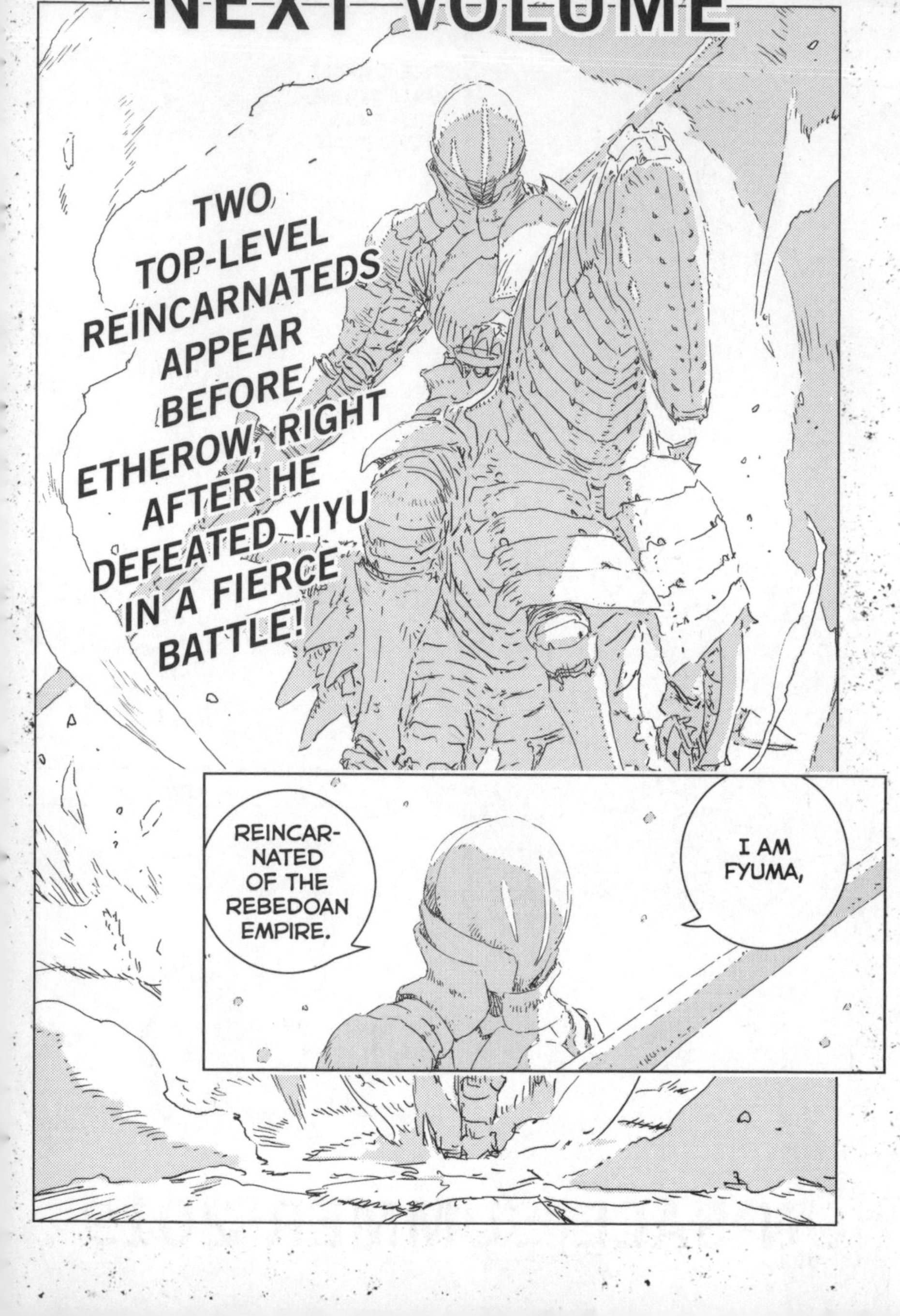
TWO TOP-LEVEL REINCARNATEDS APPEAR BEFORE ETHEROW, RIGHT AFTER HE DEFEATED YIYU IN A FIERCE BATTLE!
I AM FYUMA,
REINCAR-NATED OF THE REBEDOAN EMPIRE.